Sefer
ORCHOT TZADIKIM

אורחות צדיקים

Ways of the Righteous

Unknown Author

There is no known book without mistakes. Therefore, I ask in every language of application if anyone has any questions, comments, clarifications, corrections, please send to: **book@simchatchaim.com**

All material used in this section may not be used for commercial purposes, but only for study and teaching.

To get this book or books and information Email me at:

book@simchatchaim.com

Copyright©All Rights Reserved to

www.simchatchaim.com

YB"S©All rights reserved to the Editor

First Edition 2023

Sefer

ORCHOT TZADIKIM

Ways of the Righteous

TABLE OF CONTENTS

Page	Contents
3	About Orchot Tzadikim
6	Introduction of the Rabbi
21	Chapter One: ON PRIDE
40	Chapter Two: ON MODESTY
56	Chapter Three: ON SHAME
67	Chapter Four: ON IMPUDENCE
70	Chapter Five: ON LOVE
91	Chapter Six: ON HATRED
96	Chapter Seven: ON MERCY
101	Chapter Eight: ON CRUELTY
112	Chapter Nine: ON JOY
146	Chapter Ten: ON WORRY
153	Chapter Eleven: ON REMORSE
156	Chapter Twelve: ON ANGER
166	Chapter Thirteen: ON GRACIOUSNESS
175	Chapter Fourteen: ON ENVY
187	Chapter Fifteen: ON ZEAL
194	Chapter Sixteen: ON LAZINESS
201	Chapter Seventeen: ON GENEROSITY
209	Chapter Eighteen: ON MISERLINESS
212	Chapter Nineteen: ON REMEMBERING
231	Chapter Twenty: ON FORGETFULNESS

ORCHOT TZADIKIM — TABLE OF CONTENTS

234	Chapter Twenty-One: ON SILENCE
247	Chapter Twenty-Two: ON FALSEHOOD
256	Chapter Twenty-Three: ON TRUTH
264	Chapter Twenty-Four: ON FLATTERY
280	Chapter Twenty-Five: ON GOSSIP
298	Chapter Twenty-Six: ON REPENTANCE
337	Chapter Twenty-Seven: ON TORAH
390	Chapter Twenty-Eight: FEAR OF HEAVEN

Sefer

ORCHOT TZADIKIM

Ways of the Righteous

About Orchot Tzadikim

Orchot Tzaddikim - Ways of the Righteous, is a book on Jewish ethics written in Germany in the 15th century, entitled Sefer ha-Middot by the author, but called Orḥot Ẓaddiḳim by a later copyist. Under this title a Yiddish translation, from which the last chapter and some other passages were omitted, was printed at Isny in 1542, although the Hebrew original did not appear until some years later (Prague, 1581). Subsequently, however, the book was frequently printed in both languages. The author of the work is unknown, although Güdemann (Gesch. 3. 223) advances the very plausible hypothesis that he was Lipmann Mühlhausen.

Most of the book is not original writing; it is following the order of "The Improvement of the Moral Qualities" by Solomon ibn Gabirol, adding paragraphs from many of Maimonides' works, and ideas from the famous ethical writings "Shaarei Tshuva" (by Rabbenu Yona of Gerona) and Chovot HaLevavot.

ORCHOT TZADIKIM About the book

The Orḥot Ẓaddiḳim, which was designed to be a very popular code of ethics, contains the following maxims among others:

"It is evil pride to despise others, and to regard one's own opinion as the best, since such an attitude bars progress, while egotism increases bitterness toward others and decreases thine own capability of improvement" (ch. 1).

"Be just and modest in association with others, and practice humility even toward the members of the household, toward the poor, and toward dependents. The more property thou hast, the greater should be thy humility, and thy honor and beneficence toward mankind" (ch. 2).

"Be kind to thy non-Jewish servants; make not their burdens heavy, nor treat them scornfully with contemptuous words or blows" (ch. 8).

"Forget not the good qualities thou lackest, and note thy faults; but forget the good that thou hast done, and the injuries thou hast received" (ch. 20).

"Abash not him who hath a bodily blemish, or in whose family there is some stain. If one hath done evil and repented, name not his deed in his presence, even in jest, nor refer to a quarrel which has been ended, lest the dead embers be rekindled" (ch. 21).

In ch. 27. the author bitterly attacks the pilpul method of study, reproves his countrymen who engage in this

ORCHOT TZADIKIM

method of Talmud study, and reproaches those who neglect the study of the Bible and of all sciences.

According to Rabbi Gil Student, "Orechos Tzadikim is an anonymous mussar sefer that has enjoyed a lasting impact on Judaism. It is surprising that the sefer was never attributed to anyone...we can state with certainty is that the author lived in or after the early 14th century. Despite being influenced by the German Chasidim, he was a follower of the French Ba'alei Ha-Tosafos. We can suggest that the author lived in the late 14th century in France or among French exiles, but not in Germany or Spain.

There is speculation that the book was authored by a female, owing to the author's heavy reliance on biblical passages as sources and choosing to publish anonymously, though publishing anonymously may merely indicate the author's very example of character development.

Sefer

ORCHOT TZADIKIM

Ways of the Righteous

Introduction of the Rabbi

"The end of the matter, all having been heard: fear God, and keep His commandments; for this is the whole man." (Eccl. 12: 13).

Solomon was the wisest and greatest of all men. He was king over earthly and celestial beings. After he had seen every sort of activity, tried all things and made known all sorts of wisdom, he concluded all of his words by saying, "The end of every matter is fear of the Lord." And thus, he began, "The fear of the Lord is the beginning of knowledge" (Prov. 1:7), and he ends, "A woman that feareth the Lord, she shall be praised" (Prov. 31:30).

And Solomon was the richest of all men, as it is written, "And the king made silver to be in Jerusalem as stones" (I Kings 10:27). For him it was proper to say "Vanity of vanities, all is vanity" (Eccl. 1:2), and one ought not to busy himself with anything save for the reverence of Heaven. And thus, did Moses, our teacher, peace be upon him, say: "And now, Israel, what doth the Lord thy God require of thee, but to fear the Lord thy God" (Deut. 10:12). And thus, did David, the King, peace be upon him, say: "The fear of the Lord is the beginning of wisdom" (Ps. 111:10).

And because we see that man is the choicest of the creatures of the Creator in the lower world and that he is perfected in his form and that there is within him the soul that contemplates the secret of the highest heights and of the lowest places and that he is the chief object of all intentions in the world, and that everything that was created in this world, all of it, is for his need. And, in addition to this, there has been given to man a Torah of Truth, to teach him the righteous way, for man is very dear to the Lord, since we see that even the angels serve in supplying the needs of a righteous man as we have found in the case of Abraham, our father and Isaac and Jacob: "The angel who hath redeemed me from all evil, bless the lads" (Gen. 48:16), and "So he strove with an angel, and prevailed" (Hos. 12:5).

And we have seen that an angel came to their help as it is written. It came to pass that night, that the angel of the Lord went forth, and smote in the camp of the Assyrians" (II Kings 19:35). And there are many instances like these.

We have long known that there is a man who has greater excellence over other men even though they are all created in one form and all of them have one foundation. Except that the soul of one man has ascended to the spiritual heights for he caused his wisdom to rule over his desire, while the other man has caused his desire to rule over his wisdom. And therefore, he walks all his days in darkness and feels his way like a blind man in the thick darkness.

There are five senses in man. The first is the sense of hearing; the second is the sense of seeing; the third is the sense of smell; the fourth is the sense of taste; the fifth is the sense of feeling or that which a man senses when he touches anything. These five senses are all functions of man and no work is done without at least one of these five senses. And the mind works through them, for the five senses bring to the mind every matter, and every deed and every thought are influenced by them. The mind has many characteristics, for example, pride, humility, memory, forgetfulness, sorrow, joy, shame and impudence. And like unto these there are many more. And all of these thoughts or qualities are strengthened by the one possessing all five senses, for the blind man cannot pride himself as though he could see.

Therefore, , every man who reflects should try with all his might to attain the final good, for if a man reaches a good state or elevation then he will always desire to ascend to the degree which is higher until he will finally attain the ultimate good and in this manner he will reach the "world of reward" which is the world to come. Long ago David longed to attain the good of the world to come, when he said: "Oh, how abundant is Thy goodness, which Thou hast laid up for them that fear Thee" (Ps. 31:20), and he said: "They are abundantly satisfied with the fatness of Thy house, and Thou makest them drink of the river of Thy pleasures" (Ps. 36:9). And this degree no one can attain except he be worthy of it, as he said: "Who shall sojourn in Thy tabernacle? Who shall dwell upon Thy holy mountain? He that walketh uprightly, and worketh righteousness" (Ps. 15:1). And the rest of the matter which is said there.

And inasmuch as we have mentioned the advantage of the qualities of man, it is only fitting for us to

ORCHOT TZADIKIM — Introduction

explain their importance and their blame, their goodness and their evil until there will stretch in front of the intelligent person a straight path, and he will reach the courtyard of the King if his soul will choose good qualities with all its might, for inasmuch as a man has choice, he may throw aside the husk and take the fine flour. How can this be?

There is a certain type of man that is a man of wrath, that is always angry, and then there is a man who is calm and never gets angry at all, and if he does get angry it is a very little anger and occurs once in many years. And there is a man that is exceedingly proud of heart and there is another man who is exceedingly humble. And there is a man who lusts and his soul is never satisfied with following his desire, and there is another man, very pure of heart, who does not desire even the few things that the body needs. And there is a man with so many desires that his soul would not be satisfied with all the money in the world, like the matter that is spoken: "He that loveth silver shall not be satisfied with silver" (Eccl. 5:9).

And there is one whose desire is so limited that everything is enough for him even in the smallest quantity and he does not seek to obtain all his needs. And there are times when he afflicts himself with hunger and gathers each morsel and does not eat a penny's worth that belongs to him except with great anguish, and there are times when he throws away his money with his own hands knowingly. And in this vein, there are the rest of the Characteristics. For example, one glad, one sorrowful, one miserly, one liberal, one cruel, one merciful, one tender of heart and one brave of heart, and all similar traits. And of all of these characteristics there are some which a man has from the moment of his creation according to his physical nature. And there are also characteristics which the nature of this particular man is more prepared and more ready to receive quickly in the future than other characteristics And there are those qualities that do not belong to a man from the beginning of his creation but he learns them from others or he turns to them himself according to an inclination that occurs to his mind. There is a certain trait that one must use in many places and there is a trait which one should use only a little. And all of this is like one preparing a dish for which he needs vegetables, meat, water and salt and pepper. Now of all of these ingredients he must take from each one a certain measure, from this ingredient a little and from this ingredient much. If he puts in too little meat the dish will be meager and if he puts in too much salt then the dish cannot be eaten because it is too salty. And thus it is with all traits; if he puts in too little of what he requires much, and puts in too much of what he requires but little, then the food will be spoiled. And the expert is the one who can take of every ingredient the proper measure. Then the food will be pleasant and sweet to those who eat of it. In a similar manner are the qualities of a man. There are qualities of which he ought to take much, for example, modesty, embarrassment, and their like. And there are qualities of which he must take only a little, for example, pride, impudence, and cruelty. Therefore, , when a man weighs his qualities in the balance of the scales, let him take from every quality its proper measure. He should not take less and he should not add. In this way he will reach the ultimate goodness.

You should know and you should understand that if he whose nature inclines him towards an evil quality or one who is accustomed to an evil quality does not take it to heart to repent of it but always permits it to grow stronger, that this will bring him to a state where he will reject and loath good qualities.

And just as much pain and anguish and troubles are the sickness of the body so are most of the evil traits the sickness of the soul. And just as the sickness of the body tastes the bitter as sweet and the sweet as bitter and there is, among those who are ill, one that longs for food that is not good for him and hates good food, and all of this depends upon the extent of his sickness, so do people whose souls are sick, long for and love evil traits and they hate the good path or are too lazy to walk on it, and it is very hard for them according to the extent of their sickness. And thus, Isaiah says concerning these men, "Woe unto them that call evil good, and good evil; that change darkness into light, and light into darkness; that change bitter into sweet, and sweet into bitter" (Is. 5:20). And concerning them it is said, "Who leave the paths of uprightness, to walk in the ways of darkness" (Prov. 2:13).

Now how and what is the correction for the sickness of the soul? Let them go to the wise men who are the healers of souls and they will heal their illnesses with the traits that they will teach them until they will restore them to the good path. And concerning those people who know their evil traits but do not go to the

ORCHOT TZADIKIM — Introduction

wise men to heal them Solomon said: "The foolish despise wisdom and discipline" (Prov. 1:7).

There are many people whose desire it is to take hold of the good path but they do not know what is good for them and they plan each day to attain the loftiest heights but they do not reach it in all of their days. And this circumstance arises out of two causes: First, he does not know wherein he is lacking and does not perceive clearly his ugly ways. And he is like Reuben who seeks for Simon but would not recognize him even if he saw him. Even if he should seek for him all day, he will not find him, for though he approaches him several times he will not recognize him. Such is the case with this man. Even though he always thinks about what he ought to do and seeks to do the good deed he will not attain it for he does not know what he lacks. And there is a man who knows the bad qualities he possesses and plans to abandon them and take hold of good qualities. This man, too, will never attain the righteous path. For he is too lazy to seek out the good qualities properly. And he is like Reuben who seeks Simon and does know him and nevertheless does not find him because he does not seek him in the proper manner. And concerning this type of man, it is said: "The tongue of the righteous is as choice silver" (Prov. 10:20).

He who loans money to his companion and the borrower comes to pay him silver by weight, if the lender does not know the accuracy of the scale and the justness of the balance or if he knows everything about the scale, but does not know the properties of silver, then he is very near to being injured in the matter of weight and money, for at times he will

ORCHOT TZADIKIM

refuse the silver and take the dross, or he may take less than the weight which is properly his, for if he takes too light a weight or puts the silver on the heavy side of the scale, through all of these types of ignorance he is bound to make an error. Or even if he is an expert in recognizing silver and in weighing it, if he does not look at it as carefully as he should then it is possible that dross will be mixed in with his silver. But if he is an expert in all things, in weighing, and in recognizing silver and he looks at it as he should, then he will be paid as he should be, with pure silver and complete weight. Therefore, , he has compared the "tongue of the righteous" to "the best of silver." For the righteous man must recognize the good and the bad and should know all of the qualities, and he should look and examine them as is proper, and he must exert his body and his wisdom to leave off folly and to take hold of understanding and to remove the mixtures of dross from himself. Then will his soul be purged and purified before God, as it is written: "Take away the dross from the silver, and there cometh forth a vessel for the refiner" (Prov. 25:4). When the dross is removed then the vessel is purged.

Then there is a man who changes his habits and is not stable. At one time he clings to this quality and at another time he departs from that habit and takes hold of another habit and thus he keeps doing always, and he is like a man who wants to get to a city but does not know the way to it, nor does he know any of the paths that will lead him to the highway. Therefore, he is bewildered. One time he goes by one path and he strays, so he comes back and tries another path, and thus he does with a third path and with a fourth. Concerning such men, the wise man said: "The labour of fools wearieth every one of them, for he knoweth not how to go to the city" (Eccl. 10:15).

Therefore, , we must have pity on the people who are sunk in the nothingness of vanity and we must teach them the importance of the just weight and the correctness of the scales, to let them know how silver is tested and to teach them the path of the righteous in order that a man should choose, at the very outset of his being tested, a path that will bring him to a place that is fresh and fertile where all that is good can be found and by "good" we mean reverence of God, which is the goal of all of deeds. And this is the question which the Lord. Blessed be His Name, asks every man, as it is written: "What doth the Lord thy God require of thee, but to fear the Lord thy God" (Deut. 10:12).

And no deed is considered worthy unless it contains pure reverence. Therefore, it is necessary to make known to everyone that every man who wants to bring his soul towards the attainment of good qualities must mingle reverence to Heaven with each and every quality. For it is fear of the Lord, reverence of God, that strengthens all of our qualities. And fear of the Lord or reverence of God is like the thread which we run through the holes of pearls and then we tie a knot at its end so that it will firmly hold all the pearls. There is no doubt that if the knot should tear, all of the pearls will fall. Such is the reverence of Heaven. It strengthens all of the qualities and if you will undo the knot of reverence, then all your good qualities will depart from you, and when you have no

ORCHOT TZADIKIM — Introduction

good qualities within you then you have neither Torah nor Commandments. For the whole Torah depends on the constant improvement of the qualities. As regards the qualities, the good and the bad, the wise man can make good ones of bad ones but the fool can make evil qualities out of good ones. As for him who walks in the darkness, and does not consider the improvement of his qualities, it is possible that one quality will destroy all of his merit. For example, one who takes great pride in his deeds and boasts and preens himself always with the shame of his companions, and seeks to obtain honor through his companion's disgrace, such a man is like one who fills a barrel with fine wine, but there is in the bottom of the barrel a little hole. There is no doubt that all of the fine wine will be lost because of the small hole, if he does not stop it up. So, this man who is arrogant, even though he is filled with Torah, will lose everything through this evil quality if he does not hasten to repair it.

There are so few in the world who recognize the truth. There are those who are not wise enough to recognize it. Just as a man whose two legs are amputated cannot ascend a ladder, neither can such a one ascends the stairway of wisdom if he has no understanding. But there is also a man who is wise, but has been impressed with the lusts of the world from his youth until he directs all of his wisdom to attaining his desire and to do the will of his evil desire for he has been accustomed from his youth to do evil deeds until they are firmly fixed in his soul. Thus it is very difficult for him to escape from the trap and snare of his sins: Then there is the man who does have the wisdom to recognize what is right and has also the desire to walk in good paths, but he has never been in the presence of the wise to hear from them instruction concerning wisdom and the righteous path and, because of this, he walks in the darkness, and he is like a man who has a hidden treasure in his house and does not know about the hidden treasure, and he sells the house to another.

Consider then that if a man has many differing and dissimilar qualities that each and every quality will tear at the mind of the man. This one pulls him here and this one pulls him there. And in this struggle the evil desire helps a man choose the lowliest one. And this is like a man who walks in the wilderness and bears, lions, leopards, wolves and many other beasts of prey confront him. This man should open his eyes and fight against each one, for if he averts his eyes for one moment, these harmful beasts will tear him to bits. So is it with man. His evil qualities like lust, arrogance, hate, anger and similar ones keep rolling about in his heart always. And, if he blinds himself to them and does not correct them, then he will root out from his heart the light of truth and grope about in thick darkness. And concerning this it is said: "I have set the Lord always before me" (Ps. 16:8).

When a man is born, he is in his body and in his wisdom weaker than all other creatures. For all creatures from the very day, they were born can walk, eat and help themselves. But man requires much in his physical needs. And he needs even more correction in his soul, to adjust his wisdom and to understand the good paths. For man at his beginning, without someone to teach him, conducts himself like one of the cattle, but his heart is like a tablet which is ready to be written upon. If this tablet is in the hands of a fool, then he will scribble upon it until he spoils the tablet and it has no further worth. But the wise man will write upon it the correct order of his affairs and his needs and his obligations. And from the information written on this tablet he will be enabled to feed and support his children and attain great worth. Such is a heart of man! The fools draw upon its drawings of falsehood and write upon its engravings of wrong-doing. And they fill their hearts with thoughts of folly and emptiness while the intelligent people write upon the tablet of their hearts, the writing of God, which is the foundation of the Torah and the Commandments, the wisdom of attaining noble qualities, until their souls shine like the radiance of the firmament. And this was the intention and meaning of Solomon when he said: "Bind them upon thy fingers, write them upon the table of thy heart" (Prov. 7:3).

This too did Solomon say: "Even a child is known by his doing, whether his work be pure, and whether it be right" (Prov. 20:11). This verse was said concerning the ability of the young to distinguish values, for their qualities or traits can be recognized in their youth. You can discern in some youths the quality of modesty and embarrassment, while in others impudence is apparent, and some incline themselves toward lust while some incline themselves towards good qualities. And know concerning all the qualities that you see in a man in the days of young manhood and in old age that they were there in the days of his childhood and dawning youth, except that in those days he did not have the strength to show them and to exhibit them in deeds. And as for the youths with whom folly has become great, it is still possible for a man to swerve them to the good path, for it is easy for youth to learn and they have not the strength or the wisdom to depart or to flee from beneath the hand of the one that corrects them, and so they must bear it. But in the days of old age, people cannot be swerved from their paths easily or from those traits which were in them in the days of their youth. And they are like a silver tray that was hidden in the soil and became coated with a thick tarnish during the long time that it was hidden there. Such silver needs to be polished and republished until the silver returns to its original beautiful appearance. Thus is it with a man who has followed his own way and his habit and has become deeply sunk in the depths of inferior qualities, it becomes necessary to polish his intelligence so that he can distinguish between that which is unclean and that which is clean and to continue this task until the good qualities are impressed and bound in his heart.

This book of qualities was written and sealed with the seal of wisdom in order to teach man knowledge and to be a valuable utensil in the hand of every man so as to correct through its use his traits and his deeds. For a craftsman who has the tool of his craft in his hand can do his work but if he does not have the tool of his art, he can do nothing. Therefore, hearken to correction and take the tool of your art into your hands in order to correct your qualities. Can you not see that he who has all sort of coins, small ones and large ones but does not know the worth of every coin,

ORCHOT TZADIKIM — Introduction

will not know what to buy with each one until he knows the value of each coin. And he also must know which coin the king has voided and decreed concerning it that it should not be minted. And after he has weighed every single coin and appraised its worth, then he will know how to purchase with each coin whatever he needs at its proper value. And as for the coin which the king decreed that it should not be minted, he will be careful not to circulate it except in a manner where he will not be deserving of punishment. We will then find that this type of man will attain goodness and joy with every single coin. But the fool who does not weigh and does not know the value of the coin and circulates what the king has declared void, there can be no doubt that he will suffer great harm. But you, my son, accept this parable which has been told you about the many qualities that are within you, the great and the small. And weigh every single quality in the balance-scale of your wisdom until you learn to know the value of every quality, and you will know those qualities which the Great King has declared void and you will guard yourself against them so that they will not appear in you and will not be found in you except under such circumstances where you will not receive injury or punishment. And in this way, you will attain complete fulfillment, and you will be an artist with the proper tool of your art in your hand.

Now we desire to make known the roots of man's qualities and their branches, their worth and their harm. And it is our intention to turn natural powers of man from folly to love of correction so that even the simple will try to know the traits of the wise. And

ORCHOT TZADIKIM

from God, may the mention of His Name be Exalted, we shall ask help that He may let us know the righteous paths and the ways of justice so that we may teach the tribes of Jeshurun — the Congregation of loving-kindness.

Sefer
ORCHOT TZADIKIM
Ways of the Righteous

Chapter One

ON PRIDE

In the first chapter we shall speak about the quality of pride. How good it is that it occurs at the very beginning of all the chapters because of the obligation of man to separate himself from it! For pride is the doorway to many evils and we have seen nothing as evil as arrogance in all of the qualities. Therefore, a man must be wise and lead pride along paths that are worthy, and thrust it away from the place where it is not proper for it to be.

Pride is the coin which the Great King. Blessed be He, voided, and about which He warned us in His Torah, as it is said: "Take care lest you forget the Lord your God and fail to keep His commandments" (Deut. 8:11). For the arrogant person forgets his Maker, as it is written, "… and (when) your herds and flocks have multiplied, and your silver and gold have increased, and everything you own has prospered, beware lest your heart grow haughty and you forget the Lord your God … and you say to yourselves, 'My own power and the might of my own hand have won this wealth for me'" (Ibid. 8:13-18). And in the case of a king, it is said: "Thus he will not act haughtily towards his fellows or deviate from the Instruction to the right or to the left..." (Ibid. 17:20). If the Torah warned against pride even in the case of a king, so much more does it warn ordinary men that they should not attempt to lord over one another.

Arrogance may be divided into two types. One: the pride of a man in his body; Two: the pride of a man in his intellectual attainments and in his deeds.

The pride of a man in his body or person is, in turn, divided into two classifications, one good and one evil. And this is the pride of a man in his body which is evil. When arrogance becomes strong in the heart of a man, then it rules over him from the top of his head to the soles of his feet. In his head and in his throat, as it is written: "Because the daughters of Zion are haughty, and walk with stretched-forth necks..." (Is. 3:16). In his hands and in his feet, as it is written: "Let not the foot of pride overtake me, and let not the hand of the wicked drive me away" (Ps. 36:12).

And it was because of the "foot of pride" that the daughter of Rabbi Hanina ben Teradion was punished, for it was decreed that she dwell in a brothel because on one occasion, when she was walking before the great men of Rome, she heard them say, "How beautiful are the steps of this maiden!" Whereupon, she took particular care of her step (Abodah Zarah 18a).

With eyes, as it is written: "Haughty eyes" (Prov. 6:17).

A person can be haughty with his ears when he does not hear the cries of the wretched poor. A person can be haughty with his nose when he stands near the poor or when he enters their houses and they smell bad to him. And he can be haughty with his speech when he speaks impudently and with pride against the righteous.

Pride can also be recognized in his food and drink, and in his wearing of proud garments — the garments of a heathen — and against this we are warned in the Torah of Moses, as it is said: "You shall not follow the practices of the nation ..." (Lev. 20:23), and it is also written: "... Neither shall ye walk in their statues ..." (Ibid. 18:3), and it is further said: "Take heed to thyself that thou be not ensnared to follow them ..." (Deut. 12:30). All of these precepts concern one matter — warning that Israel should be distinguished from the nations in its garments, speech and customs, and thus it says: "... for I have set you apart from the peoples" (Lev. 20:26).

Arrogant people are disgusting in the eyes of the Lord, as it is said: "Every one that is proud in heart is an abomination to the Lord" (Prov. 16:5). And such a one is easily surrendered into the power of his evil impulse, for God's help is not with him since he is abominable to the Lord. And even though he does not lord it over any man by word or deed but in his heart alone, he is called "abominable" for it says, "Every one that is proud in heart is an abomination to the Lord," that is to say, even if he has no arrogance except in his heart.

Our Rabbis said: "Every man who is impudent or proud of spirit it is as though he were an idolator" (Sotah 4b), for it is written, "Every one that is proud in heart is an abomination to the Lord" (Prov. 16:5) and it is written there: "You must not bring an abhorrent thing (idol) into your house ..." (Deut. 7:26). And there are those who say it is as though he violated all the laws against sexual license, for it is written: "For all these abominations were done by the people who were in the land before you and the land became defiled ..." (Lev. 18:27). And there are those who say, "It is as though he built a place for idolatry." And they said in Sotah 5a, "Every man who is arrogant of spirit becomes less in the end as it is said: 'They are exalted for a little while' (Job 24:25). And such a one is deserving to be hewn down like a grove planted for idol worship, as it is said: 'And the high ones of stature shall be hewn down' (Is. 10:33). And his dust shall not awaken and the Spirit of God laments over him. The Holy One Blessed be He, said, 'I and he cannot live in the same world,' as it is said: 'Whoso is haughty of eye and proud of heart, him will I not suffer'" (Ps. 101:5).

And they said in Baba Batra 98a, "He who is arrogant — even the people of his own household will not accept him," as it is said: "The haughty man abideth not..." (Hab. 2:5) which can be translated, "The man who is haughty abideth not even in his own abode."

Arrogance leads to the pursuit of wealth in order to lord over people. You already know what happened to Korah and his band because of his arrogance, for he sought to make himself great and to assume greatness that had not been given to him by Heaven, and from this he entered into controversy and from the controversy came jealousy and hatred. All of these qualities are very demeaning qualities, as shall, with God's help, be explained.

ORCHOT TZADIKIM   Chapter One

The end of the matter is that every one who adorns his body in order to lord it over others forgets the Lord, Blessed be He, and will not concern himself with the commandments, and will not pursue good deeds, for all his intent is concentrated on himself — to adorn his ephemeral body whose end is worms. And he who concentrates on adorning his person is near to committing immoral acts, for he will display himself before women to win favor in their eyes and this will lead him to draw close to them and he will engage in laughter and levity.

Also, the woman who adorns herself to display herself before men arouses their desire and puts unworthy thoughts in their minds and for this her punishment is very great for she places a stumbling block before many. Did not our Sages forbid men to gaze at the gaily colored garments of women when these garments are spread out upon the wall, even when she is not dressed in them, all the more so is there great punishment for a woman who adorns herself for men who ogle her.

And moreover, arrogance leads to lust, for the heart of the arrogant person is open wide to every temptation and desires everything. And lust is the worst quality of all, for because of his pride, a person will lust to wear expensive garments and build big palaces and eat tasty food, for the proud person longs always for "big things" and if he finds he cannot attain them, legitimately, he comes to steal and rob. For the arrogant person lusts to fill his purse and grow wealthy. He is never satisfied with his destiny, for all that he has seems too little for him, especially with the many expenses which his lust costs him. And, moreover, pride causes him to be impatient with the disciplines of society. It is not necessary to dwell upon the unworthiness of the impatient, for this is known to all.

And there is a sort of personal pride or pride in one's person that is good and necessary. Otherwise, a man might say, "Since arrogance is so evil a quality I shall separate myself from pride even more." And then he denies himself meat, drinks no wine, does not marry, does not live in a nice dwelling, does not put on a nice garment, but wears sackloth and coarse wool, and torn, soiled clothes, uses soiled and ugly dishes and utensils, does not wash his face, hands and feet until his appearance becomes more bedraggled than the appearance of other men and he does all this so as to remove himself from pride as far as is possible.

One who follows this course is called a "sinner", for lo it is said of a Nazarite: "and make expiation on his behalf for the guilt that he has incurred through the corpse" (Numbers 6:11). The Sages said, "If one who denies himself only wine is called a sinner how much more he who denies himself all pleasure" (Ta'anith 11a). The Sages said, "Is it not enough for you that the Torah has forbidden that you wish to forbid yourself other things?" (T.P. Nedarim 9:1). And on this subject and similar one, Solomon said, "Be not righteous overmuch: neither make thyself overwise; why shouldest thou destroy thyself?" (Eccl. 7:16).

The proper way for man is to be clean in all matters, for cleanliness is the fence that guards good deeds. How shall he conduct himself? He should wear garments of moderate worth, and not expensive and splendid clothes that invite everyone's attention. Nor shall he wear poor or shabby garments that shame the wearer, but garments of moderate worth, lovely and clean, according to his means. And it is forbidden that a spot or a stain be found on his garments. They should not be torn and they shall not be styled as the vulgar sometimes do.

His food should be clean and he should not eat "royal dainties" but ordinary food and ordinary drink according to his means. He should not eat nor drink out of repugnant dishes lest he transgress the commandment: "You shall not draw abomination upon yourselves..." (Lev. 11:43), but everything shall be with cleanliness.

His table and his bed shall be clean and all things that pertain to him shall be clean. His own body or person shall be clean not loathe some and he should be careful to wash his face, hands and feet and all his body at frequent times. As we find that "When Hillel the elder took leave of his disciples they said to him, 'Whither you go?' And he said to them, 'To fulfill a precept!' Then they asked him. 'Which precept is Hillel about to fulfill?' He said to them, 'To bathe in the bathhouse.' They asked, 'Is this a precept?' He said to them, 'Yes! If you consider that the statues of kings which are set up in theatres and circuses are scrubbed and cleaned by the one delegated to this task, and this man receives sustenance for this and is among the honored men of the kingdom, should we who are created in the image of God (Gen. 9:6) have less regard for our bodies?' " (Leviticus Rabbah 34:3).

Moreover, as it is written: "The Lord made everything for His own purpose" (Prov. 16:4) (Sabbath 50b).

ORCHOT TZADIKIM — Chapter One

And all who are careful to observe these matters for the sake of the command and not merely to make themselves attractive and proud, even though this care of the body may seem like conceit — as long as it is his intention to serve God through cleanliness, there is great merit in him.

Pride in Wisdom and Good Deeds may be divided into two types — one good and the other bad. The pride that is bad is when a man despises others in his heart and with his mouth, and when all people aside from himself are small and lacking in his eyes, and he constantly praises himself that he is all wise and is Therefore, often tempted to deny a truth because he is too conceited to admit that he could be wrong. Such a person always believes that his words, advice and deeds are better than the words, advice and deeds of his friends and companions. Such a one boasts constantly of his wisdom and deeds for he desires praise and honor for all the good things he does. And covering this sort of person, Solomon says, "Let a stranger praise you and not your own mouth!" (Prov. 27:2).

The arrogant person will always take all credit for himself and thus will not trouble himself to study Torah, for he cares nothing for the Glory of God but desires only that the world shall praise him and call him a good and wise man. Such a man always rejoices when others stumble for lack of knowledge and feels himself exalted when his companions are disgraced. And this fault is one of the 24 things which prevent repentance. (Alfasi Yoma Ch. 8). A man, all of whose deeds are good, but who boasts about them in order to attain honor is like a very fine dish, seasoned with the finest seasonings and spices, but standing near the fire so long that is becomes overcooked and emits a bad odor — until it cannot be eaten because of the burnt taste caused by the fire. Similarly the man who boasts about his deeds overcooks and causes a bad odor by his self-praise even of his admittedly good deeds. As for him who boasts of his wisdom and deeds when he has neither, there is no worse quality than this and none to equal it. And our sages have said: "If people honor a man because they believe that he knows two tractates of the Talmud when he knows only one, he should tell them he does not know more than one tractate" (T.P. Shebi'ith 10:8). All the more so must he not deceive people into holding him in high regard for qualities or knowledge he does not possess.

And know this — that we are obligated that all our deeds, public or private, be dedicated to God's Holy Name, may He be Exalted, and the whole purpose of service to God should be to attain His will and approval alone and not the approval of men, so as to gather praise and honor for one's deeds. But a person should do all for the sake of God who looks to the heart as it is written: "I the Lord search the mind and examine the heart" (Jer. 17:10), and it is said: "The secret things are known to the Lord our God" (Deut. 29:28).

Therefore, if a man does not constantly guard himself with wisdom and alertness to be saved from arrogance, even though he possesses much knowledge of the Torah and many good deeds, he will inherit Gehenna. For the evil desire always lies in ambush for him, and brings reasons and proofs in order to make him arrogant, for the whole mission of the evil desire is to destroy a man. Therefore, a man should not be too idle to conquer the evil desire daily. And this is a great battle, as we have found in the case of one of the saintly who met men returning from war with plunder. He said to them, "You have returned from a small war; you must face a great war." They asked him, "What kind of war?" He said to them, "The evil inclination and its hosts, for every other enemy when you conquer him one, two or three times, he will let you be, but the evil desire will not desist from you even if he is conquered a hundred times, as our sages said: "And do not believe in yourself until the day of your death" (Aboth 2:4), for all your days he will be in ambush for you, hoping that perhaps you will turn your attention away from him. And if he defeats you in the smallest matter, he will in the end defeat you in the most serious matters. And since arrogance is the root of many unworthy qualities and since the evil desire participates and mingles in all that goes on in the heart of a man, and the entire purpose of evil desire is to falsify Truth and make the Lie seem true, he teaches man to be proud and brings arguments to justify arrogance, Therefore, you must arm yourself to deal wisely in your struggle against him.

The first of the schemes of the evil desire is to harden the heart and exalt it and to sweeten arrogance and other evil qualities, and even though a man knows clearly that there is sin and wrong in his arrogance, he still transgresses willfully and continues to be arrogant, for the evil desire causes the heart to be drawn after honor until it does not feel the sin of it.

However, in the case of a man who is pure in his deeds and does not boast or vaunt himself since he knows that there is sin in this matter, then the evil desire comes and conducts a war to the death, to overthrow and capture him in his net, and teaches that that which is forbidden is really permitted and presents opinions and citations to the effect that he will be following the commandment and will receive reward for his self honor and boasting. And thus the evil desire says, "You have already attained the heights of wisdom and piety, and it is proper for you to conciliate yourself with a natural desire and try to be liked by people even though you may have to fawn upon them and reveal to them your wisdom and righteousness in order to win their love." The evil desire will even bring proof from the words of our Sages: "Everyone whom people like, God also likes" (Aboth 3:10). But all this is false proof, for this type of reasoning is already a branch of arrogance. But the truth of the matter is, as it is written: "When a man's ways please the Lord, He makes even his enemies to be at peace with him" (Prov. 16:7). And the meaning of this verse is, 'If a man does not boast before others and does not try to be liked by them because of his good deeds, and yet people like him, this is great evidence that the Holy One, Blessed be He, loves him, and has sown (the seeds of) love for him in the hearts of people and has made him a good name on their tongues. In truth there are some individuals who are loved by people and the Holy One Blessed be He hates them, for they do not fulfill His Commandments. For the Holy One Blessed be He loves only those who study the Torah and fulfill its precepts.

After attempting what has been mentioned, the evil desire will entice you to reveal your piety and good deeds before the public and will bring as proof that by doing so you will be influencing others to do good likewise. This feeling also comes from arrogance. Although we have seen some of our great sages, who praised their own conduct, they did this only before their disciples and companions in study, in order that their disciples and companions be drawn after them and emulate their deeds. Certainly, this is a great good deed to make dear to them the performance of good works, but even before his disciples and companions he should not feel proud in his heart when he says, "This I know!" or "This I do!" But before people generally, it is forbidden to expose your good deeds or display your wisdom.

Even though you be modest and pray at length and study Torah at set times, your evil desire will entice you to be proud and say to you, "Now the people who see you will deem you important and honor you because of your good ways. And there is much to be gained, because since you are important in their eyes, they will receive your moral teaching and rebuke."

All this is nothing! When you do good deeds for the sake of the Creator alone, Blessed be He, your words of rebuke will be eagerly welcomed by people, even if you do not think so, for the willingness of people to accept correction from you does not depend on your thoughts.

Now if you can avoid the temptation to display your goodness, the evil desire may tempt you to the other extreme and say to you. "You cannot serve God completely unless you avoid the flatterer altogether. Therefore, conceal your good deeds and do the opposite of what you were previously tempted to do — Pray briefly, and when you study any form of wisdom do it privately and let no one know of your prayer and study other than the Creator alone. And let there not be seen in you any good quality. On the contrary, let there be apparent an idleness or laziness in your Service to God in order that you be not esteemed and thus lose your Heavenly reward, and do not warn people against evil and direct people to do good, and do not let people know that you have wisdom and do not teach it to others and do not show any sign of one who reveres God, as for example, the Tefillin, the Mezuzah and the Tzizit, but on the contrary go along with the crowd and mingle with them in their food, drink and gaiety, and hilarious laughter." All this is the scheme of the evil desire to trap men in his net and he who does these things, believing them to be the performance of God's command, his loss is a million times greater than his reward and he is like one who escapes a small fire into a big fire.

The right way is for him to pray with intent and at length and direct others to do good and warn them against evil and do good deeds both openly and in secret. And if people honor and esteem him — in this no harm is done, since he did not intend to win honor and esteem when he did these things. Therefore, when you do your good deed, consider in your soul from whom you expect a reward. If from God — then your act is completely good; if from another source, your

ORCHOT TZADIKIM

act is not completely good. You should also analyze if the good deed which you do publicly you would do in the extremist privacy and anonymity with the same zeal with which you do it publicly. And if it is clear to you that you would, then your good deed is wholly good.

All that we have recounted here regarding the evil desire is but a drop in the ocean in view of how greatly we must be warned against him, for in everything, in every deed and in every good quality the evil desire comes to destroy and to spoil. We have simply opened the door slightly to inform those who do not know the beginning of their ways, concerning the evil desire. And the wise will understand and hasten to thrust him from within himself as it is written: "And he that has clean hands increases strength" (Job 17:9).

The pride in the attainment of wisdom is praiseworthy, as it is said: "But let him that boasts boast of this — that he understands and knows Me" (Jer. 9:23). Such a one will increase his thanks to the Creator, Blessed be He, and will also increase prayers for wisdom, of which this is an example: "I thank Thee that Thou hast assigned my lot among those who sit in the House of Study and not in the market place," or "Happy are we and how goodly is our portion and how pleasant is our lot!" And on this subject, it is said, "And his heart was lifted up in the ways of the Lord" (II Chron. 17:6). For the man who prizes Wisdom will be of high spiritual worth and lofty of heart concerning all matters pertaining to the world to come, and he will not be contented with what comes to him by chance and he will not be satisfied with what knowledge or wisdom he himself acquires, but he will minimize in his own eyes all his deeds and his soul will strive higher continually, and he will find fault with his soul as though it offers too little in the Service of God, Blessed be He. This type of pride does not harm modesty, but, on the contrary, helps him to rejoice in all good qualities and to be glad when his companions are honored and to concern himself with their honor.

And arrogance against the wicked is exceedingly to be praised, to rebuke them and to shame them, and he must never humble himself to them, and he must command them concerning the good and warn them, as much as lies in his power, against evil. Even though his preaching to them may seem in the eyes of the world like lording over others and boasting, since his intention is for the sake of God he is to be praised. And he should not humble himself before the wicked, following the example of Mordecai who refused to bow before Haman. And wherever he has to perform a commandment of God, let him not bow at all to the wicked to leave the good thing he intends to do, merely because he will be lower in their eyes. And this in itself requires wisdom as to when he should lord it over them in the matter of performing a good deed. For there are times when it is not worthwhile to oppose them, since if he opposes them in his attempt to perform one precept, he may lose the opportunity of persuading them to perform a hundred precepts.

For this reason, the wise person should consider carefully the importance of the matter at issue and the time, and only in accordance with these factors should he plan his actions. For there are matters

ORCHOT TZADIKIM — Chapter One

which it would be better to abandon for their sake and there are matters where he can make no concession at all and must stand up to them with his body and all his might and not yield to them at all. All this applies to the case of God's command being the issue. But, where the difference of opinion or quarrel is about a business matter, he should yield to them and do to them in any secular matter even more than the law requires. And this is a great good deed!

Whoever has the quality of arrogance ought to try and turn away from it for it is very base, and the damage caused by it is great and ever-present, and the worth that is in it is very little. Therefore, , we must distance ourselves from it with all our might, for arrogance brings man to ruin and to humiliation, as it is said: "Pride goes before destruction" (Prov. 16:18), and it is also said: "A man's pride shall bring him low" (Prov. 29:23). And you already know what happened to Pharaoh when he said, "Who is the Lord, that I should hearken unto His voice to let Israel go?" (Exod. 5:2), and to Goliath, the Phillistine, who said: "I do taunt the armies of Israel this day" (I Sam. 17:10), and to Sennacherib, who said, "Who are they among all the gods of these countries that have delivered their country out of my hand?" (Is. 36:20). And Nebeuchadnezzar, when he said, "And who is the god that shall deliver you from my hand?" (Dan. 3:15), and similar instances of those who spoke thusly, and their end was shame and disgrace. And whoever clings to this quality is not saved from sin and wrongdoing, as the Sage said, "A proud and haughty man, scorner is his name. Even he that dealeth in overbearing pride" (Prov. 21:24).

ORCHOT TZADIKIM — Chapter One

And since our words have reached this far on the subject of Arrogance, listen to the words of the Sages. One wise man said: "Who is the one who is never free from worry? He who seeks to attain a height that is too high for him." And they also said: "He who thinks that he knows everything, him people will designate as a fool." And they said further, "Evil deeds are near to Arrogance, and he who has in him a leaning towards evil deeds will incur the hatred of all men." And one Sage said: "As a pleasant countenance is the light of the body so are pleasant qualities the light of the soul."

And he said further: "There is nothing to be gained for himself when a king is arrogant, how much more it is important that other people do not behave so with each other," And he said, "There was once a king, sitting on his kingly throne, who observed his nobles sitting on thrones one higher than the other. So the king said to them, 'How did you dare seat yourselves thus, one above the other without my permission?' The one seated on the highest throne answered, 'The greatness of the pedigree of my family entitles me to sit on a higher place than my companions.' The second one said, 'I deserve my higher throne because of my great wisdom.' The third one answered, 'The humiliation of my soul and my crushed heart have seated me below the others.' Thereupon the king raised him and made him great." And in this connection it is said: "For it is better that it be said to you, 'Come up hither' than that you should be lowered in the presence of the prince" (Prov. 25:7).

When a man sees that the quality of arrogance is growing stronger within him, he should think of things that will frighten his heart, "That he come from a fetid drop and will return to a place of dust and worms, and that he will be compelled to render an accounting before the King of Kings, the Holy One Blessed be He." And he should reflect upon how many arrogant individuals strutted boastfully for a moment and then disappeared from the world, forgotten as though they had never existed, and what did their arrogance gain for them?

Make a fence to restrain yourself at a distance from arrogance and the other evil qualities.

He who desires to root out haughtiness from his heart completely cannot do this by thought alone, but must at first depart from arrogance to its furthest extremity. How? A man who was accustomed to dressing himself in the finest garments such as the haughtiest people wear and wants to turn from this ostentation must overcorrect his defect. If he should wear ordinary clothes in an attempt to correct his fault he will not eradicate his haughtiness from his heart. Or if his custom was to boast and to exalt himself to win honor by words or deeds. There is no means of correcting this unless he goes to the other extreme and conducts himself with the greatest humiliation, sitting below everyone or far to the rear, and wears worn and shabby clothes that disgrace their wearer, and does similar things until he roots out his haughtiness to heart.

The same is true of a man with a hot temper who is angry often. At first, he should conduct himself so that even if they beat him and curse him, he should not feel it at all. He must continue in this manner for a long time until he roots out the very roots of anger from his heart. When he has achieved this, he can then take the middle road and follow it all his life. One should follow this procedure with all evil qualities. At first one should withdraw to the furthest extreme and act thusly for a long time. Afterwards he should take the middle road. And this method of procedure is a complete healing in connection with all evil qualities. And he whose intention continually is to serve the Creator Blessed be He, with every part of himself and in the best manner, will place this path before himself and before his companion. And concerning this it is said: "And to him that ordereth his way aright will I show the salvation of God." (Ps. 50:23).

Sefer
ORCHOT TZADIKIM
Ways of the Righteous

Chapter Two

ON MODESTY

Modesty is indeed a good quality and is the opposite of arrogance. And he who possesses this quality has already turned away his soul from all sorts of evils, and he who has reached this honored lofty degree performs a precept and receives his reward according to the greatness of his humility. For Modesty is the root of Service to God, and a small deed done with Modesty is received by God, Blessed be He, a thousand times more readily than a great deed performed with arrogance. And thus did our Sages say: "The one who sacrifices much and the one who sacrifices little have the same merit, provided that the heart is directed to heaven" (Berakoth 5b Menahoth, 110:a). But a work done with arrogance is not welcomed by God, Blessed be He, for it is an abomination to His Spirit, as it is said: "Every one that is proud in heart is an abomination to the Lord" (Proverbs 16:5). "And because of this he cries and is not answered, as it is said: "Yea, when ye make many prayers, I will not hear" (Isaiah 1:15). And a man of arrogance may perform the precepts and they tear them to pieces before his eyes, as it is said: "Oh, that there were even one among you that would shut the doors (of the Temple so that the arrogant would not presume to serve Me!)" (Mal. 1:10). And when an arrogant person brings a sacrifice, it is not received, as it is said: "Who hath required this at your hands, to trample My courts?" (Is. 1:12). And, it is said: "Add your burnt offerings unto your sacrifices and eat ye flesh" (Jer. 7:21). (That is to say. "Don't offer your burnt offerings to Me; I do not want them.")

But a man with the quality of modesty and humility attains all good for it is said: "But unto the humble He giveth grace" (Prov. 3:34). And, inasmuch as he has grace in the eyes of the Holy One, Blessed is He, when he cries out, he is answered at once, as it is said: "Before they call, I will answer" (Is. 65:24). And when a humble man performs the precepts, they are received with pleasure and joy, and it is said: "For God hath already accepted thy works" (Eccl. 9:7), and not only this, for God longs for them, as it is said: "Then shall the offering of Judah and Jerusalem be pleasant with the Lord" (Mal. 3:4).

And what really is modesty? It is humility and lowliness of the spirit, regarding oneself as nothing. And a man must feel this constantly — to be low in his own eyes, humble of soul, tender of heart, and broken in spirit. The root of modesty is that he shall consider, while he is at peace and quiet, healthy and rich, that the Creator, Blessed be He, has done much good to him, and that he is undeserving of all that God has given him. And he should think about the greatness of God and the exaltation of His glory, and should consider, "What am I? Am I not a small humble creature and I am in a lowly transitory world." And he should further think, "All the good deeds that I am able to do are nothing but a drop in the ocean in contrast with what I ought to do." And he must do all of his deeds for the honor of Heaven, and not to flatter any man, or for the sake of pleasure, but he must do everything for the sake of God's Great Name. This is the root of modesty

But a person who feels humility before the Creator, Blessed be He, only when he becomes ill in body or in any limb, or when his children or friends die, or when he loses his wealth or high position, or when he grows old, this may belong to the realm of modesty and humility, and is accepted by God, Blessed be He, but does not reach the essence of modesty.

And he must conduct himself in his dealings with people and in money matters with even greater care for their interests than the law demands (beyond the letter of the law), and all his transactions with people should be with humility and gentleness. And the essence of modesty is that he should be humble before those who are in a lower position than he. For example, to his help and his household, and to those poor who obtain their sustenance or benefit from him — to those from whom he never needs or expects any favors, and whom he does not fear.

He who is humble before widows and strangers and bears their troubles and burdens, and he who hears shameful insults but does not retort because of the greatness of his modesty — this is modesty indeed!

There is still another excellent modesty; for example, one who is humble before his Rabbi or Teacher and before the wise and before the righteous ones who follow the paths of righteousness, and thinks in his heart, "These are the servants of God, Blessed be He — His ministers and those who love Him." And because of this he humbles himself before them and honors them. This too is excellent modesty — that he should think, "I will be humble before the wise in order that they should bring me near to them and teach me and correct me and guide me in the way of the Lord, Blessed is He." And there is another excellent modesty — that he should be humble before his pupils and that he should explain every hidden meaning, to the more apt pupil according to his ability, and to the less able pupil according to his ability. And let him explain and explain again and again with a pleasant expression and demeanor until the pupil understands the matter, and he should not say, "How can I stay with him until he understands; his mind is like a rock." And he, the teacher, should clearly outline and arrange the lesson pleasantly many times. Surely, you already know the reward of Rabbi Pereda who reviewed one lesson with a pupil four hundred times (Erubin 54b).

And there is another excellent modesty — to study in the presence of the very young and ask them to explain something that he, the teacher, does not understand. And he should not say, "How can I study in the presence of youngsters and how can I seek and expect to find an answer from him when he is younger than I?" And on this subject, it is said: "From all my mentors I have learned" (Ps. 119:99). And further did our Sages say: "Be exceedingly humble" (Aboth 4:4), in the presence of all men. Not before the great alone must one be humble in spirit, but also before the small.

And he who walks in this path will cause the many to be meritorious, for he will be liked by all who see him and all his deeds and the manner of them will be acceptable to them. And always will they praise him and every man will bless his son that he be like this modest man. And thus, he sanctifies the Name of God, Blessed be He. But he who vaunts himself, profanes the Name of God, Blessed be He, and causes others to sin, such a person can be compared to a carcass that is cast out into the street and every passerby puts his hand to his nose until he passes by. Thus, is the arrogant man — he puts the Torah to shame and those who study it, and causes people to shun the Torah, for they say, "What worth is there in the Torah if those who study it are evil?". And reasoning thus, they turn away from Torah.

Modesty can be recognized in a man in six ways:

1. When a man can restrain his anger as, for example, when another shames him exceedingly by words or deeds and he is tempted to avenge the insult, but he controls his wrath and forgives the offender because of the Creator, Blessed be He. That is a sign of modesty. There are times, however, when it is forbidden to forgive an offender, as in the case of a wise scholar whom someone shames in public. In that case, the offender should appease the scholar he has insulted.

2. The second is when a man suffers a great loss —or his children die — and he declares his faith in the Justice of God, Blessed be He, and receives His Judgment with love, as it is said: "And Aaron was silent" (Lev. 10:3). And this certainly teaches what humble and modest conduct is.

3. If a man should hear that everyone praises him because of his wisdom and his good deeds, he should not rejoice at this but think that his good deeds are few compared to what he should do, and that they are nothing but a drop in the sea.

And, of course, if people credit him with good deeds he did not do, he should not rejoice at this but on the contrary feel great pain in his heart that he should have gotten credit for something he did not do. Also, in the case where somebody told evil tales concerning him — if these are true — he should not seek to twist the truth and thus clear himself, but do as Judah who said: "She is more in the right than I" (Gen. 38:26). And he should not try to contradict the man that told these tales, nor should he hate him because he revealed the matter, but he should bow humbly before the Creator, Blessed be He, that he has revealed a little of much that could have been revealed, in order to rebuke him and correct him that he might return to God.

Now, if what the man told about him is false, he should not shame the accuser or quarrel angrily with him. There was one of the Sages about whom a man spoke evil falsely. And when the pious Sage learned of this, he sent the maligner a gift with this written message: "You sent me a gift out of your merits, and now I reward you with this gift, which I send you herewith." For on the Day of Judgment they will display before many people good deeds that they did not perform, and these people will say, "But we did not perform these precepts." Then the Court of Heaven will answer them, "Those people who spoke evil of you performed these good deeds and we are taking them away from them and giving them to you." And, in the same way, they will show evil deeds to the wicked — evil deeds that those wicked people did not do. And when the wicked protest, "We did not commit these particular wicked deeds," the Heavenly Court will answer, "These sins were committed by those against whom you gossiped, and these sins have Therefore, been taken from them and added to yours." And this is the meaning of what is said: "And render unto our neighbors (who gossip against us) sevenfold into their bosom their reproach, wherewith they have reproached Thee, O Lord!" (Ps. 79:12). For anyone who reviles a righteous man, it is as though he reviles the Lord, Blessed be He. For the enemies of Israel are called the "enemies of God" in many places. And in connection with speaking against the righteous, the Torah has warned us: "Remember what the Lord your God did to Miriam on the journey ..." (Deut. 24:9).

Therefore, one who bears insult and is silent is recognized to be truly modest. And so have we found in Shabbath 31b concerning Hillel the Prince, when a man insulted him and said, "Let there not be many like you in Israel," that Hillel did not fly into a temper. And there is a statement in the Midrash, "No one can be called modest unless he can hear himself reviled and not answer as if it is written: 'And Miriam and Aaron spoke against Moses! (And it does not say that Moses responded). And following this it is written: And the man Moses was exceedingly modest'."

And concerning these that are not worried about their own honor but love God, it is written in Judges 5:31 and commented upon in Shabbath 88b: "But they that love Him be as the sun when he goeth forth in his might." (Our Rabbis taught: "Those who are insulted but do not insult, hear themselves reviled without answering, act through love and rejoice in suffering.")

4. The fourth manifestation of true modesty is if the Creator, Blessed be He, deals well with a man in giving him wealth and children, and also gives him great wisdom, understanding and honor. That man should become even more modest and humble before the Creator, Blessed be He, and honor men and do good to them more than before. As in the case of Abraham when the Holy One, Blessed be He, said to him: "Shall I hide from Abraham what I am about to do, since Abraham is to become a great and populous nation..." (Gen. 18:17-18). Abraham responded, "And I am dust and ashes."

Much of the wisdom and much of the wealth that we see multiplying in the hands of some people in this world come to them for one of three reasons:

The first is as a goodness sent by the Holy One, Blessed be He. The second is as a trial or temptation. The third is wealth acquired as an act of vengeance.

The first reason — wealth and wisdom as the benificence of God, can be evidenced by the fact that this rich man harms no man with his money, nor does the wise man use his wisdom to harm any man. And when this man with his wisdom and this man with his wealth add to the Service of the Holy One, Blessed be He, in accordance with their interest, then you may be sure that this wealth and wisdom come from the Holy One, Blessed be He.

The sign of wealth or wisdom as temptation is that the possessor of the wealth is occupied with guarding his wealth, and is constantly concerned about losing his money and does not enjoy his wealth to obtain power or to consume what it buys. The possessor does no harm to anyone with his wealth, and does not boast of it, but bothers constantly to gather more wealth and worries about guarding it. He does not give alms and does not show pity to the poor. He does not feed them and he does not clothe them. And so is it with the wise man who devotes most of his wisdom to temporary worldly matters and desires to fill the needs of the moment but does not use his wisdom for an evil or good purpose. These are certainly trials.

And the third is wealth acquired and held as an act of vengeance. And the sign of this is that the owner of the money harms others with his wealth and boasts of it, and does not give charity, and is fully occupied with enjoying it as it is written: "And behold joy and gladness, slaying oxen and killing sheep" (Is. 22:13), and it says further: "And the harp and the psaltery, the tabret and the pipe, and wine are in their feasts" (Ibid. 5:12). And he does not pay of all his wealth that which is due to the Holy One, Blessed be He. On this it is said: "Riches kept by the owner thereof to his hurt" (Eccl. 5:12). And thus, it is with the wise when he schemes to do evil deeds and not good deeds with his wisdom, as it is said: "They are wise to do evil, but to do good they have no knowledge" (Jer. 4:22). Then his wisdom is a stumbling block to him.

Therefore, the intelligent person will do with his wealth and his wisdom the good he can, according to the extent of his wealth and wisdom, and will add to his modesty and humility and his heart will not grow haughty and he will always worry whether this wealth is not his sole reward. Such a person belongs to those who fear that their wealth may destroy them and of whom it is said: "But who instantly requites with distraction those who reject him" (Deut. 7:10). The wise man, too, will worry whether he is among those of whom it is said: "They are wise to do evil and do not know how to do good" (Jer. 4:22). And every man is obligated to grow wiser and to understand more clearly and continue to attain through his wisdom good deeds until his wisdom can achieve no more.

5. The fifth way in which modesty could be recognized in a man is when he rebukes himself because of some evil he has done to someone through deeds or words, and although he has no need whatever of the friendship of that man and never expects to receive some benefit from him, he, nevertheless, voluntarily and without any one urging him, goes to the person he has offended and asks his forgiveness, humbles himself before him and corrects what he has done wrong and speaks words of supplication and pleading to him he has offended. This, too, is a sign of true modesty.

6. The sixth way in which true modesty can be recognized is if a man customarily speaks soft words, as it is said: "A soft answer turneth away wrath" (Prov. 15:1), and with a low voice, for this speaks of humility as it is said: "And you shall be humbled and shall speak from the ground and your speech shall be low out of the dust" (Is. 29:4). And he should not occupy himself with the beauty of clothes and ornaments, as it is said: "For He saves the humble-eyed person" (Job 22:29). And he should not occupy himself with the pursuit of pleasure, as it is said: "The righteous eats to satisfy his soul" (Prov. 13:25), and not more. All these are the signs of Modesty.

Modesty is a ladder by which one ascends to the ways of the Holy One, Blessed be He, as it is said: "He guides the humble in justice and He teaches the humble His way" (Ps. 25:9). Through humility he attains the reverence of God, Blessed be He, as it is said: "The reward of humility is fear" (Prov. 22:4). The Shekinah dwells on the humble as it is said: "I dwell... with him that is of a contrite and humble spirit" (Is. 57:15). The Holy One, Blessed be He, ignored all the high mountains and hills and inclined His Spirit to Mount Sinai and descended to this lowly mountain. And it is written: "Awake and sing, ye that dwell in the dust — for thy dew is as the dew of light" (Is. 26:19). He that lives in the dust in his earthy life will live in the world to come.

And it is written: "For though the Lord be high, yet He regards the lowly" (Ps. 138:6) (See Sotah 5a).

And he who makes his heart as nothing but flesh — his prayer will be heard, as it is written: "All flesh will come to bow before Me, said the Lord" (Is. 66:23) (See Sotah 5a). And it is written: "O Thou that hearest prayer, unto Thee does all flesh come" (Ps. 65:3).

Rabbi Joshua ben Levi said, "Come and see how great before the Holy One, Blessed be He, are the lowly in spirit. When the Temple was still standing, if a man offered a burnt offering, he received the reward of a burnt offering; if he offered a meal offering, he received the reward of a meal offering; but he whose spirit is humble is said by Scripture to be as though he had offered all of the sacrifices, for it is said: "The sacrifices of God are a broken spirit" (Ps. 51:19). Not only this but his prayer is not rejected for it is also said in the same verse: "A broken and contrite heart, O God, Thou will not despise." (And this is commented upon in Sotah 5b.)

Many good branches sprout from the root of modesty. The modest person is patient and from patience comes peace and with humility one can quiet the wrath of a man who is angry with him, as it is said: "A soft answer turns away wrath" (Prov. 15:1), and seeking peace is a very good quality indeed.

The modest person has charm, as it is said: "And He gives grace to the humble" (Prov. 3:34). The prayer of the modest person is received before the Holy One, Blessed be He, for he, the modest person, is always generous and waives his claims against others. And it is because of this that the prayer of Rabbi Akiba was received when he began, "Our Father, our King" as is commented upon in Ta'anith 25b. The modest man merits increasing wisdom, for he is humble in the presence of the wise and sits at their feet, as it is said: "He that walks with wise men shall be wise" (Prov. 13:20). Heaven has mercy upon the humble person, as it is said: "He who confesses his wrongs and forsakes them shall obtain mercy" (Prov. 28:13).

The modest person flees from greatness and from honor and it is on this that the modesty of a person really depends, as it is said: "And to walk humbly with thy God" (Michah 6:8).

The modest person is happy with the portion that the Holy One, Blessed be He, has allotted him, whether it be great or small, as it is said: "Better is a little that the righteous has" (Ps. 37:16). And with his rejoicing in his portion, he quiets his heart from the hustle-

ORCHOT TZADIKIM   Chapter Two

bustle of this world, and thus his heart is left open to search wisdom and to the service of the Holy One, Blessed be He.

The modest person judges every man favorably. An example of this is when they asked one of the pious: "By what means did you merit to become the master of the wise of your generation?". He responded: "Because I credited every man, I saw with being better than I. If he were wiser than I, I said, 'He is also more reverent to God than I because of his greater wisdom,' and if he were less wise than I, I would say, 'Any fault he commits he does unknowingly, but I, whatever sin I commit, do so knowingly.' If he were older than I, I would say, 'He has amassed more merits than I,' but if I were older than he, I would say, 'His sins are less than mine,' and if he were like me in wisdom and in years, I would say, 'His heart is better directed to God than mine, for I know the sins I have committed and I do not know the sins he has committed.' And if he were richer than I, I would say, 'He gives more charity than I,' and if he were poorer than I, I would say 'he is more crushed and lowly in spirit than I and is better than I.' And for these reasons I honored all men and humbled myself before them."

The faults of a humble person are quickly forgotten because people seek to honor such a person, and the modest person finds many helpers. For example, they said of a certain king who was lodging with many people one night that he himself arose and adjusted the lamp so that it should not be extinguished. His followers said to him, "Why did you not command us to do this?" He said to them, "As king I felt it to be my duty" (noblesse oblige).

And the sages said, "Every virtue is envied except modesty," and they said further, "He who is lowly in his own eyes is great in the eyes of others."

But in exercising the quality of humility we ought to shun being submissive and modest before the wicked, and on this subject Scripture has said: "As a troubled fountain and a corrupted spring, so is a righteous man that gives way before the wicked" (Prov. 25:26). And if he has the power, he should avenge the wickedness of the wicked, for the honor of God's Name, and add strength to his rebuke against them and stand against them like a roaring lion to save the plundered from the plunderer. And let him teach others the true Service of the Holy One, Blessed be He, and rebuke them with all his might, according to his wisdom — first gently, and, if this does not succeed then he must shame them. He must constantly command them to do good and warn them away from evil, with mouth and tongue, according to his wisdom, and he must hasten to exact what is due to God and not be submissive or humble in this.

There is a modesty which is as evil as arrogance, as in the case of the false prophets who used to dress in the humble garments of the prophets of truth in order that people should accept their lies and falsehoods, as it is said: "Neither shall they wear a hairy mantle to deceive" (Zech. 13:4).

Therefore, , those who are modest in their dress and speak gently and conduct themselves as pious and just in order that others should believe them and depend upon their works, and flatter those who should not be flattered, and make secret schemes and do not worry about fulfilling the commandments except when they are in the public eye and not when they are alone, and thus deceive the people — these are profaners of God, Blessed be He, more than all others — for they cause people to disbelieve the good teachers and prophets, for these latter are then suspected by people who say, "Perhaps these men are like those who deceived us." When anyone recognizes a false and lying prophet, he should spread this abroad and let everyone know, as our Sages said: "We must publicly expose those who are flatterers" (Yoma 86b).

Therefore, arouse yourself and do not be reluctant to weaken the temptation within you to exalt yourself and to deceive. And do not hold back because you see many of your contemporaries still clinging to these qualities and not attempting to eradicate them, and they say to those who rebuke them, "Who is the man without some pride, and who is the man who is constantly upright in his business dealings, never taking advantage of a person, and all of whose deeds are faultless? Surely there are many people better and greater than I that do such and such. Therefore, I will do as they do and whatever happens to them in the world to come will also happen to me." Those who think thus are guilty of unequalled folly. As an analogy, take the case of one whose eyes pain him greatly and he has a certain remedy that is excellent for healing the eye, and all people know the positive worth of this remedy, it is not wise to say, "I will apply no medicine, and if I become blind what of it? There are a lot of blind people in the world and what happens to them will happen to me." Surely, this type of reasoning is nonsense and to be scorned by everyone.

Therefore, scrutinize well your soul and try with all your power not to let your eyes dwell on those who are below you in wisdom and in Service to God — for then you, yourself, will be lessened in the service of the Holy One, Blessed is He, and in the quality of wisdom. But rather, pay heed with your eyes and your heart to him who is above you, and try to follow his example and to emulate him according to your ability in exercising wisdom and in the service of the Holy One, Blessed be He. And on this subject, it is said in Hosea 6:3: "And let us know — eagerly strive to know the Lord, His going forth is as sure as the morning, and He shall come unto us as the rain, as the latter rain that watered (instructs) the earth".

Sefer

ORCHOT TZADIKIM

Ways of the Righteous

Chapter Three

ON SHAME

The Sages have said: "Intelligence is a sense of shame and a sense of shame is intelligence." For regarding Adam and Eve, it is said: "The two of them were naked and yet they felt no shame" (Gen. 2:25). And they did not understand what modesty is and they could not distinguish between good and evil. But, after they had eaten of the Tree of Knowledge, it is said: "Then the eyes of both of them were opened" (Gen. 3:7).

And thus, with all living creatures outside of man there is no sense of shame, since they have no wisdom. Every one wise of heart knows the worth of the virtue of intelligence and wisdom, for through this virtue he attains the truth of things and also the concept of the oneness of his Creator, Blessed is He, and how to serve Him — and in serving God man can be like the angels.

And since the virtue of wisdom is so great it is necessary that her companion, a sense of shame, who resembles wisdom, should be ever near to her. And the proof of the matter is that you have never seen a man with a sense of shame who is not an intelligent and knowing person, and conversely, you have never seen an intelligent and knowing person who is without the sense of shame. Therefore, it is fitting for every person to try and find pleasure in the exercise of this important virtue, and to cleave to it until it becomes fixed and established in his soul. He must make it the strongest quality in his nature, and it must be in his eyes the most important quality he possesses, for through it he will attain most of the other virtues and will be restrained from sins and from all ugly qualities.

The quality of shame is a fence and an iron partition between a man and all manner of sins, for a man may commit many sins in private that he would be ashamed to do in public. An example cited by our Sages: "When Rabbi Johanan ben Zakkai was about to expire, his disciples said to him, 'Our teacher, bless us!' And he said to them, 'May the fear of Heaven be upon you as much as you fear human beings!' They asked in wonder, 'Shall we indeed fear God only as much as we fear human beings and no more?' Whereupon, he said to them, 'Would that it was so, if only you would realize that when a man commits a sin he thinks "I hope no one sees me,"' (Berachoth 28b). All because he is afraid of being disgraced in the eyes of people, and this fear of disgrace often restrains him from doing a sinful act. Eventually, he will refrain from doing a sinful act from nobler motives (Pesahim 50b).

But the highest form of the virtue of shame is that he should be ashamed before the Holy One, Blessed is He, as it is said: "O my God, I am ashamed and blush to lift up my face to Thee" (Ezra 9:6). And if you should think, "How can I be ashamed before Him whom I cannot see with my eyes?" you should truly know that even though the Holy One, Blessed is He, is hidden from the eyes of all the living, He is found in our hearts and is revealed in our thoughts. Man can attain a higher degree in his sense of shame if he meditates in solitude on the greatness of God, Blessed is He, and if he remembers constantly the Holy One, Blessed is He, who sees his deeds and searches the reins and sees his thoughts. As an example, one of our Sages said, "If you have guarded yourself all your days not to sin, do not take credit for yourself because the beginning of turning away from sin lies in your being ashamed of what people will think of you." Therefore, a person should be very careful to guard against this motive and to keep in his heart when he avoids sin that he does not refrain from sin because of shame from his fellows, for the evil desire prompts him to concern himself with the opinion of his fellows, saying, "If you do this people will hold you in contempt." Therefore, a man should place as first above all — that he must know his Creator, recognize His power, and decide in his heart whom he wishes to serve and whom he fears, whose command he wishes to obey and who has warned him. As David said to Solomon, his son: "Know thou the God of thy father and serve Him with a whole heart and with a willing mind" (I Chron. 28:9). In this way he will attain to the degree where he is ashamed only before God.

It is clearly known that all people do many things in secret, speak many things in secret, and think many thoughts, and the only thing they fear is that these matters will become known. If all their deeds that they did from their youth and all the words they spoke and all the thoughts they thought were to be exposed and revealed before everyone, they would suffer the greatest embarrassment. Then how much more ought one to be ashamed before the Holy One, Blessed is He, who looks into the hearts of men and sees their thoughts and knows all the deeds, words and thoughts that a man has done all his life long, and does not forget — how much more ought we to be ashamed before Him!

There are four stages in a sense of shame. The first is a person who is ashamed to do sins in public and sins in secret. Such a person insults God for he shows that he cares more for people's opinion than he does for God's opinion, and his transgression is a great one.

The second is a person who is ashamed to do wrong publicly and holds back from sinning even privately because he feels that somehow his sin will become known and then he will be ashamed before God, Blessed is He, and man (for his fault will be a profanation of the Name.) Of this person our Sages said: "From a base motive he will arrive at following a precept for its own sake" (Pesahim 50b).

The third is a person who thinks, "How shall I do this evil in secret and show more shame before a servant (human beings) than before the master (God) and thereby attempt to deceive God." Thus, he holds back from the transgression. This is a good virtue.

The fourth is a person who is ashamed before God alone, Blessed is He, for anything wrong he does publicly or privately. There is no quality above this virtue.

Our Sages said: "Anyone who does a transgression and is ashamed of his deed is forgiven for all his sins" (Berakoth 12b). And they said further, "He who has a sense of shame is destined for Paradise" (Aboth 5:42). And our Sages said, "Faith and a sense of shame are linked together, for the one who is ashamed before people shows that he believes in people. If he did not believe in the importance and worth of people he would not care for their opinion and Therefore, would not be ashamed before them." The wise man said, "If it brings you no shame do all that you desire."

A man should accustom himself not to do anything that will embarrass his companion and make him too ashamed to protest — as, for example, if he should suddenly enter into the privacy of his companion uninvited or stay as a house guest; and his companion is painfully ashamed to tell him to leave. Or if he reads from the diary, letters or other private papers of his companion and his companion is too embarrassed to tell him not to read his personal papers, and similar instances.

And he should be careful not to impose upon his companion in any way by asking him for something, a gift — or requesting him to loan him some utensils or money when he knows his companion does not do these things willingly but is ashamed to turn the petitioner away empty handed.

He who has the quality of shame will find it difficult to bear the fact that his companion is put to shame because of him. On this subject the wise man said, "Love that friend who clearly shows that he cannot do without your help, even though you need his help more than he needs yours, and who forgives you if you wrong him in such a manner that it would appear that he was in the wrong, and asks of your things he does not need in order that you may not be embarassed to ask him for things that you do need."

He who wishes to accustom himself to having a sense of shame should sit constantly in the presence of those of whom he is ashamed of doing anything wrong in their presence.

A man should not lose his dignity by constantly begging favors of people, for if you do lose your dignity, you will find it difficult to find some one who will restore it.

There is a man who brings shame on his friend not because he hates him but because he wants to free himself from a sense of shame. Such a man says, "What did I do? So and so did the same thing I did." In this way he makes light of his wrongful act. From these great evils follow: First he brings others to shame because he feels less guilty by making light of his sin. Second, he will find it difficult to repent for he thinks, "What did I do? So and so did likewise." And third, he causes others to sin because as long as he removes his own feeling of guilt, he will excuse the act in others and even induce them to do likewise. And if he lies about others in order to make his guilt and shame seem less, then his guilt is exceedingly great for he ascribes disgrace and shame to good people. And many more evils result from this.

There is a person who is ashamed of keeping away from sins. For example, where his fellow citizens commit certain sin — as to ogle at women who pass by and similar lewd conduct, and they mock anyone who does not do likewise. In such a case a man ought to strengthen himself to bear the shame they heap upon him and resist sinning no matter how they belittle him for clinging to his morals.

And there is he who is ashamed when he follows certain commandments of the Torah that many people no longer follow, and these people laugh at him for following these "outmoded precepts". He should bear their mockery and fulfill the commandment. And a person should never abandon any precept or religious practice because he is ashamed to perform it before people, for he should rather be ashamed before the Creator, may He be Blessed, who commanded the performance of these precepts.

For it is clear that the servant of a king will not abandon the king's command though he bears much shame from everyone who may laugh at him for performing that which his king commanded him. And he who cannot bear the shame in performing the precept and is ashamed to fulfill the command of God — and thus forsakes the path of good out of fear of shame — this kind of shame is very evil. And thus, if he is ashamed to admit the truth, this too is an evil disease. And thus, if he is too shy to rebuke people and command them to do good. And thus, if he sits before his teacher and is too ashamed to ask what he does not know, whether it be a small matter or a big matter, such an attitude is very ugly. In these cases, Scripture says: "Do not act foolishly by exalting yourself nor by cunningly keeping silent" (Prov. 30:32). And our Sages of Blessed Memory said: "The one who is ashamed (to ask questions) does not learn" (Aboth 2:5). The proper way is never to be ashamed to ask concerning what one does not know whether it be a small matter or a large one. Did you not see that David, King of Israel, said in Psalms 119:46: "And I will speak of Thy testimonies before kings and I shall not be ashamed."

A pious man is so called because he has a sense of shame, for the word 'hassid' or 'pious' means 'white', for the translation of 'stork' (Hassidah) in Aramaic is " hawaeita " meaning "the white one", as you note in Leviticus 11:19, and similarly in Isaiah 29:22: "Neither shall his face now become white" (with shame), and the Aramaic translation of "herpah" (shame) is hisda (same as Hassid), as you will note in Genesis 34:14. And all of this for what reason? That the Hassid or pious person must bear shame in order to fulfill the Torah, and he must remove shame from his face at performing any precept. Then he is called a Hassid or "pious one", and thus he attains to prophecy as it is written: "Then didst Thou speak in vision to Thy pious ones" (Ps. 89:20). And through his sense of shame, he will attain to true reverence of God, as it is written: "In order that His awe be upon your faces and you do not sin" (Exod. 20:20). What kind of awe or fear of God can be seen in a person's face? You must surely say, "A sense of shame" (which causes the face to change color) (Nedarim 20a).

And one should be very careful not to shame any man for the Sages said: "He who whitens (shames) the face of another in public has no portion in the world to come" (Baba Mezià 59a). To whiten another's face is like murder, for the red departs and the white comes (thus one is spilling the blood of the shamed one within him) (Ibid., 58b). And the Sage said further:

The pain of shame is worse than death. A person should allow himself to be burnt alive and not shame his fellow in public. And they learned this from Tamar who, even though they brought her forth to be burned, did not want to shame Judah (Berakoth 43b). And even when you are required to rebuke another the Torah says: "You shall surely rebuke your neighbor and not bear sin because of him" (Lev. 19:17). How shall you rebuke? At first, secretly and gently. However, if you rebuke him at the beginning in public and shame him, then you have sinned because of this, (Arakin 16b). And this is all the truer where one shames another where no rebuke is called for.

And the destruction of Jerusalem was caused because of the shaming of Bar Kamtzah (Gittin 58b).

Therefore, one should be most careful not to do anything that will cause anyone in the world shame. Even when he discusses Torah with another and hears his companion make a mistake, he should not say to him, "You made a mistake!" or "You don't understand!" or any similar expression, so that his companion be not shamed, but he should pretend that he is not aware that his companion made a mistake. Nor in conversing should he directly refer by nickname to a man so as not to embarrass him. But if he wants to speak with someone who has a nickname, or even about him out of his presence, he should say, "So and so, from such and such a place" or "the son of so and so" or mention a few characteristics that will identify him without using the nickname.

And a man should never say publicly or privately, "This one (naming him) wanted to give me his daughter as a wife but I did not want her." For in this way he honors himself and shames another. And thus, he must be extremely careful in every matter that no shame should be borne by another because of his words.

Let a man always be among the shamed ones rather than among those who shame others, and among those who hear insults and do not respond, for of them it is said in Judges 5:31 "But they that love Him shall be as the sun when he goes forth in his might". This is commented on in Shabbath 88b: "Measure for measure! Because he heard insult and his face turned pallid (and yet he was silent) God will cause his face to shine more than the light of the sun, as it is similarly said in Isaiah 60:1, 'And the glory of the Lord has shone upon thee.' "

From the sense of shame, one reaches humility, for he humbles himself before people because of his sense of shame. And one reaches the state of sincere modesty, since one with a sense of shame will not do any wrong acts openly. The Sages said, "Of good children — a sense of shame is written on their faces, for he who has a sense of shame — it is a sign that he is from the seed of Abraham, Issac and Jacob" (Yebamoth 79a). The Sages said, "A sense of shame is known at a time of anger" (when even his wrath does not cause a man to do or say something of which he will be ashamed.) And they also said, "Easier it is to bear the hatred of a person with a sense of shame than the love of a fool." A man should have a sense of shame before any man and place upon his face the mask of shame that shows his feelings clearly. As you know of in the case of Saul, when he hid because of his modesty, as it is said: "Behold he has hid himself among the baggage" (I Sam. 10:22). And God chose him to be king, as it is said: "Have you seen him whom the Lord has chosen?" (I Sam. 10:24). The Sages said, "This quality of modesty is among the best qualities of a precious soul."

And it perfects the nature of a truly pious man as complete physical health perfects the body. And he who has the sense of shame is of greater worth. The rest you will seek and understand more clearly.

Sefer ORCHOT TZADIKIM
Ways of the Righteous

Chapter Four

ON IMPUDENCE

Impudence, or shamelessness, is a most inferior trait in all of its manifestations. It is the opposite of modesty, for the one who is humble and has a sense of shame is generous, compassionate, forgiving and pardoning. But he who is impudent does not feel shame before any man, but stands rudely before all men, does every evil thing, without shame, but on the contrary, clings obstinately to his evil and grows harder in his transgressions. Concerning this type of person, it is said: "They have made their faces harder than a rock! They have refused to repent" (Jer. 5:3). And it is said: "And the children are brazen-faced and hard-hearted" (Ezek. 2:4).

And the opposite of all good traits that appear in the modest person are found in the impudent. When a man persists in this quality and increases in impudence, he becomes very disgusting in the eyes of all people, no matter how wise he is. Many evils follow in the train of impudence. He who deals impudently with others will not be free from quarrels, hatred and jealousy. And he who is of the impudent ones denies the uniqueness of God. Such a person cannot bear the presence of a great man and cannot be gracious to the old, and all the transgressions in the Torah are trivial in his eyes — all because of his great impudence. And of him it is said: "The impudent to Gehenna!" (Aboth 5:20).

The impudent person is called wicked, as it is said: "A wicked man hardens his face" (Prov. 21:29). And the wicked are ugly and despicable before the Lord, Blessed He be. And the name of the wicked is ugly, as it is written: "But the name of the wicked shall rot" (Prov. 10:7). On the quality of a sense of shame it is said: "And He teaches the humble His way" (Ps. 25:9). And concerning the wicked impudent it is said: "But the way of the wicked He makes crooked" (Ps. 146:9).

He who has the trait of impudence commits sins in great quantities and yet considers himself righteous. And it is in this vein that we confess our sins by declaring, "We are not impudent and stiff-necked to say before Thee O Lord our Lord 'We are altogether righteous and we have not sinned.' " And this is a very wretched and evil quality — one who is wicked and yet says "I have not sinned." And for this the Holy One, Blessed is He, judges him and has no mercy upon him, as it is written: "Behold I will enter into judgment with you because you say 'I have not sinned' "(Jer. 2:35). And He has said: "He that covers his transgressions shall not prosper, but who so confesses and forsakes them shall obtain mercy" (Prov. 28:13). And this path of the hard and impudent is far indeed from the paths of repentance. And of the harlot it is said in Proverbs 7:13: "With an impudent face she said to him...". This quality is very evil, for it brings man to shaming his companion and the poor, as it is said: "The poor pleads but the rich answer impudently" (Prov. 18:23). And how much eviller is it when he shames his teachers and acts impudently towards them, and hardens his neck to those who rebuke him because of his excessive rudeness — then this evil quality can remove him from the world. It is proper that a man should far remove any touch of impudence from his soul.

But this very quality of impudence is very praiseworthy in connection with the Torah and Service to God — to be impudent towards the wicked and stiffen the neck against them in order not to listen to their counsel, and not to accept their lies and abominations and not to flatter them. And a man should have a touch of impudence in observing the commandments if people laugh at him for doing so. He must "harden his face", be bold towards his teachers, to ask what he does not know and not be ashamed in doing this, and he must "harden his face" or be bold in rebuking people and in revealing to them their sins.

And a man should strengthen himself in connection with this quality — to subdue it where it would be shameful to assume it, and to strengthen himself over it according to his strength. For it is very difficult to completely escape from this evil quality if he does not pit the maximum of his strength and the very might of his power against it to conquer it and remove it from his presence in the place where it would be sinful to use it, and to set it up within him and in his face in such a place where he would receive a reward for his obstinance.

Sefer

ORCHOT TZADIKIM

Ways of the Righteous

Chapter Five

ON LOVE
The quality of love involves more deeds than all the other qualities. And when a man uses the quality of love for evil there is not a single quality so evil. But when a man uses the quality of his love for good, then that quality is higher than all others, as it is written: "And you shall love the Lord your God" (Deut. 6:5). And there is no greater virtue in the Service of the Creator than he who serves Him out of love.

And now listen how love can spoil good deeds when his love is stronger than his wisdom. For there are all sorts of different kinds of love. One love is the love of a man for his children, and because of his great love, he may not correct them and guide them to the good path, and he permits them to go in the obstinacy of their evil hearts, and out of this can come great harm.

The second love is the love for money, and because of his great desire for money, his business dealings may not be honest and he covets, plunders, and robs, in order to amass wealth. And because of his great longing for wealth, he closes his hand from giving alms and is miserly.

The third love is the love of men for their wives. And if a man has a bad wife — conceited and self-centered — she may remove from his heart the desire to fulfill the commandments and draw him after her. And because of his great love for her he is not firm with her and listens to her counsel, and she can bring him to evil acts. And it can also happen that a man, because of his great love of women, will gaze at them constantly and speak disgraceful things and come to immoral conduct.

The fourth love is the love of a man for his relatives — his father and his mother, his brothers and his sisters and the rest of his kind, friends and companions, and because of his love for them he helps them in their quarrels, and does not feel, nor does he ascertain whether or not his relatives did wrong against the other party of the quarrel, but always helps, protects and shelters them. And even if they have broken forth into wild and boisterous conduct, he protects them. And he may even listen to their advice, and even if the advice is not good, he will not turn away from their words. He may even want to raise them to positions for which they are not fitted — for example, to make them rulers and leaders of their generations, to dominate and govern the people. And even if they are wicked, he does not sense it, for love blinds his eyes and makes deaf his ears, and there is, in this nepotism, great damage, for they will cause others to go astray in this same folly.

The fifth love is the love for long life, and because he loves mere existence so much, he will not stand up in a trial that involves danger.

The sixth love is the love of honor, and he who loves honor will not do his good deeds for the sake of God, but in all the commandments, or good deeds he does — whether it be philanthropy or studying or supporting Torah, or the value of the commandments, his thoughts and intentions will be fixed on receiving praise and honor and he will want people to give him a crown and greatness, and this is a great flaw in the Service of God. Even he who has great knowledge of the Torah and many good deeds — the pursuit of honor removes him from the world. How much uglier is the pursuit of honor by one who is devoid of Torah and good deeds.

And there is a seventh love — which is the worst of all loves — and that is the love of pleasure and amusement — like eating, drinking, and other pleasures of the senses like immoral conduct and pleasure excursions. And it is not necessary to dwell on this matter because he who loves wine to the point of drunkenness and eats only the daintiest of foods and goes constantly to parties and feasts will undoubtedly forget his Creator, as it is written: "And (when) you shall eat and drink ... guard yourself lest you forget the Lord" (Deut. 6:11-12). "And (when) you shall eat and be satisfied ... guard yourself lest your heart be deceived and you turn aside and serve other gods" (Ibid. 11:15-16). And it is written: "But where Jeshurun grew fat he kicked" (Ibid., 32:15).

He who wishes to escape from the fowler's net of all these loves will need great wisdom and much courage, lest he be caught in their pit for all of these various loves surround the heart of a person, and if he succeeds in thrusting away one or two of these loves from within him, then will the remaining loves still thrust him from the light to the darkness. Therefore, it is necessary to teach you that you should be careful and alert as to how to deal with all of these loves and always be mindful in combatting them of the ways of the Lord, Blessed is He, according to the tenor of what is said: "In all your paths know Him (Prov. 3:6). A real love for one's children must be in this path — that he thinks always to guide his children in the paths of Justice, and teach them the manner of serving God. Blessed is He, according to what is said: "The father shall make known to the children Thy truth" (Is. 38:19). And it is written: "And you shall make known (the lessons of Sinai) to your children and your children's children" (Deut. 4:9). And, as it is said concerning Abraham, "For I know him to the end that he should command his children and his household after him" (Gen. 18:19).

And love of money should be in this manner: — that he should love his own money in order not to covet the money of others, and not find it necessary to steal, rob, or be compelled to receive alms, but shall able to provide for others out of his own, and clothe the poor and feed them, and strengthen with his money those who study the Torah and revere the Lord. And, also, because of his money, he can free himself from many involvements in this material world and set definite times for Torah and the fulfillment of God's commands, inasmuch as he has sufficient for his material needs. But he should not find security in his great wealth and vaunt himself with it but should purchase with his transitory wealth the eternal life of the world to come.

And the love of a wife should be in this manner — that he should have it in mind that his wife saves him from sin and separates him far from immoral conduct, and, through his wife he fulfills the command of "Be fruitful and multiply," and it is his wife that raises his children and she works for him all her days, and prepares his food and all the other needs of the household, and because of her devotion and work he has time to study Torah and concern himself with God's commands, and thus she aids him to serve the Creator, may His Name be Blessed.

And love for father and mother should be in this manner — that he should be ever mindful that they reared him and exerted themselves to teach him the ways of the Lord, may He be Blessed, and instructed him and educated him as to Torah and Commandments, and it is through them that he can fulfill the command of the Creator, may He be Blessed, as it is written: "Honor your father and your mother" (Exod. 20:12).

And his brothers, sisters and other relatives he should love in this manner — that he should assume and have it in mind that they are attempting to bring him to virtues that are dedicated to the service of the Creator, may He be Blessed, and that he should similarly interest himself in them to teach them and correct them and not show them many special privileges or partiality in a matter involving others. For this there is great reward for him, since this fair conduct is a great virtue, as it is written: "And he has not done a shameful thing to favor his relative" (Ps. 15:3).

And there is much advantage to a man in his relatives, as we found in the case of Lot whom Abraham, his uncle, saved from the warring kings, and fought for his sake, and also from the destruction of Sodom, Lot was saved because of the merit of Abraham.

A man should love his friends and all those near to him as well as the rest of Israel with a complete love to fulfill what is said: "And you shall love your neighbor as yourself" (Lev. 19:18). And this is a great general rule in the Torah: "That which is hateful to you do not due to your neighbor" (Shabbath 31a). And even more pertinent is the verse: "For in the image of God made He man" (Gen. 9:6). (This is commented upon in T.P. Nedarim 9:4.)

And there is a great benefit to one who conducts himself with love and friendship with people.

One gain is in this world — if he conducts himself with love for everyone, everyone will help him. If he should fall, many are they who will help him and support him, and if a man rises against him to quarrel with him, then many will silence those who speak evil against him and abuse him. And if trouble comes upon him, all will feel his pain and will extend a hand to him. And if he should come to distress and poverty, many will be compassionate with him and show it by their gifts.

As for his gain in the world to come — because he is beloved by all, his words are listened to and he has the power to rebuke people that they should improve their deeds. And also because of his love for all he will be at peace and secure and free to study and to do good deeds. And also, from the depths of their love people will help him and he will do his work more easily and they will protect him, and he will find more leisure to serve the Creator, may He be Blessed, with complete service. And because of this love for all others, he finds favor in the eyes of all who observe him, and his good deeds will be welcomed by all and everyone will long to do as he does.

And how can a man reach that stage of loving all men? I will make you grasp it and enlighten you!

The way to do this is that he should help all others with his life and with his money according to his ability.

"With his life" means that he should minister to everyone whether he be poor or rich and should trouble himself for their sakes.

"Help with his money" means that he should loan to the rich when the rich need funds, and similarly, he should loan to the poor in the time of their distress, and remember the poor with a gift in accordance with his ability to give, and in extreme cases he should send portions and gifts also to the rich. And he should be liberal and open-handed out of his substance. If he has dealings with people every transaction must be in complete faith and honesty, and he should not be strict with his companion in small matters. He should always desire that his companion should receive some joy or gain from him and let him not try to gain profit out of his companion. And let his words be gentle with all people. If a man has shamed him, let him not shame his abuser. If a man has deceived him, let him not deceive his deceiver. Let him bear upon his neck the yoke of the world, and let him not cause trouble to others. Let him avoid argument with others and let him welcome everyone with joy and with a smiling countenance, for his welcome reception strengthens love. And he must deal with another for the other's good. He must comfort and try to help every man out of his grief and worry. If someone has revealed a secret to him, he must not reveal it to others even if the man who told him the secret enrages him. He must never speak evil of a person nor listen when others speak evil of anyone, and he should always try to find something good and pure in a person wherever this is possible, and in this connection, he must be most earnest and careful. Then he will surely be loved by all. He must honor every man by his deeds and his words, and let him not vaunt himself over any person at all, but let him be humble before every man. And all of these things he must do with the intent to serve God. And he must be careful to avoid the companionship of people that are not respectable, so that he will not learn from their deeds, and he must always separate himself from cynics and scoffers.

And the wise man said to his son, "If it should occur to you to make friends or companions, then make friends with a wise person as it is written: 'He that walks with the wise shall be wise' (Prov. 13:20). And it is said: 'Give knowledge to a wise man and he will be yet wiser' (Prov. 9:9). And so, if you wish to grow in wisdom be a companion to the wise, for if you do act wisely your wise friend will praise you and not question your wisdom, and then you will know that you can rely on your wisdom. If they honor him, he will honor you; if they praise him, he will praise you. If you need his help, he will help you, and in the things, you say he will declare you to be in the right. If you grow angry, he will have patience with you, and you will learn from his good deeds. And be a companion to every person from whom you can learn things that will bring you to the Service of God, Blessed may He be!" And the Sages said, "If you wish to become a friend of a man get him angry with you and if he will still admit and confess the truth of what you say even in his wrath then become his companion and friend. If not, leave him. But, when you choose a friend, choose one who knows his own worth, for if he does not know himself his wisdom is of no good. Acquire a friend who will rebuke you when you do something that is not proper and who will teach you to do the good, and who will help you with his might and money — and such a friend will be faithful. But a friend who flatters you and smooths over your mistakes and errors and comforts you when you have done evil things — separate yourself from such a one. And similarly, a friend who will take from you whatever he needs and cause you much harm for the little benefit he will gain from the transaction — quickly turn away from such a friend. And do not make friends with those who "go along with the crowd" and who always agree that there is an injustice, as it is said, "Do not say 'Conspiracy!' just because this people say 'Conspiracy!' " (Is. 8:12).

And it is forbidden to associate with a wicked man in business or social or community affairs, as it is said: "Because you have joined yourself with Ahaziah the Lord has made a breach in your works!" (II Chron. 20:37).

And even in fulfilling a commandment it is forbidden to join with the wicked, as it is said: "Do not envy the man of violence and do not choose any of his ways" (Prov. 3:31). And the sages said: "Do not join with the wicked even in fulfilling a command" (Aboth de

R. Nathan, chap. a), and many are the ways that lead to death when one is in the companionship of the wicked.

And if a man is careful in guarding himself from these things and if his words are gentle with all people and he is pleasant and sociable with them, is abused by them but does not abuse them, honors them — even those who make light of him — and deals with every person honestly and does not spend too much time in the gatherings of the ignorant and their parties, and is not seen flitting about, but occupies himself with Torah, wrapped in his fringed Tallit and crowned with his Tefillin, and does more than is required of him by the letter of the law, but at the same time, does not separate himself utterly from the community and make himself a hermit, and if as a result of his behavior every one will praise him and love him and long to emulate his deeds — such a person sanctifies the Name of God and about him Scripture says! "And he said to me 'You are my servant Israel through whom I will be glorified' " (Is. 49:3).

And the love of long life should be in this manner — that he should love the days of his life not for eating and drinking and the frivolous pleasures of life, but he should think, "The work of following the Torah and its commandments is exceedingly great, and if the length of my life were doubled and redoubled many times over I would not be able to complete the requirements of the Torah and reach the heights and goals set by the Torah through which a true servant of God pleases his Master." And in this manner, he will truly love the days of his life for with them he acquires the means of serving the Creator, Blessed be

ORCHOT TZADIKIM — Chapter Five

He, with purest reverence, and love, and he thus acquires provisions in this fleeting world which he can convey to the world to come, and he can acquire in the transitory world and its vanishing days a world that will endure and a joy that will never, never cease. And he will always fear death for this reason only — that perhaps he has not attained the limits of the perfection that lie in his power to attain. And every day he will increase love and reverence for God.

But a life that has no reverence of God in it cannot be called life. And a person should be disgusted with and reject a life that is against the will of the Creator, may He be Blessed, as is said of Rebecca: "And Rebecca said to Isaac, 'I am weary of my life because of the daughters of Heth. If Jacob takes a wife of the daughters of Heth, such as these daughters of the land, then of what good is my life to me?'" (Gen. 27:46). Therefore, in a place where there is desecration of God's Name he should not worry about his life and always let his heart be ready to surrender himself for the Sanctification of God's Name in all of the commandments, be they light or of great importance.

Love of honor is very bad. Therefore, a man should separate himself far from the love of honor with all his might. And if a man should separate himself from two things — the love of honor and receiving of pleasure by the adultation and gifts of others, then he will be near to all the good virtues, for the love of honor spoils all good deeds, for in the things he does he has in mind to be honored, and even if he does not care about honor but seeks to receive gain from others by his good deeds, then all of his deeds are spoiled because his heart always inclines him to make profit out of everything. Therefore, he must put it in his heart to distance himself from honor and also from getting benefits from others through his good deeds.

But there are times when it is a good deed to pursue honor, as when he is a righteous and wise man and people hold him cheaply and make fun of him because of his good deeds and because of this his words are disdained and not listened to. Then if it is in his power to compel men to do him honor and listen to his rebukes, it is commendable to pursue honor in order to correct and rebuke the people. Similarly, if people have shamed him publicly, he should not forgive them until they have entreated and appeased him. But in most cases, he must go away from honor and flee from it. Did not the Sages say: "Jealousy, lust and the pursuit of honor take a man out of this world" (Aboth 4:28). And a man ought not to learn or to do any good thing in order to be honored, but should do the good deed for the sake of the Creator, may He be Blessed, and in the end the honor will come.

As for the love of pleasure, such as eating, drinking and sleeping, know that man must direct his heart and all his deeds only to know the Lord, Blessed is He. So, a man's sitting, arising and his speech should all be centered on this. How? When he does business or works at a job for pay, let there not be in his heart the thought of gathering money for its own sake; but to do so in order that he may secure the things his body needs — food, drink, a dwelling place, and marriage. And when he does eat, drink and enjoy connubial pleasures, he should not put it in his heart to do these things solely for his pleasure until he is not able to eat and drink anything except the foods that are sweet to his palate, and he marries only for pleasure. But he must put it into his heart that he must eat for the health of his body and limbs. Therefore, he should not eat everything the palate longs for as does a dog or a donkey, but should eat those foods which are good for the body, whether they be bitter or sweet. And he should not eat things which are bad for the body even if they are sweet to the taste. He must accustom himself to this habit and determine in his heart that his body shall be completely well and strong, in order that his soul may be upright and firm to know the Lord, may He be Blessed. For it is impossible for him to understand and grow wise in the Torah and commandments if he is hungry or sick or one of his limbs pains him. Therefore, it is not good to fast always, lest his strength grow weak and his intelligence grow less. Therefore, he should arrange and direct all his matters to the service of the Creator, may He be Blessed. If he fills his stomach then he may grow heavy in body, and if he eats too little he will be weak, so it would be good for you to have less of the trimmings at a meal and depend on one dish if you can, and let that suffice for you in modest quantity. Intend that this food shall reach your stomach for the sake of nourishing you and not merely to delight your taste, and accustom your appetite on a few occasions to do without delicacies, so as to discipline your nature so that it will be easy for you when you cannot obtain these foods. If possible, abandon those foods or dishes which take much time and trouble to prepare and let your meals during the day be lighter than your evening meal, and accustom yourself to eating twice a day so that the functioning of your limbs may be light and easy and in this way your studies of the Torah will come easier. And accustom yourself to drink water unless your intention is to drink wine for your health's sake, or to drive away worry, and be very careful not to drink too much wine for it saturates and washes away Torah.

This is the general rule that should always remain with you: A man should not satisfy all of his desires in eating and drinking, but he should eat and drink enough to keep his body in a healthy state and should refrain from reaching for a surplus of food. A man should not love this world for the sake of eating, drinking and having pleasure. For example, the wise man says: "I will eat in order to live." And the statement of the fool is "I will live in order to eat." On this subject it is said: "The righteous eat to the point of satisfying their desire, but the stomach of the wicked is always wanting no matter how much they eat" (Prov. 13:25).

And so, with a man who marries. Let him be mindful that this is in obedience to Divine command, that he should fulfill the command of "Be fruitful and multiply" and that he should have children who will serve the Lord, may He be Blessed, and revere God. Or he should be mindful that he satisfies his desires and quiets his passion with his wife and is Therefore, not tempted by other women, or to be considerate of his wife when he senses that she longs for his embrace so that she be not tempted by other men, or he may have regard to the health of his body which requires normal sex habits for its health. But he who indulges too frequently will suffer many ills.

He who walks in the path described above serves the Lord, may He Be Blessed, always, even when he is engaged in doing business, even when he lives with his wife, for his intention is to fulfill his bodily needs so that he can serve God, Blessed be He. And even when he sleeps, if he sleeps, so that his mind will be refreshed and his body rested, so that he does not become ill and therefore, not be able to serve the Lord, Blessed is He, because of his illness — that sleep with this intent is considered service to God, Blessed be He. And on this subject our Sages commanded and said: "Let all your deeds be for the sake of Heaven (God)" (Aboth 2:17). And this is what Solomon said in his wisdom: "In all thy ways, know Him and He will direct your paths" (Prov. 3:6).

Let a man abandon all other loves and cleave to love of the Creator, Blessed be He. For the Love of God, Blessed be He, is the goal of all good qualities, and the final purpose of all worthy traits in the ladder of ascent of all men who serve God and of those with generous souls among men of kindness and mercy and of the Prophets and the Pharisees — yes, this is the ultimate goal and there is no goal that is higher than this.

Many times, the Torah sets fear of God before love of Him, as it is said: "And now O Israel, what does the Lord your God ask of you except to revere and to love Him" (Deut. 10:12). And since the love of fellow men is the goal of all who separate themselves in order to lead holy lives and this love is the closest rung to the rung of the love of God, in the ladder of our upward climb, love of God must be more than the love of a man for mankind. And a man can reach that highest rung only through fear and reverence of God. That is why reverence or fear in the verse referred to precedes love of God.

And what is this love? It is the yearning of the soul and its own upward inclination towards the Creator, may He be exalted, in order that it may cleave to His highest illumination and light. This soul is the source of knowledge and is clean and pure and the Creator binds her in the body for His desire is great to try her and see if she will go in the ways of the Lord. And because man is clothed in a body which was created with the nature of animals there is not sufficient power in the soul created by God to have in constant mind her Creator, for she is mingled with all fleshly desire of the body. And all the days of man's petty strivings he seeks nothing and asks nothing but the gratification of his lusts, and his hunger for pleasures of this world which is a world of vanity and falsehood, and because of his desire to gather much wealth, there is no strength in the soul to keep in mind the Creator, may He be Blessed, for the soul is clothed in frivolous nothings. But after the soul senses that it can aspire to something nobler by itself without the participation of the body, then she longs to seek rest from the ills of the body as the sick person earnestly seeks a doctor. And when the soul is healed from its illnesses then she possesses light in her very self and strength in her spirit, and the soul is then truly filled with love and this love is bound up with joy. And this joy causes the pleasures of the body, and delight in mere physical life to flee from his heart, and that joy is strong and is in control of his heart, and all the pleasures of the world are as nothing compared with the mighty joy in the Lord, Blessed is He. And all his love and delight at the playing of his children are as though they had never been when compared with the mighty joy in the Lord, Blessed is He.

And with all his thoughts he should meditate how to do the will of the Creator, and purify the many others to do likewise, and to sanctify the Name of God and to surrender himself completely in the love of God, Blessed be He. And this is the love of God, Blessed is He, that is written in the Torah, as in the case of Phineas who risked his life for the sake of the Creator, may He be Blessed (Num. 25), and as in the case of Abraham, our father, who said: "I have lifted my hand to the Lord, the most High God, Creator of heaven and earth, that I will not take from a thread or a shoestring nor will I take anything of yours" (Gen. 14:22-23). And, as in the case of Elisha who did not wish to take anything from Naaman (II Kings 5:16).

And a man ought not to waste his time away from Torah because he loves to sport and play with his children, or enjoys much visiting and conversation. And he also ought to avoid promenading about. But let him sing sweet hymns so that he fills his heart with the joy of the love of God, Blessed is He.

He who serves God out of love occupies himself with the Torah and the Commandments, and walks in the paths of wisdom. Have you seen how he will carry out all the mitzvoth out of love and how he will love God, Blessed be He with a great love, for no worldly reason — not out of fear of evil befalling him, and not out of expectation of good resulting from his conduct, but doing the true deed because it is true, and the good will come in the end. This virtue is very great indeed and not every man can attain it. And this was the virtue of Abraham our father, whom the Holy One, Blessed is He, called "My loving friend" (Is. 41:8) for he served God only out of love. This is the quality that the Holy One, Blessed be He, commanded us to attain through Moses our Teacher, upon him is peace, as is said: "And you shall love the Lord, your God with all your heart and with all your soul and with all your might" (Deut. 6:5). And when a man loves the Lord, Blessed is He, with the proper love, he will, at once, do all the commandments out of love.

And what is "the proper love"? It is that he must love the Lord with a great, mighty and supreme love until his very soul is bound up in the love of the Lord, may He be Blessed, and he is in the ecstasy of that love always, as though he were love sick and his mind cannot for a moment be free, as when a man is infatuated with a woman, and he thinks of her with constant ecstasy, where sitting, rising, eating or drinking. Even more than this must the love of the Lord, Blessed be He, be in the heart of those who love him, ecstatic with longing for Him, as He commanded: "with all your heart and with all your soul" (Ibid.). And this is what Solomon said by way of a parable in the song of Songs: "For I am love sick" (2:5) and the entire Song of Songs is a parable of this love of God.

It is clear and well known that the love for the Holy One, Blessed be He, is not securely bound in the heart of a man until he feels its ecstasy constantly as indeed, he should, and he forsakes all else in the world outside of it as He commanded and said "With all your heart and with all your soul" (Deut. 6:5). And he loves the Holy One, Blessed be He, through knowing His ways and according to his knowledge of God is his love whether it be little or great. Therefore, a man must concentrate on understanding and grasping mentally those wisdoms and insights which make him know his Creator as much as it lies within the power of man to understand and attain.

God glorious and awesome — it is a command to love and revere Him, as it is said: "And you shall love the Lord your God" (Ibid.), and it is further said: "The Lord your God you shall revere" (Ibid: 13). And this is the way to attain to love of the Lord, Blessed is He : When a person contemplates the great and wondrous works and creations and sees from them how God's wisdom is unparalleled, and infinite, he, at once, loves God, Blessed be He, and praises and extols Him and is filled with a great longing to know His Great Name, as David said "My soul thirsts for God — for the living God" (Ps. 42:3). And when he considers these things profoundly, he immediately trembles and is startled, he is fearful and terrified, and he realizes that he is a small, lowly, obscure creature, standing with his little, finite mind before the Perfect in All Knowledge, as David said: "When I behold Thy Heavens, the work of Thy fingers, the moon and the stars which Thou hast established, what is man that Thou art mindful of him?" (Ibid. 8:4-5).

And when a man contemplates these great and marvelous things and comes to recognize all God's creatures from angel to planets sweeping through their orbs [and man] and he perceives something of the wisdom of the Holy One Blessed be He in all formed and created things and beings, he increases his love for God, Blessed be He, and his soul will thirst and his flesh yearn to love the Omnipresent, Blessed be He, and he is awed and fearful at his own low, poor and slight status when he compares himself with any one of the holy bodies which the Lord, Blessed is He, has created.

And in another place in Scripture, it is said: "One that feared God" (Job 1:1), and the Sages explained this, to mean that he feared the punishment of Heaven, of Gehenna, and the punishments of this world as well (Sotah 27b and 31a). And this quality is very far from true love for God. For a man should fear the Lord, may He be Blessed, like a man who loves his wife and she loves him and he fears to do anything against her lest he forfeit her love. So is this — and such is the meaning of the word Reshăfihă it's (love's) flames — the flames of the fire of love for the Creator may He be Exalted. Let a person fear to transgress God's commands lest he lose the love of the Creator, may He be Blessed.

And this is what is meant: "Serve the Lord with fear" (Ps. 2:11) — the fear of losing His love" and rejoice with trembling out of this great fear of losing the love of the Creator, rejoice that you have the opportunity to do His will.

Thus, this "fear" is really "love" and it is of this that Isaiah says: "And the fear of the Lord is his treasure" (Is. 33:6).

And such a love cannot endure except in one who resolves to perform all the commandments according to their proper requirements, for one who does not know the commandments which the Creator of All commanded him to observe, cannot be called a true lover of God. Therefore, should a man love everything which brings him closer to love for the Creator, Blessed be He, and Blessed be His Name. And he who does so — it is well for him in this world and in the world to come.

Sefer ORCHOT TZADIKIM

Ways of the Righteous

Chapter Six

ON HATRED

Concerning the quality of Hatred, we see in it the firm prohibition "You shall not!" As it is written: "You shall not hate your brother in your heart" (Lev. 19:17), and with this verse we have been warned to remove from our souls the trait of hatred. This trait causes many sins — such as gossip, for he who hates his companion tells it to the world because of his hatred, accuses him, and always seeks and desires evil to happen to him, and rejoices at his misfortune, and tries to harm him whenever he can, and seeks vengeance upon him, and nurses a grudge against him and has no pity upon him though he be in great distress. And because of his hatred, he slanders all the good deeds of the one he hates and makes them hateful in his own eyes and in the eyes of others. The hater withholds the good that is due to the hated and will not admit the truth of anything his victim says or does, and if the victim owes him anything, the hater oppresses him.

There are several kinds of hatred. There is one who hates his companion because he harmed him in money matters or struck him, or shamed him, or slandered him. For all of these and similar causes, a person should not hate his companion and be silent about his grievance as it is said in connection with the wicked: "And Absalom did not speak with Amnon either bad or good for Absalom hated Amnon" (II Sam. 13:22). But it is a mitzvah that he let his companion know that he feels he has been wronged and say to him, "Why did you do thus and thus to me?". As it is said: "You shall surely rebuke your neighbor" (Lev. 19:17). And if the offender repents and asks the person who was wronged to forgive him, he must forgive him and the one who forgives should not be cruel it is said: "And Abraham prayed to God" (on behalf of Abimelech who had wronged him) (Gen. 20:17). And even if the offender does not ask him to forgive him, the one offended should not hate him but should conduct himself towards him with love, and in the end, it will come to this — that the one in the wrong will correct what he has spoiled.

There is an evil which is grievous, indeed, and that is hatred without cause, and it is that evil which caused the destruction of the Second Temple. Then there is hatred arising from jealousy, which is even worse, and it is proper for a person to reprove his soul to separate itself far from these evils. And there is one who hates his companion because he does not deal kindly with him, or does not give him a gift that he wants, or does not loan him money when he is in distress. It is proper for a person to separate himself from all these and similar evils and receive with love all that the Creator, Blessed be He, decrees for him. And he should not place his trust in man but should think, "If I were indeed worthy in the eyes of God,

Blessed is He, He would give my needs to me notwithstanding the refusal of man to give or loan me anything." And if he is in poverty and in distress or if he is ill and severely pained by great pains, he should think that the Creator has decreed this for his good that he might learn to receive God's will with love. And there is no doubt that, when he does this, all hatred will depart from his heart, and this acceptance of God's will with love is a great foundation and mighty pillar for Torah and Commandments.

And he who disciplines himself thus to receive everything with love and to say at every occasion and mischance, "This, too, is for good" (Ta'anith 21a), and meaning this in his heart, and rejoices in the judgment of the Creator, may He be Blessed, will be saved from hatred, enmity and jealousy.

And even the hatred which a person often feels for those in his craft or profession — all this is folly and a great evil, for he should be mindful that no person can earn more than what the Creator has decreed for him.

The worst at all kinds of hatred, the one most difficult to eradicate is that which people feel towards those who rebuke or correct them in order to teach them the righteous path, as in the case of which Amos speaks: "They hate him that reproves them in the gate" (Amos 5:10). And there is a hatred eviller than this; namely, when people hate those who do good and pursue justice, as it is said: "They oppose me viciously because I follow the thing that is good" (Ps. 38:21). And those who follow this path hate the Lord Himself for they hate those that He loves and they hate the

Torah and Commandments since they abhor, reject and hate those who fulfill its commands.

The Sage said, "If you want your companion to hate you, keep visiting him constantly, and if you want him to love you, visit him after long intervals." And on this subject, it is said: "Let your foot be seldom in your neighbor's house lest he be sated with you and hate you" (Prov. 25:17).

And it is necessary for you to know that he who hates others — they, too, will hate him, and he who increases hatred in his heart will bring evil upon himself. And where there is love that is not for the sake of Heaven, it can turn into very great hatred, as it is said concerning Amnon: "Then Amnon hatred her with exceeding great hatred for the hatred wherewith he hated her was greater than the love wherewith he had loved her" (II Sam. 13:15).

Do not believe the counsel of one who hates and is inimical, as it is said: "But the kisses of an enemy are importunate" (Prov. 27:6). And know that many people express love with their words but it is possible that they are total enemies in their heart, and it is necessary that you recognize them and do not put your faith in them as it is said: "He that hates dissembles with his lips while he lays up treachery within him" (Ibid. 26:24). And even though he speaks to you with a smooth tongue and speaks tender words, do not incline your heart to him as it is said: "When he speaks graciously, do not believe him for there are seven abominations in his heart" (Prov. 26:25). And this is the type of conduct that Joab showed to Abner, son of Ner (II Sam. 3:27) and to Amasa, son of Yeter (II Sam. 20:9-10) (peace and love) until he killed them, and as Ishmael son of Nethaniah did with Gedaliah, son of Ahikam until he slew him (Jer. 41:1-2). One of the Sages said: "The best plan of those you can plot against your enemy is to turn him to your love (to make a friend of him) if you can."

There is a hatred that is a mitzvah: for example, a wicked man who will not accept correction — it is a command of the Torah to hate him, as it is said: "The fear of the Lord is to hate evil" (Prov. 8:13). And it says: "Lo, I hate them O Lord that hate Thee and I strive with those that rise up against Thee, I hate them with the utmost hatred; they are my enemies" (Ps. 139:21-22). And a man should hate lies and falsehood. The end of the matter is this — that a man should hate everything which separates him and holds him back from loving the Creator of All, as it is said: "I hate every false way" (Ibid. 119:128). And this is a great general rule, that a man should hate every false thing, and every act which will increase hatred for false ways will increase love for Torah" (Ibid 163). And let each person love truth and peace as it is written: "Therefore, love ye truth and peace" (Zech. 8:19).

Sefer
ORCHOT TZADIKIM
Ways of the Righteous

Chapter Seven

ON MERCY

Mercy is a most praiseworthy quality and is one of the thirteen attributes associated with the Holy One, Blessed be He, as it is written: "Merciful and Gracious" (Exod. 34:6). A man should do as much as he can to conduct himself in this quality. And just as a person desires people to have mercy upon him in the hour of his need, so it is proper for him that he should have mercy upon anyone who is in need, as Scripture says: "And you shall love your neighbor as yourself" (Lev. 19:18).

The Creator, may He be Blessed, apportioned this quality to the righteous and to His servants so that through this quality they might be identified, as you learn in the case of Joseph, "whose mercies were kindled" (Gen. 43:30). And it is fitting for the intelligent person that the quality of Mercy and Graciousness should be firmly fixed and present in his heart at all times.

There are several kinds of mercy and each rather far apart from the other. The mercy of a father on his child — this is a mercy that comes from the very nature of all creatures that live, as in the case of dogs and cattle. And then there is the case of the master who has mercy on his servant and the man who has mercy on his friend. Even though he expects some benefit from his act, nevertheless, it is very good that he should grasp and hold in his heart the quality of mercy. But the best and most lofty manifestation of the quality of mercy is when a man has mercy upon his son in order to bring him to the service of the Creator, may He be Blessed, as it is written; "The father shall make known Thy truth to his children" (Is. 38:19), and has more mercy upon his son's soul than upon his body. For it is necessary to strike him with the rod of chastisement in order to make him walk in the right path, yes, even if he chastises him harshly, for this apparently cruel conduct is in reality sublime mercy. And if he should withhold the rod of chastisement from his son because he feels too much pity for him to strike him and lets his son go on in the hardness of his evil heart — then this type of mercy drives out and destroys the son from life in the world to come. And even one who raises an orphan of whom it is said: "Ye shall not afflict any widow or fatherless child" (Exod. 22:21), it is a commandment to give stripes even to him in order to make him go upright in the upright path. Nevertheless, he must, in spite of this command, (to correct the orphan) conduct himself with this orphan with more mercy than with all others, but he must not permit him to go on in the obduracy of his heart.

And it is also necessary that he not indulge in too much self pity, but that he reproves himself and bend his evil desire.

And he should have mercy on his relatives, as it is written: "And that you hide not yourself from your own flesh" (Is. 58:7).

And, also, on the poor must one have mercy, and especially on those who revere God. And this is the principal manifestation of mercy — that he should be gracious and show mercy to those who serve God, and do His will.

But there is a kind of mercy that is worse than cruelty. For example, when one has mercy on the wicked and strengthens them. And there is a great stumbling block before the one who raises up the wicked and gives them his hand and abases and rejects the good, and on this it is said in the Torah: "Neither shall thine eye pity him, neither shalt thou spare, neither shalt thou conceal him" (Deut. 13:9). Nor shall one have mercy upon the poor in the course of a law suit, but judge the case fairly, as it is written: "Neither shall you favor a poor man in his cause" (Exodus 23:3), which means that he should not prevert justice because of sympathy with the poor man's distress. And there is mercy which is cruelty. For example, when one gives alms to a poor man and afterwards burdens the poor man by saying, "I gave you this and this; now you must do something for me and serve me just like all that I did for you." And of this type of mercy, it is said: "The mercies of the wicked are cruel" (Prov. 12:10).

One must also have pity on animals for it is forbidden to cause pain to living creatures and on this subject the Torah has said: "Thou shalt surely help him lift him (the animal) up" (Deut. 22:4). And one must feed one's animals before he himself sits down to eat (Berakoth 40a).

The quality of mercy identifies the descendants of Abraham our father — the seed of Israel as it is written in Deuteronomy 13:18: "And He shall show you mercy and have mercy upon you and multiply you" i.e. (God will give you the quality of mercy). Therefore, everyone should accustom himself to speak all his words with the language of petition and mercy. Also, when he prays, his prayer should be in the tone of plea and petition. And great indeed is the reward that a man will receive from his words of mercy when he speaks to the heart of the poor.

Many know the commands that lie behind these precepts. You surely see that our Rabbis said: "He who gives a penny to the poor is blessed with six blessings, and he who appeases him with words of kindness is blessed with eleven blessings, Therefore, , his alms should be clothed in merciful words that will speak kindly to the poor and let his words be gentle to the one in need. And let him comfort him with his deeds and the effort of his hands and honor him and lift him" (Baba Bathra 9b).

And you, O son of man, have mercy on your soul which endures forever! Bring it to a wondrous joy that no eye has seen and let not your many lusts bring you to sin and you be thus thrust from light to darkness. Have pity on yourself and be merciful to your own soul and do not profane the splendor of your soul with the vein frivolities of idle pleasure. The wise man has said, "From his deeds of charity does a man attain the quality of mercy." And in the words of Solomon, it is commanded concerning mercy and grace when he says: "Save those that are being taken to death and those near to be slain" (Prov. 24:11).

And you will discern and understand the great virtue of this quality of mercy in that the Creator conducts Himself with that quality with all His creatures, as it is said: "And His tender mercies are over all His works" (Ps. 145:9).

Sefer
ORCHOT TZADIKIM
Ways of the Righteous

Chapter Eight

ON CRUELTY

Cruelty is the opposite of Mercy as it is written: "They are cruel and have no compassion" (Jer. 50:42). And this trait of cruelty is not found in righteous people but in the souls of the wicked as it is written: "The tender mercies of the wicked are cruel" (Prov. 12:10). This quality is also found in the impudent as it is written: "An impudent nation that shall have no regard for the person of the old and show no mercy to the young" (Deut. 28:50). And you already know the evil of the trait of impudence. Go forth and learn the evil nature and the punishment of cruelty, for in the matter of the reward of a wicked man — rebellious and disobedient — it is said: "A rebellious man seeks only evil, Therefore, a cruel messenger shall be sent against him" (Prov. 12:11). Every cruel person has no quality of kindness in his make up, even towards himself, as it is written: "The merciful man does kindness to his own soul, but he that is cruel troubles his own flesh" (Ibid. 11:17).

The cruel person is very far from all good qualities, for he has no pity on the poor, and will not loan to them in the time of their distress and gives them nothing. And it is written: "He that is gracious to the poor lends to the Lord" (Ibid. 19:7). And it is further said: "Well is it with the man that deals graciously and lends, and orders his affairs justly" and it says (Ps. 112:5), "Happy is he that considers the poor. In the day of evil the Lord will deliver him" (Ibid. 41:2). And all these instances are the opposite of cruelty and are not found in the cruel person.

For the cruel person feels no pain at the troubles of his companions, as you see in contrast with David who said: "As for me, when they were sick, my clothing was sackcloth, I afflicted my soul with fasting, and as for my prayer for them — may it return to my own bosom" (Ps. 35:13). And in the Book of Job it is written: "If I have not wept for him that was in trouble and if my soul grieved not for the needy" (Job 30:25). And all this is very far from the cruel man. This trait of cruelty is found only in people whose natures are like the nature of lions that prey and violently rend. When the spirit of wrath takes strong hold of a man then the quality of mercy flees, and Cruelty grows powerful to ruin and destroy as it is written: "Wrath is cruel and anger is overwhelming" (Prov. 27:4). There is no wrath like the anger of Cruelty. In the attributes of the Creator, may He be Blessed, you will find: "In wrath remember Compassion" (Hab. 3:2). But this is far from man's ability — to have mercy in the midst of his anger. And there is this aspect of the quality of Cruelty in the soul of man — to avenge himself on his enemies as it is written: "And he will not spare in the day of vengeance" (Prov. 6:14). The meaning of this verse is that where there is the desire for vengeance there is no compassion, only cruelty. And Scripture says: "You shall not avenge nor bear a grudge" (Lev 19:18). We are warned not to bear a grudge even in our heart — all the more so not to do any deed with the hands to hurt a companion. Even when your enemy has fallen through no fault of yours, you must not rejoice as it is written: "Rejoice not when your enemy falls and when he stumbles let not your heart be glad" (Prov. 24:17). The avenger or the grudge-holder never overlooks a grievance and never forgives his companions who have wronged him, and this attitude drags after it quarrels and hatred, and you already know how good and how pleasant is the quality of peace.

And in the general scope of cruelty is included him who robs his companion of anything and therefore, caused him pain. And there is a great punishment in store for him who robs the poor — and one who does so is deserving of death as it is written: "Rob not the weak because he is weak" (Ibid. 22:22). And it is written: "For the Lord will plead their cause, and despoil of life those that despoil them" (Ibid. 22:23). And even though there be greater and more severe sins than robbery the punishment for robbing is very grievous, as it is written about the generation of the flood, "The end of all flesh is come before me; for the earth is filled with violence through them" (Gen. 6:13). Our Rabbis said, "If there is a box filled with sins — there is no more severe accuser among them than robbery" (Sanhedrin 108a). And he who causes pain to an orphan or a widow through robbing them or shaming them or any kind of malicious pain is worthy of death through the power of Heaven. This is also true of judges who have the power to save them from the hand of their oppressors and do not fairly judge the case of the orphan or the widow — they are deserving of death as it is written: "You shall not afflict any widow or fatherless child" (Exod. 22:21). And it is further written: "If you afflict him in any way, for if he comes unto me, I will surely hear his cry" (Ibid.: 22). And it is written: "My wrath shall burn and I will slay you with the sword and your wives will be widows and your children will be orphans" (Ibid.:23). Measure for measure: "Your wives shall be widows" for "afflicting widows" and "your sons shall be orphans" for afflicting orphans."

And anyone who causes pain to a fellow Jew transgresses a prohibitive command, as it is said: "And you shall not wrong one another but you shall fear the Lord" (Lev. 25:17), and this phrase "you shall not wrong" is said concerning wronging by words (Baba Mezi'a 58b). And our Rabbis, of blessed memory, said: "All gates are closed to hearing accusations against the repentant except the gate of wronging a fellow Jew" (Ibid. 59a). Therefore, , should one be very careful not to cause pain to his companion in any way — not by deeds and not by words.

He who robs from his companion it is as though he slew him — even if he robs him of a trifle such as only a penny, he is deserving of the death penalty. Also, this crime belongs under Cruelty — one who spreads slander about his companion and, thus, causes him pain and shame. And he who slanders the morality of a man's family, (such as attacking the legitimacy of his birth) there is no atonement for such a crime to all eternity.

"You shall not deal with him as a creditor does" (Exodus 22:24), means not to cause pain to the borrower. And the lender should even avoid walking by the borrower when he knows that the borrower has no money with which to pay back the loan, (Baba Mezi'a 15) for the lender distresses the borrower with this kind of conduct. And we have been warned to remove from our souls the quality of cruelty, as it is written: "You shall not afflict any widow or fatherless child" (Exod. 22:21), and it is written: "And you shall not wrong one another and you shall fear your God" (Lev. 25:17). We are commanded to return to the poor his pledged article as is written: "If you take the garment of the poor in pledge you shall restore it to him before the sun goes down" (Exod. 22:25), as it is said: "And it shall be when he cries unto me that I will hear for I am gracious." And it is said: (Ibid: 26) "And you shall not wrong nor oppress a stranger."

Even from an animal he must keep cruelly far away, as it is written: "A righteous man knows the needs and capacity of his animal" (Prov. 12:10), so as not to burden it too much and not to let it hunger, and so it is written: "When you see the donkey of one who hates you lying under his burden you shall restrain yourself from passing by; you shall surely work with him to release the animal" (Exod. 23:5). And our rabbis said: "The laws against causing pain to living creatures are from the Torah" (Baba Mezi'a 32b). And if you are a man who inspires fear, and the fear of you is upon other human beings so that they are afraid to refuse your requests, be very careful not to overburden them even by asking them to warm a flask of water or sending them on an errand to the market square to buy merely a loaf of bread. And on this subject, it is said in the Torah: "But over your brothers the children of Israel you shall not rule one over another harshly" (Lev. 25:46). And as to this precept we have been warned that a man should not cause his companion to work at hard labor and not command him to anything unless he does it willingly and knowingly. A Canaanite slave may be directed to do hard labor, yet even in this latter case the pious way is to be merciful to him and not to make the yoke too heavy and not shame him, not by a blow and not by words, for Scripture has permitted you to receive his labor but not to shame him (Niddah 47a). And the master must speak quietly to his Canaanite slave even though there is a quarrel between them, and he must listen to his slave's complaints, and so did Job say: "If I did despise the cause of my man servant or of my maid servant when they contended with me — What then shall I do when God rises up and when He remembers some wrong, He claims I did to a slave, what shall I answer him. Did not he that made me in the womb make him (the Canaanite slave) also? And did not the One fashion us (both) in the womb?" (Job 31:13-15).

Our Sages of the first generations used to give their slaves food of every single dish that was served them (Ketuboth 61a). They would always feed the animals and their slaves before their own meal for lo he says: "Behold, as the eyes of servants unto the hand of their master, as the eyes of a maiden unto the hand of her mistress, so our eyes look unto the Lord our God" (Ps.

123:2). And the truly pious, before he himself would eat, would give to his slave from every single dish that was to be served to him — and for the merit of this act Elijah would speak to him sooner. (See Kethuboth 61a).

The Torah says: "And you shall love your neighbor as yourself" (Lev. 19:18), and one who has within himself the quality of cruelty is very far from this. This cruel person is not liked by his fellow men, and there is no kind regard for him in the eyes of the world.

Even when it becomes necessary to rebuke someone we have been warned not to rebuke with cruelty, as it is written: "You shall surely rebuke your neighbor but not bear sin because of him" (Lev. 19:17), which means "Do not rebuke him strongly and with cruelty to shame him and thus be guilty of sinning against him."

Until now we have told of the evils of cruelty, but there are places where it is necessary to conduct one's self with cruelty against the wicked, as Job said: "And I broke the jaws of the unrighteous, and plucked the prey out of his teeth" (Job 29:17), and as the Torah itself has commanded us to execute the wicked and to lash them. And thus did our rabbis say: "He who does not want to build a Sukkah, nor make fringes for his tallit ... nor fix a Mezuzah on his doorpost deserves to be beaten within an inch of his life" (Ketuboth 86a). And all this requires cruelty of a sort — to pursue the wicked and to press heavily upon them in order to restore them to good conduct.

And it is necessary to be cruel in judgment in order not to favor relatives, friends and the poor, but to decide according to the law. And our Rabbis said further: "In whom do you find the words of the Torah? In him who makes himself as cruel as the raven to his children, as Rabbi Adda bar Matna who was going to the House of Study and his wife said to him, 'What shall I do for your children' (to feed them if you go to study Torah instead of to work)? He responded, 'There are vegetables in the swamp' " (Erubin 22a).

For this is clear, he who has much pity for his children thinks chiefly how to earn money for their needs but does not reflect on how this money will come to him — illegally or legitimately, for the love (he bears his children) blinds him to honest appraisal ("spoils the straight line"). Then too because of absorption, in that he is busy day and night to secure, in large quantity, their foods and their other needs, he has no time for the words of the Torah, for he makes his business the important thing, and from this wrong emphasis all his deeds are confused.

And a man should be cruel in his battle against the wicked and not have mercy upon them. And our Rabbis said: "Everyone who becomes merciful when cruelty is needed will in the end become cruel when mercy is required" (Koheleth Rabbah 7). And so, you find in the case of King Saul. Because he had mercy on Agag there came forth from Agag, Haman, who became an oppressor of Israel. A person should also be cruel to his body to trouble it always to do the will of the Creator, may He be Blessed, and not to have mercy on his body by pampering it and pursuing these vain things with obduracy, but he should make himself cruel over himself to bend his evil desire to live a life of pain and to occupy one's self with Torah and to fulfil the commandments even if it is very difficult for him to do so. But he should not be so cruel to himself as to harm his body, but let him adopt the middle road.

And you, son of man, examine yourself and be far from cruelty and have mercy upon the poor and the needy and let the poor be as the members of your family. "Then the Lord ... will show you mercy and have compassion upon you and multiply you" (Deut. 13:18). Everyone who has mercy on his fellow creatures will have mercy shown him from heaven (Shabbath 151b). Therefore, do not remove mercy from you but guard yourself against the quality of cruelty. And Solomon said: "Lest you give to others your vigour and your years unto the cruel (to being cruel)" (Prov. 5:9). And guard yourself against the desire for vengeance which itself stems from cruelty. If you wish to truly avenge yourself on your enemy then add to your good qualities and walk in the path of the upright, and in this way, you will be avenged on him who hates you, for he will writhe in pain because of your good qualities and good repute and mourn when he hears good of you. But if you do ugly deeds then your enemy will rejoice over your shame and disgrace and thus avenge himself against you.

And if you wish to have mercy on your children and kin and to honor them with a great honor, then you must occupy yourself with Torah and good deeds and kindly acts of charity and this will be the best for them — that they should be honored through you and not bear reproach because of you. For there is no greater shame than that one should have parents and relatives who are wicked people. And he whose father is a thief or robber or had done other notorious deeds that are ugly in the eyes of the world, all his descendants are made ugly after him for many generations, for people say of them, "These are the descendants of that wicked one." And for the sins of parent's children die, as it is written: "Visiting the iniquity of the fathers upon the children unto the third and fourth generation of them that hate me" (Exod. 20:5). See and understand this — is there a crueller man than one whose children die because of his sin? And there is none who shows greater mercy to his children than the righteous man, for his merit continues for a thousand generations (and his descendants are blessed and honored because of him.)

Abraham bound his son, and the Holy One, Blessed is He, swore to remember this merit to the credit of his children for generations and generations. When Israel sinned with the golden calf, Moses, upon him is peace, stood in prayer and said: "Remember the deeds of Abraham, Isaac and Israel thy servants" (Exod. 32:31), and so Solomon prayed: "Remember the good deeds of David Thy Servant" (II Chron. 6:42), and their prayers were answered. And thus, we mention every day the merits of the fathers (in our daily prayers).

Therefore, you must know that there are none so cruel as those who commit transgressions, for through the sin of hatred for no good reason the Second Temple was destroyed and all manners of troubles come upon the world because of sins, as our Rabbis, upon them is peace, stated: "Because of the sin of failure to give Hallah there is no blessing in the harvest" (Shabbath

32b). And, "Because of the sin of failure to give Terumah and Tithes the Heavens withhold their blessing" (Ibid). And, "For the sin of twisting, falsifying and degrading the law the sword, great plunder, plague and drought come" (Ibid.: 33a), and there are many similar instances. And in truth those who cause these troubles are the really cruel ones against themselves, their children and the people of their generation, as it is said that all the people were sustained through the merit of Hanina ben Dosa (Berakoth 17b).

This is also an answer to the poor who say: "With what can we do good?" We have nothing to give as justice (alms) to the poor." Such statements are nonsense, for the poor man can give the righteousness of his good deeds and of fulfilling the commandments, — his care in giving Service to the Creator, may He be Blessed, with all his ability. It is through the merit of the good and the righteous that the Holy One, Blessed is He, does good to the world and sustains it. Is there greater justice or alms or charity than this? But even the poor man can give some alms, even though he himself sustains himself through alms he receives, and his reward is doubled and redoubled, for the little he gives is as important as the great contributions of the rich man. And so did our Rabbis say: "Whether one gives much or another gives little — the important thing is that the heart be directed to Heaven" (Berakoth 5b) [Menachoth 110b].

Sefer

ORCHOT TZADIKIM

Ways of the Righteous

Chapter Nine

ON JOY

The quality of Joy comes to a man out of the peace and security in his heart without an evil happening clouding it. And a man who achieves his desire without a sad event to mar it will be happy always, and his face will glow and his radiance will gleam, and his body will be healthy and old age will not quickly come upon him, as it is said: "A merry heart is good (healing) medicine" (Prov. 17:22). From joy will come laughter, but it is not fitting for an intelligent man to laugh too much, for with too much laughter goes a frivolous mind, as it is said: "For as the crackling of thorns under a pot so is the laughter of the fool" (Eccl. 7:6). And it has already been said that one of the signs of a fool is that he laughs when and where laughter is not proper. And it is not fitting for one who has the obligation of correcting others to conduct himself laughingly at meetings or gatherings, for the sages have said concerning him, "He who laughs much loses the respect of others, for when he laughs, another is unable to revere him (with the reverence due his teacher i.e.) with the fear of

Heaven. The concept involved here is that when one receives a teacher with reverence, it is as though he had received the Divine Presence. Therefore, a man should reprove and strengthen himself not to laugh at the slightest pretext, nor should he acquire a teacher or companion who is given to much laughter, as it is said: "I did not sit in the assembly of them that make merry and rejoice" (Jer. 15:17). And it is written: "In all sadness there is some profit" (Prov. 14:23) (something to be learned or gained).

There are many evils in too much rejoicing and in too much laughter, as for instance one who rejoices when his companion stumbles or when some evil mischance of the tragic happenings that afflict the world comes upon him. And concerning this it is said: "When your enemy falls do not rejoice" (Ibid. 24:17). And there is a joy that is even worse than this — as when a man rejoices because his companion made errors in the Service of the Creator, may He be blessed, or rejoices at the lack of knowledge of his companion. The following parable you should easily understand: a servant who ministers to his king faithfully is pained when he sees people rebelling against his master and abusing him [and he should rebuke them to their faces and let them know the extent of their vile conduct], but when a servant is happy when he sees the service of his master being spoiled and his master's consequent shame, then he is not a faithful servant [he is a comrade to the destroyer and will have to bear his guilt]. And behold Scripture says: "The Lord desires those that revere Him" (Ps. 147:11). And he who rejoices when his companion stumbles — his desire is not like the desire of the

Creator, may He be Blessed. Therefore, Rabbi Nehunia ben Hakanah prayed: "And let not my fellows err in a point of law and I be happy with this" (Berakoth 28b). Therefore, Rabbi Nehunia ben Hakanah prayed to be free from this fault for he saw that it was common that one rejoices in the mistake of his companion in order that he should feel triumphant over his companion and have that fame. And how many important people there are who do not take care in this connection. Therefore, every man whose will is the will of God feels great pain when the will of God is not accomplished by men. A man should pray that even his enemy should serve the Creator, Blessed be He. And he should intend in his prayers — when he comes to the Benedictions of "Thou art Gracious" and "Restore Us" and "Forgive Us" — to include all of Israel, those that love him and those that hate him. And so, should it be with all his Benedictions. For how could it be true that he should pray for "the healing of his people Israel" and the other Benedictions, and not want his companion to be healed or become wiser?

And because this desire to triumph over an enemy is very common in the hearts of people and one may not sense it within himself, Therefore, we write to warn those who revere the Lord to direct their hearts to God with true and complete devotion — to pour out their souls towards the presence of the Lord in prayer for all Jews — those who love him and those who hate him, and thus fulfill the commandment : "And you shall love your neighbor as yourself" (Lev. 19:18). "And he that has clean hands becomes stronger" (Job 17:9).

There is another kind of joy and laughter that is very evil, for example, he who laughs at one who is very careful and pious in the way he serves God, may He be Blessed, and fulfills His commandments, and in this there are four evils:

The first is that he darkens his own soul from the light of the commandments when he rejects or laughs at those who fulfill them — and he makes the Commandments ugly in his own eyes.

The second evil is that perhaps with his mocking laughter he can dissuade the righteous man from his righteous deeds for the later may not be able to bear the laughter.

The third is that people who have never tried to walk in the ways of God, may He be Blessed, may not, because of this laughter, ever repent, and will walk in darkness all their days. Then it is clear that the scoffer does not only hold back his fellow from the great good that is treasured up for the righteous but thrusts him down into the lowest pit. This scoffer falls within the guilt category of those who cause others to sin.

The fourth evil is that the scoffer is like a bandit that stands at the crossroads and cuts off the legs of those who come bringing gifts to the king. Such a one is a hater and an enemy of the king and his wickedness is very great.

There is another joy whose effect is as bitter as wormwood — for instance the joy of those who pursue immorality and robbery and all other sins and rejoice when they attain their evil lusts. Concerning these it is said: "Who rejoice to do evil and delight in the forwardness of evil" (Prov. 2:14). Their guilt is great and brings them to the lowest pit.

And there is yet another confusing joy that casts smoke over all the Commandments and causes reverence for the Lord, may He be Blessed, to be forgotten from the hearts of men, for instance — those who get themselves drunk and rejoice in the banquet houses. And after this type of joy comes sorrow, for much hurt comes from drinking feasts. And who in wisdom was as wise as Solomon, the son of David, who said: "Who cries 'Woe!' Who cries 'Alas!' Who has quarrels? Who has ravings? Who has wounds without cause? Who has red eyes? They that tarry long at the wine; they that constantly try mixed drinks" (Ibid. 23:29, 30). Also, the prophet said: 'Woe unto them that rise early in the morning that they may pursue strong drink. They tarry late into the night till the wine inflames them" (Is. 5:11). And he said further: "And the harp and the psaltery, the taboret and the pipe and wine are in their feasts, but the work of the Lord they do not regard and the work of His hands they have not seen" (Ibid.: 12). And he said: "Therefore, my people are gone into captivity for want of knowledge, and their honorable men are famished and their multitude are parched with thirst" (Ibid.: 13). And he said: "Therefore, has the netherworld enlarged her desire, and opened her mouth without measure and down go their glory and their tumult and their uproar and he that rejoices, among them " (Ibid.: 14). And he said: "But these also reel through wine and stagger through strong drink, the priest and the prophet reel through strong drink; they are confused because of wine, they stagger because of strong drink, they reel in vision; they totter in judgment" (Ibid. 28:7). See how much harm comes from the wine! And it is written: "Wine is a mocker, strong drink is riotous and whoever reels thereby is not wise" (Prov. 20:1).

Behold, wine causes one to become a scoffer and a mocker and to be riotous and quarrelsome. And everyone who transgresses through it is not very wise. Our teacher, Moses Maimonides wrote: "A gathering for drinking intoxicating liquor deserves greater shame among you that when naked people gather exposing their nakedness. And drunkenness is an evil deed for it causes one to lose the intelligence which the Lord, may He be Blessed, breathed into man's nostrils." In truth, the drinking of wine is very good if one drinks like an intelligent person, as under the circumstances and in the manner of which Solomon said: "Give strong drink to him that is ready to perish and wine to the bitter in soul. Let him drink and forget his poverty and remember his misery no more" (Prov. 31:6-7). And more is said about wine: "Wine which cheers God and man" (Judges 9:13). And it is written: "And wine that makes glad the heart of man" (Ps. 104:15). Also, Scripture says: "For thy love is better than wine" (Ecel. 1:2), and it also is said: "And the roof of thy mouth is like the best wine" (Ibid. 7:10).

From all of these citations we can know the praise of wine when it is drunk according to the measure of the wise who drink a specified amount — so that the intelligence may be stronger than the wine and not the wine be stronger than the intelligence, and who drink at a set time, together, and not with those barren of knowledge, vain and empty. For wine adds deep wisdom, a tree of life for those that hold it. And wine adds wisdom to the intelligent person, but doubles the folly of the fool. It revives the love of a friend but stirs up the enmity of a foe. It opens the hand of the generous and hardens the heart of a miser.

And thus, should be the manner of one who drinks wine. He should use the wine as a healing for his worry and thus strengthen himself in Torah to study it with joy, for when a man is plunged in grief he cannot study and even judges of courts of law, when they are grieved, cannot give a clear judgment. Grief also disturbs the concentration of the mind on one's prayer.

Also, when a man is plunged in pain or grief, he has not the strength to fulfill the request of someone who is speaking to him or is asking him for a favor. And it is written: "In an acceptable time have I answered you" (Is. 49:8).

Therefore, an intelligent person should direct himself in drinking wine in this manner — that he should remember not to drink too much so as to be compelled by his condition to neglect his work and his affairs. And, moreover, he must guard himself from drinking so much that he neglects his study of the Torah and his prayers, or until he becomes too frivolous and light headed. And he should not drink to the extent that he reveals his secrets or the secrets of others. And if you will drink in this moderate measure, wine will not become loathsome to you.

Even on Holidays and Festivals, of which it is written: "And you shall rejoice before the Lord your God" (Deut. 12:18), one should not prolong his drinking more than is proper, as it is said: "Because you did not serve the Lord your God with joyfulness and with gladness of heart" (Ibid. 28:47). From this you learn

ORCHOT TZADIKIM — Chapter Nine

that we have not been commanded to rejoice in a manner that the Creator of all is forgotten. For it is impossible to serve the Lord, may He be Blessed, out of light headedness, or laughter, or drunkenness.

In the quality of joy there is a positive command to accept all that happens to one with a conviction of God's justice, as it is said: "And you shall consider in your heart that just as a man chastises his son, so does the Lord chasten you" (Ibid. 8:5), i.e., for his own good.

And if, after a man repents, his affairs are not as good as they were at first, it is a command that he think in his heart that for his own ultimate good has his project turned bad — that before that man repented, the Holy One, Blessed be He, was paying him the reward of whatever good deeds he had done in order to drive him forth from sharing in the world to come, as it is said: "And He pays him who hates Him to his face (quickly and completely) so as to bar him" (from sharing in the world to come) (Ibid. 7:19). And just as He deals with those that hate Him, so does he mete out the punishment for the sins of those that love Him in this world, so that they will be pure and perfect in the world to come. And all this is dependent upon the quality of joy, for he (the good person) rejoices in the portion that God, may He be Blessed, has allotted to him.

Now the way in which a man should be happy with his portion and receive with joy the evil as well as the good - this way is divided into several paths:

First: A large fence is needed to hedge him securely in his trust in God.

Second: A firm faith — the will to believe.

Third: Intelligence — that understands that a blessing may come of pain.

Fourth: Self sufficiency that needs no approval but God's.

The wise man said: Every man needs a fence and support in order that his good deeds should be brought to fulfillment. And what is the fence? It is complete trust — to always trust in God, may He be Blessed, as it is said: "Cast your burden upon the Lord and He will sustain you" (Ps. 55:23).

And what is the fence of trust? What is it that causes a man to trust in God? It is the quality of Faith. From the fact that he believes in the Creator and that all his good fortune in this world and in the world to come is from Him and that there is none beside Him, he firmly sets his mind to love Him with all his heart.

And what is the fence of faith? What thing brings a man to complete faith? It is that he should not sway or tremble before a bad happening but receive all that happens to him with joy. And this is like the case of a servant who knows his master well, — knows that his master is generous, merciful and pays a large reward to those who do his will and carry out his bidding. And though he sometimes assigns hard work to his servants, he rewards them with great rewards, and makes them great and important. They become the men with whom he counsels, and they eat at his table and he causes them to ride in a carriage second only to his own and sets them up as administrators over his land. There is no doubt that a servant who knows this about his master, would leave any other interest he has in the world and do the will of his master with joy, even though the work is very difficult for him, when he has in mind the good which will be his because of this work. But the servant who sees that his master holds back the wages of his servants, and knows in his heart that his master is a miser, and that his troubles as a worker are much greater than his wages, such a servant can exert himself only with great sorrow.

So is this matter! He who believes with complete faith in his Creator, that He does good and shows Mercy more than any merciful one, that He is a true Judge, and that all that God does to him is for his good and in order to give him great reward for all that he bears for the sake of His great Name and for every service and ministry that he does for the sake of Heaven, — such a one will attain for himself great pleasantness in the world that is forever pleasant, as we found in the matter of Nebuchadnezzar, who, because he took four steps in honor of God, may He be blessed, merited greatness and honor (Sanhedrin 96a), and as we found in the matter of Esau, who, because he was scrupulous about honoring his father merited greatness in this world, he and his seed after him, and so there are many similar cases. There is no doubt that when a man believes all this with a perfect heart, he will certainly rejoice with all the judgments of God, may He be Blessed, for who would not rejoice when someone takes from him copper pennies and gives him in their stead a talent of gold?

He who believes in God with a perfect heart and trusts in Him with a strong trust, his trust will bring him to the point where he will never fear man or evil circumstance and he will never serve a man in order to please him and he will never place his hope in man, and he will never agree with people in a matter that is contrary to the Service of the Creator, may He be Blessed, and none of their affairs will frighten him and he will not fear their quarrels and if he rebukes them will not worry about their pride and if he finds it necessary to shame them he will not be shy before them, and he will not make their falsehood beautiful or acceptable as the Prophet said : "For the Lord God will help me, Therefore, , am I not confounded, Therefore, have I set my face like flint, and I know that I shall not be ashamed" (Is. 50:7).

He who trusts in God — his trust will bring him to cleanse his heart from worldly matters and to devote himself solely to matters concerning Torah and Worship. And a man ought to search out the ideas that take hold of his heart so as to trust in God completely. His first thought should be that he should know with a clear knowledge that God has mercy upon man more than any merciful being and that He watches over him in secret and openly. And at times when he does not take such care as he should, God has mercy on him and guards him from evil happenings as it is said on this subject, "The Lord guards the simple" (Ps. 116:6).

His second thought should be that all the good which comes to him from his father, mother, his brothers and his other relatives and friends are all from the Lord, may He be Blessed, and these people are simply the messengers of God, Blessed is He.

The third thought should be that all the good that comes to him is the result of God's kindness, not that he deserves it, and the Holy One, Blessed be He, is not doing him good because He needs him, but it is God's voluntary and gracious gift and kindness.

The fourth thought should be that in all his matters and achievements there is a boundary and limit, and no human being can add or detract to what the Creator, may He be Exalted, has decreed. And if the Holy One, Blessed is He, has decreed his portion should be small, then man cannot increase the little or lessen the much. And what God has decreed to come later no man can advance nor, can be delay what God has decreed to come early, for all is in accordance with the decree of the Highest and His will.

The fifth thought is that he should know that the Creator, may He be Blessed, sees his heart and knows whether his trust in Him is a complete trust without guile. For a servant who ministers to a human being is able to deceive his master so that the master should believe that the servant loves him with all his heart, though in fact, he hates him, and the master will deal well with him under the conviction that his servant loves him. But all this can not be true of the Creator, may He be Blessed, for He knows the desire of the heart and the thought within it and He knows all that is above and below, his faith and his unbelief. Therefore, one cannot walk before Him with attempt to deceive.

The sixth thought is that he should take it into his heart to fulfill what God has commanded him and to avoid all that He has warned him not to do. If a man desires that the Creator, may He be Exalted, should do that which he depends upon Him to do, then he must act according to the words of the Sages: "Make His will thy will in order that He shall do thy will as

His will. Nullify your will before His will in order that He should nullify the will of others before your will" (Aboth 2:4). But he who trusts and depends on the Lord, may He be Exalted, and does not fulfill what He has commanded him — what a simpleton and fool is he! And of this it is said: "For what is the life of the flatterer, though he gets profit or gain, when God takes away his soul? Will God hear his cry?" (Job 27:8,9). And it says: "Will you steal, murder, and commit adultery and swear falsely and offer unto Baal and walk after other gods whom you have not known, and come and stand before Me in this house upon which My name is called?" (Jer. 7:9-10). And it says: "Has this house wherein My name is called become a den of robbers in your eyes?" (Ibid: 11).

The seventh thought which leads to rejoicing is that he should know that the Creator, Blessed is He, created man for many labors and provided food for him to obtain through much exertion and work and that if all these things like food and clothes were prepared for man without any trouble at all on his part there would be a number of commandments that would not exist — for instance Charity — laws prohibiting robbery, theft, covetousness, and many similar commandments. Then too, if all were provided, man would have no need to trust in God. And for this reason, Hezekiah the King of Judea hid the Book of Healings (Berakoth 10b) in order that the sick person should trust in God, may He be Exalted, and not merely in drugs. Moreover, if a man were freed from the necessity of work and did not have to trouble himself about his sustenance, he would kick out against all restraint and pursue wrongdoing as it is written: "When Jeshurun prospered, he kicked" (Deut. 32:15). And our Sages said: "The study of the Torah is good when combined with making a living, for the exertion necessary for both activities causes one to forget all thought of sinning" (Aboth 2:2).

So now we see that the Lord, may He be Exalted, has placed two types of service in the hands of man — one — his own necessary labor for a livelihood and the second — his Service of the Torah, and a man must follow the middle road between both of these services — and devote special hours to the service of the Torah and special hours to work for the needs of this world. And you must strengthen yourself to always accomplish both for the good of yourself and your posterity. And one type of service should not be considered a loss as against the other service as it is said: "Did not your father eat and drink and do justice and righteousness? Then it was well with him" (Jer. 22:15). And it says: "It is good that you should take hold of the one and from the other not withdraw your hand" (Eccl. 7:18). And he must trust in the Lord, may He be Blessed, that He will cause him to prosper in his affairs, and he ought not to trust in his work and his occupations, but consider that his work and occupation are merely means to his support from the Lord, may He be Blessed; just as when a man splits wood with an axe, even though the axe splits the wood, the power does not come from the iron blade of the axe but from the man who wields the axe and splits the wood with it.

And a man who has a job or some occupation by which he supports his family should not think, "If not for this job I would be utterly lost." But he should trust in the Creator may He be Blessed, and think that if this work were not here to occupy him, then the Creator may He be Blessed, would provide his sustenance through some other means, because all the work of his hands and his needs are in the hands of God, and God has many messengers (of good fortune), as Scripture says : "For there is no restraint of the Lord to save by many or by few" (Samuel 14:6), and it says further : "It is He who gives power to get wealth" (Deut. 8:18), and it says : "Not by might nor by power but by My spirit says the Lord of Hosts" (Zech. 4:6).

And thus, the man, whose whole livelihood and the fulfillment of whose needs depend on another, should not in his heart put his trust in that man, but should root his trust in the very depth of his heart in the Creator, may He be Blessed. And it is not enough that he should say this merely in his heart, but he must verbally give praise and thanks to the Creator, may He be Blessed, for not having removed His kindness from him. He should accept willingly this fitting parable concerning this matter: It is like a hundred blind people walking in single file and each one's hand is on the shoulder of his companion, but at the head of all of them there is a man who sees, and it is he who leads them all. In that case each blind man knows, that even though he places his hand on the shoulder of his companion and his companion leads him, that this "leading" is not actually in the power of the man in front of him, but that all of the men in single file are being led by the man who sees and is leading the whole line, and that if this man is taken from them — they will all stumble and fall. This is what a man should say to his heart and consider, that the Holy One, Blessed is He, is the Leader and that we are all of us like the blind, and each one of us is helped and aided by a companion, but there is no power in the companion to aid if it were not for the First and Uppermost Leader who directs all of His paths in straight lines, and none can find fault with Him. And just as the one who is being supported by another human being should regard only the Holy One, Blessed is He, so should the one who supports another not vaunt himself that he supports another, but consider himself like the blind man who precedes another blind man and leads him only through the help of the First Leader, who is the one that sees.

And on this subject it is said: "And I will bring the blind by a way they knew not in paths that they knew not I will lead them" (Is. 42:16), and he says further: "And look (understand) you blind, that you may see!" (Ibid: 18). And he says further: "Who is blind, but My servant? or deaf, as My messenger that I send? Who is blind as he that is wholehearted and blind as the Lord's servant?" (Ibid: 19).

Now, all of the matters in which we trust in the Holy One, Blessed be He, may be divided into eight parts:

1. The first is his body — his general health.
2. The second is his sustenance.
3. Matters concerning his wife, relations and friends.
4. The duties of the hearts and the limbs which may help or harm him.
5. The functions of his limbs insofar as they may help or harm others.
6. His reward in this world.

7. The reward stored up for the righteous in the world to come.

8. The reward in the days of the Messiah.

The first trust — in the matter of a man's body, means, that he must submit his life and self to God's great mercy and know that there is no counsel or way of conduct except with God's permission and decree. And even though all the functioning of his limbs and the measure of his days are bound up in the decree of the Creator, may He be Blessed, nevertheless, a man must move about to earn his needs and save his life and prepare the medicine he needs and he must trust in God that he will heal him, and that the doctor and the medicine to heal him also come to him from the Lord, may He be Blessed. And he should not depend on any but God to give him the needed ability and strength. But a man should not say "Since my welfare is bound up in the decree of the Creator, may He be Blessed, I will walk into any danger and drink deadly poison."

Have we not found in the case of Samuel that he asked. "How can I go? If Saul hears of it (that he is to anoint another) he will kill me" (I Sam. 16:2). And even though Samuel said this he must not be considered as of those who have little trust in God. And the Holy One, Blessed be He, responded, "Take a heifer with you and say, 'I have come to sacrifice to the Lord' " (thus providing Samuel with a remedy in his danger).

And concerning one who deliberately places himself in danger and says, "I trust in the Lord, may He be Blessed," about him it is said: "But the fool behaves overbearingly and is confident" (Prov. 14:16). And the Torah has warned us concerning this as it is written: "You shall not try the Lord your God" (Deut. 6:16). And he who places himself in danger and kills himself through his folly, his punishment is greater than that of a man who kills others.

The second trust is concerning a livelihood. A man should have trust in the Lord, Blessed is He, that He will provide his needs and his food sufficiently. A man should not devote excessive time pursuing after many materials matters which will busy him and keep him from Torah. When he trusts in God, he will find rest for his heart and peace for his soul. And he should not attempt to earn more than he needs, but let him be content with work he can do at a specific time and the rest of his time let him busy himself to acquire the world to come.

And thus, said the sages: "Increase your study and lessen your business affairs." "Make the study of the Torah your principle aim and business secondary" (Sifre, V'etchanan). And this matter is the most severe in the trials of man — that the many affairs of this world should not trouble him to the point that he forgets his future. Therefore, he should trust in God that He will provide sufficiently for his needs so that he will have hours in which he is free to turn his heart to God.

The third trust is concerning his wife, his children, his relatives and his friends. If the one who places his trust in God is a stranger or sojourner without a wife, relative or friend, let him take God as a relative and friend as it is written: "This is my Beloved and this is my Friend" (Eccl. 5:16). And let him consider, "Everyone who has relatives will, after a little while, have to face God alone and no relative, son or friend will be able to help him, nor will any one of these be able to accompany him." And he should also consider when he withdraws to study Torah what burdens could be placed upon him by demanding relatives and consider this to his good, that if he were occupied with these and other worldly matters, he would be much bothered and would have no rest. And when he occupies himself with his future life and with matters of the commandments and uniting his heart with God, then his mind will doubtless be freer and more concentrated, because he is alone and without relatives. And, Therefore, the ascetics, who declared repeatedly the Oneness of God in their hearts, fled from their homes and relatives to the mountains in order that they might turn their hearts to God.

And if the person who trusts in God is married and has children, relatives, and loving friends, he should trust in God that He will give him the strength to give them their due and fulfill their desires, and he must trust that his mind will always be well disposed towards them. And he should teach them the paths of conduct set forth in the Torah, and the proper Service of the Creator, and all this not because he anticipates that he will receive some gain from them for this, or that they will honor him for showing them the right path, nor that he will be able to lord it over them, but he will do these things only because he wants to fulfill the command of the Creator, Blessed be He. And he must think that he is a messenger from God to teach his relatives and friends, and not take credit for himself nor permit his heart to grow lofty over them. And if he needs the help of his relatives and they fill his needs, he must think of them as the messengers of God, Blessed be He, to fill his need, and not put his trust in them at all. And if he asks them for something and they refuse him, let him not assume that they are sinning, but let him consider that there are many messengers of God who will fill his need.

The fourth thought concerning the entrusting of the heart in the care of God occurs where a man concentrates his heart through fasting, prayer and all the rest of the commandments and is thus restrained from sin. It is necessary that he go forward with all his might to fulfill the commandments, and he must pray with a faithful heart and pure thought and with firm intent to glorify His Great Name. And in doing this we are obligated to trust Him and to plead with Him to help us and to teach us the straight paths as David, peace upon him, said: "Guide me in thy truth and teach me" (Ps. 25:5). And he said: "Make me tread in the paths of thy commandments" (Ibid. 119:35), and again, "I have chosen the way of faithfulness" (Ibid: 30). And all this is proof that he chose the Service of God and prayed for two things; first, to strengthen his heart in his concentration on God so that he might separate from his heart the trouble and concern over this world. And the second thing for which he prayed was to strengthen his body and limbs so that he might be strong in his good deeds. And this is what he meant when he prayed that God should prosper him in his body and in the concentration of his heart to God.

The fifth trust is the trust of his limbs which he uses to do good to others: — for example, Charity, and by teaching wisdom to pupils and commanding them concerning the good, and to separate themselves far from evil, and to bring the wicked back to God in repentance, and to bear their shame and abuse at the time that he warns them concerning the true Service of God and awes them with descriptions of punishment and reward. And he must strive with all his might to do these things, and he must trust in God that He will help him and make possible his desire to draw near with this Service to God alone and not to acquire fame or honor among the people who benefit from his deeds, nor to expect any reward from them, and not to lord it over them. And he must be careful, as much as is possible, to do these good deeds in secret, and if he cannot keep his good deeds secret, then he must remember that all the gain and the loss that is involved does not come from God's creatures, but is the province of the Creator, may He be Blessed. And in all of this he must place his trust in the Lord, may He be Blessed. And when God, may He be Exalted, causes an opportunity for a good deed to come his way, he must consider in his heart that this is a favor from the Creator, may He be Exalted, who has dealt kindly with himin permitting him this opportunity to serve, and he should not rejoice when men praise him.

The sixth trust concerns a man's hope in this world — that he should trust God not to feed him in this world with a portion that is more proper for the coming world. And he should trust Him that He will guard him from the misfortunes of this world and from its illnesses, and from the plague and the sword and from famine and from the rest of the evils that come rushing forth upon the world.

ORCHOT TZADIKIM

And when he does trust in God, let him not do so because he feels reward is coming to him on account of his good deeds, but he should do all of his deeds for the sake of God, may He be Exalted, who has raised him and carried him in this world and dealt well with him. He must realize that there is not a moment in all the days of his life that the goodness of the Creator is not upon him. And he must consider that, if his good deeds were doubled and multiplied many times over, it would not be one ten-thousandth of what he ought to do because of God's goodness, may He be Blessed, that hovers over him every moment. And after he has thought all this, let him trust in the kindnesses of the Lord, Blessed be He, who is the One who extends kindness and who is more merciful than all the deeds of mercy of man. For God, in His mercy, gives food even to the swarming creatures, from the mighty wild ox to the eggs of lice (Shabbath 107b). And just as God has mercy on these creatures, not because of their good deeds, so will He have mercy on him.

The seventh trust is that he should confide in the King of Kings, who rules over all, Blessed be He, that He will bring, in his days, a great salvation for Israel and will establish Jerusalem and build the Temple in his days. And the intent of his trust in this salvation should not be that he may live in great security as is bound to be the case in those days, nor to eat the good fruit and to drink the finest wine, but his intent should be that he should live in those days in order to serve the Creator, may He be Blessed. For in those days God will remove the evil desire from the heart of His people and all — young and old — will know the

Lord and there will be nothing to distress them — not plague nor famine nor war nor troublesome tasks, but all people will be free, and all will attain a great concept in the knowledge of the Creator, may He be Blessed. And in those days' knowledge will increase as it is written: "For the earth shall be full of the knowledge of the Lord as the waters cover the sea" (Is. 11:9).

The eighth trust concerns the world to come that contains pleasures without end and beyond limits. And no one is able to tell the beauty of the world, and no eye can see the radiance of the glory of the righteous. And there, there is no eating and drinking. Now if this is so what kind of pleasure is to be found there? Therefore, it is necessary for you to understand and to know, that just as the bird does not know the pleasure of the fish that swims in the sea for their natures are opposite, since the bird will die in the water, and the fish will die on dry land, so anyone of this world where the soul and the body are mingled, cannot know the pleasure of the soul. For we know only the pleasure of the body, but as to a pleasure of the loftiest kind and most sublime — we cannot conceive of, nor can we know aught of it, except after much thought. And this is because we are in the physical world. Therefore, we can recognize only pleasures that disappear and cease, but the pleasures of the soul are infinite and without interruption. And there is no connection whatsoever between those pleasures and these, nor any sharing or resemblance whatever. And he who will merit that high degree of pleasure after his death, will not love these worldly pleasures anymore than a king will love to take off his glorious garments and play in the streets with children. And if, at times, a king should be young in years and the desire to participate in the follies of little children should be strong upon him so that he plays with the children and puts aside the splendor of his kingly state, then, this is because he does not have the knowledge to distinguish between the two paths, just as we often prefer the pleasure of this world over the pleasure of the world to come because of our lack of knowledge, and little ability to recognize what the spiritual world and its pleasures must be like.

Yet even in this world you can know something of what the pleasures of the soul are without the pleasure of eating and drinking. For example: men who triumph over their enemies, or the joy of being honored when people honor a man, or the joy a person feels at seeing beautiful things, or the joy a man feels when he sees his dear son whom he has not seen for a long time, or the joy he feels at hearing good news. In all these there is great pleasure without the joy of eating and drinking. And if this is so in the physical world, and we see that souls can be pleased with this, then you should be able to understand the pleasure of souls when you ascend to the highest heavens and rejoice in the radiance of the highest plane, and in the radiance, of the Shekhinah.

And there can be no account of this Divine pleasure nor any description of it, and we cannot compare it to any pleasure in this world, but as the Prophet said who wondered and marvelled at the preciousness of the world to come: "Oh how abundant is Thy goodness which Thou hast stored up for them that revere Thee!" (Ps. 31:20). And concerning the world to come, which is the desired end of man, he must place his trust in the Lord — his trust that the Lord will cause him to reach the upper world and will not cast him away from His presence.

And he cannot have such trust without good deeds. Only after he has occupied himself with these, with all his ability, can he ascend the steps of piety that are fitting for such a matter. And, of course, provided he removes the love of this world from his heart and puts in its place love of the Creator, Blessed is He, and commits himself to the Sanctification of the Name of God, may He be Blessed.

And if he does so, and trusts in the Creator, may He be Blessed, that He will deal kindly with him as He has dealt kindly with all the Prophets and pious ones, happy is he and happy is his portion! And concerning him who trusts in the Lord, may He be Blessed, this is a very good quality, and a man needs much repair and adjustment before he comes to the very essence of trust.

And he who trusts in God is invited to receive God's kindness, as it is written: "He that trusts in the Lord, loving kindness surrounds him" (Ps. 32:10). And this may be because one who trusts in the Lord must necessarily make several holes in his defenses, openings which are not good for him in this world. He must rebuke the many, even though he be afraid of them lest they injure him in body and substance. He must despair and abandon all hope in his relatives and loving friends so as not to participate with them where they do not follow the good road, and he must not flatter them. Also, he must abandon many affairs in this world in order to cleanse his heart from the follies of the world and occupy himself with Torah. And this requires great trust. Therefore, Scripture has said: "Loving kindness surrounds him."

Trust is impossible without faith, as it is written: "And they that know Thy Name will put their trust in Thee" (Ps. 9:11). For those who know His Great Name and recognize His greatness and power, and believe in Him with all their heart — only they can truly trust in Him, for trust and faith are partners; if there is no faith, there is no trust. And faith is the very beginning of the Torah, as it is written: "I am the Lord, your God; you shall have no other gods" (Exod. 20:2-3). And if a man does not believe of what good is his Torah? And where a man believes from the depths of his heart that the Creator will fulfill all that is written in the Torah, sending troubles to the sinner and paying a good reward to those who fulfill the precepts of the Torah, then he will carefully guard the Torah. For if all the thieves and robbers knew with certainty that they would be slain because of their thefts and robberies and would be unable to escape this fate, they would restrain themselves from wrong doing. But all of the thieves and robbers are sure that they will always be saved from this tragic end, and, Therefore, they do what their heart desires. And, also, in the case of the sinner, if he believed with certainty that he would be punished greatly, he would not sin. Therefore, all of the Torah is completely enclosed in faith, as it is written, "But the righteous shall live by his faith" (Hab. 2:4). And concerning Abraham, it is said: "And he believed in the Lord and He counted it to him for righteousness" (Gen. 15:6). And concerning all other good qualities such (a reward) is not written in Scripture.

And concerning Moses, it is written: "In all my house he is faithful" (Num. 12:7). And it is said in the Midrash: "Great is faith before the Holy One, Blessed is He, for because of the merit of the faith that our fathers believed there dwelt upon them the Holy Spirit and they uttered song as it is said: 'And they believed in the Lord and in Moses His servent. Then Moses and the Children of Israel sang'" (Exod. 14:31, 15:1, Exodus Rabbah 22-23).

And they were redeemed because of their faith, as it is written: "And the people believed" (Exod. 4:31). The Sages said of this verse, "Each one who takes upon himself one commandment with faith is worthy that the Holy Spirit shall dwell upon him." And the exiles are brought back through the merit of faith as it is said: "Look forth from the summit of Amanah (Faith)" (Eccl. 4:8). And it says further: "And I shall betroth thee to me with faith " (Hosea 2:22).

And now let us return to the matter of Joy. For he who believes with a complete heart and trusts in the help of the Rock (God) will always be happy and bear everything — just as a sick person eats bitter medicines in order to be healed. And he who bears problems willingly is free from the worry of the world. The one who bears all things willingly is satisfied with the little he has, for he says, "Whatever the Creator has decreed for me is enough for me."

And now look and see how Joy includes everything! For every man who worries about the material things of this world has no rest and is always planning how to make money, and he is never satisfied with what

God has apportioned to him. Therefore, the one who rejoices in his portion is rich even though he be poor, for he rejoices in the Lord who is his portion and inheritance. And so, it is written: "I have said, 'My portion is the Lord' " (Ps. 119:57). And so, he says: "Let the heart of them that seek the Lord rejoice!" (Ibid. 105:3).

And it is this quality that dwells in the souls of the righteous who derive complete pleasure in the matter of their Service to God and great joy in their separation from worldly wealth, as it is said: "Be glad with your faith in the Lord and rejoice you righteous, and shout for joy all you that are righteous in heart!" (Ibid. 32:11). And thus, he says: "Light is sown for the righteous and joy for the upright in heart!" (Ibid. 97:11).

Therefore, should a man place all his joy in the study and fulfilling of the Torah, and when he does the commandments, he should rejoice in his heart that he has merited to be a servant of the Highest King before whom all the dwellers of the Heavens bow. And thus, said David: "I rejoice at your word, as one who finds great spoil" (Ibid. 119:162). And everyone who fulfills the Commandments with joy has a thousand times the reward of one to whom the Commandments are a burden. Abraham and David would occupy themselves all day with Torah and in glorifying and praising the Holy One Blessed be He with songs and praises, raising their voices in joy.

And then he prospers in all his ways and in clarity of perception and the Holy One Blessed be He sends a spirit of Holiness within him and his heart rejoices and is filled with love of the Holy One, Blessed be

He, and his soul is united with joy and reveals secrets and new intepretations from above, and all this because he reveres God, Blessed is He and is upright. And reason enters him. And this is what Solomon said: "My soul failed me when he spoke" (Eccl. 5:16). "Yea my body will rejoice when my lips speak right things" (Prov. 23:16). And thus, said David: "Bless the Lord, O my soul" (Ps. 104:1). Because the soul which comes from above and strives upward knowing its own secret loves her Creator and eagerly assimilates His Commands, and when this soul reaches the veil (partition) and the degree which is suitable to it then she causes him (the owner) to rejoice with her hidden charms and brings him delight in her hidden chambers and at every moment his love longs for his soul and remembers it in the night as he lies upon his couch. Then God, Blessed is He, sends into her the longing for joy and the heart burns passionately from the great desire of love as it is said "I will rejoice in the Lord, my soul will be joyful in my God" (Is. 61:10). And happy is the soul that merits and experiences such joy.

The Divine Presence does not rest upon any one unless there is joy (Shabbath 30b). And all of the prophets did not prophesy at such times as they desired, but they would prepare their minds and sit joyous and glad of heart and then prophesy, for Prophecy does not dwell where idleness or sadness is found, but only where joy is. Therefore, the pupils of the Prophets would place before them lyre, drum and harp and sought by their means the gift of Prophecy, as it is written "And it came to pass, when the minstrel played, that the hand of the Lord came upon him" (II Kings 3:15).

The beauty of the soul is that she adorns herself with the beauty of the joy in that she rejoices in God and causes to gleam the light of her reverence, and the light of her majesty, and the light of her love for her Creator, an exalted and intense love that crowns itself with the crown of the beauty of clean and pure thoughts, and she sighs with the greatness of her joy and her exultation at her nearness to her Beloved, her Most High Beloved, and she binds herself to Him with the bond of love and she seeks and aspires the ascent of light — the light of life. And as she lifts herself and grows and enfolds in the Holy Knowledge of her Creator and as she cleaves with her faith to her Creator, may He be Blessed, then does she spread abroad with the renewal of joy and broadens her happiness. In that moment does the Holiness of the Holy of Holies become sanctified and then she desires and obtains grace before the King of all Kings, and in that moment, she becomes more precious and more beautiful and clothes herself in great glory — in the great might of her glory. And then the Most High acquires her to cause her light to shine, to cause her to enter in chambers of splendor and to bind her in the bond of life. And the Merciful One makes her one of his joyous servants.

There is another good in joy as in the case of two men of whom it was said that they would have a share in the world to come because they were happy men and whenever they saw a sad man, they would cheer him up, and whenever they saw two men quarreling with each other they would tell them humorous stories until they brought peace between the quarreling men. And this is true in discussions of the law, the Sages would begin with humorous words to open the mind to study with joy. Of course, this does not mean vulgar humor or nonsensical jesting, but rather words concerning the precepts of the Torah which cause the heart to rejoice as it is written: "The precepts of the Lord are right, rejoicing the heart" (Ps. 19:9). And all this pertains to the joy of fulfilling the commandments.

And thus, if a man has any kind of troubles he must rejoice even so. And thus said the Sages: "Beloved are troubles" (Berakoth 5b). And the Sages said also: "He who rejoices in his pain brings salvation to the world" (Ta'anith 8a). And a man should accustom his mouth to say: "This too is for good" (Ta'anith 21a), or "All that the merciful God has done He has done for good" (Berachot 60b). For there are many apparent evils whose end is good, and thus did our Rabbis teach and interpret this portion of Scripture, "I will give thanks unto thee, O Lord; for thou wast angry with me, thine anger is turned away, and thou comfortest me" (Is. 12:1). They explained it with a parable of two men who walked, intending to board a boat. One of them had a thorn stuck into his foot so that he could not board the boat and when his companion boarded the boat the man bruised by the thorn began to curse his "evil fortune". After a time, he heard that the boat had sunk and all the people in it had died. Then did he begin to praise the Creator, may He be Blessed, for he realized that the incident with the thorn had saved his life (Niddah 31a). Therefore, should a man rejoice with troubles and with other injuries that may befall him, for he does not know what good will be derived from them in the future. And thus, did Nahum the man of Gamzu conduct himself (Ta'anith 21a).

It is also good to cause bridegroom and bride to rejoice, as it is said, "The voice of mirth and the voice of gladness, the voice of the bridegroom and the voice of the bride" (Jer. 7:34), but one must be very careful not to amuse them with vulgar speech or jests for this type of rejoicing brings Divine Wrath. Nor should men and women mingle in the precept of causing bridegroom and bride to rejoice, for this is too frivlous. And even in mourning and during the Eulogy, the Sages said: "Let the men sit by themselves and the women by themselves! All the more is this true in rejoicings and we have learned 'Only to do justly, and to love mercy, and to walk humbly with thy God' (Micah 6:8), and "walking modestly" means — the funeral procession and bringing the bride under the Wedding Canopy" (Sukkah 49b).

It is also necessary to rejoice on Sabbaths, Festivals and on Purim because all of them are a memorial to our exodus from Egypt and of the miracles which He has done wonderously with His chosen ones. Therefore, shall one rejoice in his heart when he remembers the kindnesses of God and the great extent of his goodness with those who do His will. And for this reason, do we prepare tasty foods and precious garments and we drink wine, in order to cause the heart to rejoice. And one must be careful not to rejoice with such joy for frivolous reasons but should rejoice with such rejoicing because of his love for

God, may He be Blessed, and delight with this delight of love for the Rock, and he should rejoice and be glad in the joy of the Lord of all, who commanded him to have pleasure in that day and to rejoice. And in these Sabbath and Festival days he should be mindful of the pleasantries of the world to come which is the pleasure of all pleasures. And it is proper for a man at such times when he is enjoying pleasures that he should be mindful of the greater pleasures and desire them, as it is written "Then shalt thou delight thyself in the Lord" (Is. 58:14).

He should also rejoice when he sees the rejoicing of the wicked and the pleasures of transgressors and he should think thusly "If those who transgress God's Will can rejoice thus, then how much more will those who do His Will rejoice" (Nedarim 50b). And concerning this David says, "You have placed a joy in my heart greater than their joy in their plentiful corn and wine" (Ps. 4:8). For example, a king invited guests and when they reached the courtyard of the king, they saw the dog's eating ducks and chickens and they said: "If dogs are treated thus, then how much better will be our portion" (Shohar Tob, Midrash on Ps. 4:11).

And one should not rejoice in the good or profitable things that happen to him, and in no matter but in that which brings him closer to the Service of God.

A man should not rejoice in that which is good for him but brings an accident or loss to others. For example, a man who has much produce should not rejoice if there is a famine and consequent high prices for his food, for merely on account of his gain he should not rejoice at the loss of others. Nor should a person rejoice at the death of any man even though he gains an inheritance or other benefits through that death. The end of the matter is that one should not rejoice in the loss or downfall of any man though he gains profit from it, and on this subject, it is said: "And you shall love your neighbor as yourself" (Lev. 19:18). And a person should accustom his heart to be joyous when good things happen to others and he should especially rejoice when he sees men following God's commands in order to do the will of the Creator, may He be Blessed!

And a man should not rejoice to the point of hilarity for now all joy should be mixed with sobriety, for when our "Holy Rabbi" (Rabbi Judah the Prince) used to laugh thus, troubles came to the world (Berakoth 31a). And similarly, "Rabbi Jeremiah would bring Rabbi Zera to the point of laughter, but Rabbi Zera did not laugh" (Niddah 23a).

And when should a person rejoice greatly and laugh? When the Divine Presence returns to Zion, for this is a great joy, as it is written "Then will our mouths be filled with laughter and our tongues with song; then will they say among the nations, 'The Lord has done great things with these' " (Ps. 126:2).

Sefer
ORCHOT TZADIKIM
Ways of the Righteous

Chapter Ten

ON WORRY

Worry is a quality that is bad in all its manifestations and is easily recognized, as it is written "And(he) saw them and behold, they were sad" (Gen. 40:6). And it is also written, "Why is your appearance sad, seeing you are not sick" (Neh. 2:2).

And one of the Sages said, "I find no trace of worry in the faces of the nobler souls among men." The worry of a person who is concerned with acquiring the material and transitory things of this world is a very ugly trait and is never found in people who trust in God and believe in Him.

Worry and sadness destroy the heart and are physical ailments. And the evilest of all worries is the one wherein a person pursues vice and when he does not attain the gratification of every whim and lust of his heart, he worries and feels anguish. He who worries about the material things of this world is far from Torah, Commandments and Prayer. Therefore, one should hasten to correct this flaw and remove this evil trait from his character. There is no need to discuss at length the evil effects of worry for they are the opposite of all the benefits that come to one who is joyous.

But now consider that even in the quality of worry there is some good to be found, as the Prophet said, "Wherefore doth a living man complain — A strong man because of his sins?" (Lam. 3:29). The sinner should nurture sadness in his heart and grieve in the bitterness of his heart that he has rebelled against the Creator of all.

If a man has lost a dinar, it is hard for him to bear it. If he has lost all his fortune and is completely stripped of all property his soul mourns deeply. Thus, it is with all manner of troubles; they cause continuing pain and sorrow in his heart. But it is far more fitting that he should grieve and lament because he has rebelled against God, may He be Blessed, and has not been mindful of the kindness and favors granted to him.

Know that the levels to which a man climbs in repentance are in accordance with the extent of the sorrow he feels at his sin. For this kind of sorrow comes from the purity of his nobler soul, and, Therefore, sadness and worry are acceptable to God, may He be Blessed. Take for example, a king whose nearest and dearest members of his household angered him — and they who thus grieved him are among the most honored nobles of the land. It is clear that the king will more quickly extend grace and mercy to them than to distant offenders of lower, less virtuous degree. Therefore, God will surely have pity upon the soul that is truly in anguish and deeply worried over its sins. And thus, did David say "Lord all my desire is before Thee, and my sighing is not hiding from Thee" (Ps. 38:10).

ORCHOT TZADIKIM   Chapter Ten

Tears come from sorrow and great worry. And we have learned that "the gates of tears are not locked" (Baba Mezi'a 59a). And it is written, "Mine eyes run down with rivers of water because they observe not Thy Torah" (Ps. 119:136). And it is written, "For I do declare mine iniquity: I am full of care because of my sin" (Ps. 38:19). A man ought always to be concerned with what has passed, worry as to what lies ahead and always be fearful that perhaps he will not fulfill the full measure of repentance. "Happy is the man that feareth always" (Prov. 28:14).

Even though a person be guiltless and completely righteous he should always be fearful that a sin might come to him. And so have we found in the case of Jacob that even though the Holy One, Blessed be He, had said to him "And I will keep Thee withersoever thou goes" (Gen. 28:15), Jacob was nevertheless afraid that he had sinned (and lost the divine promise). And so, did David say "If I had not believed that I would see the goodness of the Lord, in the land of the living!" (Ps. 27:13). Even though David knew that he was a perfectly pious man he feared that sin might prevent him from receiving the pleasant reward of the righteous (Berakoth 4a).

A person should always worry whether or not his service is acceptable to God, Blessed is He, and perhaps he may be numbered among those whom God has rebuked: "Who hath required this at your hand to trample my courts" (Is. 1:12).

A man should strengthen his determination (to resist evil). There is a parable about a wise man who saw a certain person who was worried, and said to him, "If your worry is about this world, then may God lessen your worry. But if your worry is about the coming world, then may God, Blessed be He, add to your worries."

And worry is also profitable when it concerns the Torah. For then he will review it constantly lest he forget it.

Worry will also prove advantageous in avoiding unnecessary quarrel for he will be concerned lest he suffer a loss as a result of the controversy.

At night however, when a man arises to study Torah, he should not fear evil spirits but should think, "Many people walk alone at night and have never been injured." And let this man trust in God, Blessed is He, and arise, and not be afraid.

If a rabbi and Pious Man is far from his city, he should not hold himself back from going there to study because of his fear of the roads, as does the lazy man who excuses himself by saying "There is a lion without; I shall be slain in the streets" (Prov. 22:13). But a man should keep in mind that many people travel and are not injured. So, he too should not restrain himself from the journey out of fear, for those who are sent to fulfill a command of the Torah are not injured (Pesahim 8b).

The conclusion of the matter is this: In all his worries and sorrows let a man direct his concern for the sake of Heaven!

If one of his family dies, he should mourn and weep and feel anguish because the one who died may have died because of his (the survivor's) sin. And for the sins of the fathers, children may die. Thus, a man feels as though he may have slain his loved one, and will repent and abstain and plead with the Creator, may He be Blessed.

If a good and pious man dies, he should feel anguish and weep for him, for the Holy One Blessed be He counts those tears, and gathers them into His treasure house as it said "Put Thou my tears in Thy bottle; Are they not in Thy book" (Ps. 56:9), (Shabbath 105b).

And if trouble comes, such as famine, plague or other catastrophes, let him always worry lest his sins caused these events — for Achan trespassed in the matter of the dedicated spoils and several thousand Israelites fell because of his fault (Jos. 7:2-22) — and let him return to God, Blessed be He, according to his ability.

Have we not found that Elijah did not speak with Rabbi Joshua ben Levi because a lion had devoured a Jew within three parasangs of the city where Rabbi Joshua ben Levi dwelt. Rabbi Joshua ben Levi should have begged mercy of God that no misfortune occurs round about him (Makkoth 11a). Therefore, a man should always be in fear of such happenings.

And thus, we find that when there was a famine for three years in the time of David, he sought to find the sin that had caused the famine and finally discovered that because of his own conduct the famine had come (Yebamoth 78b). Therefore, in every bad happening a man should worry lest it occurred because of him.

And if a man has good fortune and security he should worry as to whether he is not receiving in this world all the reward that the future world holds for him.

If he is a poor man beset with many pains and much suffering, he should worry as to whether his poverty and suffering might not be the fruit of his wrongdoing

— with the principal punishment still awaiting him in the future world. And if he has neglected the words of the Torah because of poverty and suffering he must worry even more.

If he is wise in Torah, he should worry that perhaps his deeds are not in accordance with his wisdom. And if he is not wise then he must worry that he is not able to go to the deep roots of saintliness. And if men honor him, he must guard against rejoicing in that honor, and should worry that that honor is his total reward. But if he is wise and yet despised in the eyes of the world, let him rejoice in this; but let him worry that because he is despised people do not accept his chastisement.

There are other ways in which worry and lament may be good, as we find : Concerning every single wise man of Israel who truly knows the Torah and worries greatly because the honor of the Holy One, Blessed be He, and the honor of Israel was diminished and who longs and waits for the glory of Jerusalem and the Holy Temple and the salvation that will soon blossom forth and for the restoration of our exiled people — God, Blessed is He, causes the Holy Spirit to dwell within him (Tanna de-Be Eliyahu, chapter 4).

Therefore, , one should concern himself and weep because of the Torah which is forgotten and should lament for those who revere God, Blessed be He, and have been rejected by men, and should complain bitterly over the little piety that exists and over Israel, the people of the Lord, trodden under foot, and he should raise Jerusalem over his greatest joy and may he merit to behold her joy, as it is written : "Rejoice for joy with her; all ye that mourn for her" (Is. 66:10). May God, Blessed is He, in His great Mercy make us worthy to be among those who will behold the glory of Zion, as it is written — "For they shall see, eye to eye, the Lord returning to Zion" (Is. 52:8). And it is said, "And the glory of the Lord shall be revealed; and all flesh shall see it together; For the mouth of the Lord hath spoken it" (Is. 40:5).

Sefer
ORCHOT TZADIKIM
Ways of the Righteous

Chapter Eleven

ON REMORSE
Remorse is the quality wherein a person does something and then in retrospect regrets the deed. This is the most direct path to repentance because he who has sinned and regrets, it is as though he had not sinned.

It is impossible to repent without remorse. This means that a man's wrongs are not atoned for if he does not regret them. Even his prayer is not accepted unless he regrets his deed, for how can he say, "Forgive us our father for we have sinned" if he does not regret his sins?

For instance, a king whose servant was corrupt and seeks forgiveness from the king, if the servant does not regret his sinful deeds in his heart and repeats his evil acts daily the king will be angrier with him. Similarly concerning one who robs his fellowmen and comes every day imploring the king to forgive him while he continues to rob, there can be no doubt that this robber only increases the wrath of the king by asking for forgiveness. Therefore, he must regret his conduct, pray, confess and direct his thoughts not to repeat such wrongdoing any more, then will his prayer be received.

However, if one does a good deed and then regrets it, this is a bad quality. Therefore, you must guard yourself against regretting the good deeds you do for then you lose your reward. If you have given alms to a poor man who afterwards enrages you, guard yourself against regretting the good things you did to him, for inasmuch as your intention at the time of doing the good deed was for the sake of Heaven, your reward is assured.

A very ugly quality that is found in people is being unreliable — if a person says one thing today and regrets it on the morrow and does not keep his word; when he vows to fast or give alms or to study Torah and then regrets it, that is a very bad trait.

Even though it is a good thing to regret having done an evil thing, it is better for a man to steady himself and not be fickle in changing his traits and qualities. And this is best of all, that he should reflect in his heart and choose the good custom and the good qualities and conduct himself accordingly. And he must first deliberate on all the things he intends to do and decide if he can stand by his resolve. If so, let him cling to it and not skip from one manner of conduct to another manner of conduct, for it is a very bad quality to be unsettled and such a trait is despised by people even though he keeps jumping from one good quality to another. For then there is no stability in his dealings and one cannot rely on him.

O son of man! Repent while you still have the power to repent and do not delay until you approach the grave, for then when you regret your acts it is too late to repair the wrong.

If you have done a thing against your companion, regret it and go and appease him and if your companion has wronged you and regrets it, — welcome him. Even though you doubt that he is sorry in his heart and believe that he wants only to seem sincere in your eyes, — welcome him. If you have rebuked him with harsh words until he hates you as David said "And do I not strive with those that rise up against Thee?" (Ps. 139:21), do not regret such a quarrel and do not seek his forgiveness, for if you do express remorse and plead for forgiveness he will continue to err.

Remorse is a path to all good deeds. If he has neglected the Torah let him regret this neglect and give his heart to the study and fulfillment of the Torah with all his ability. If he did not strengthen himself to pray with complete devotion let him regret this and consider "What have I done? When I could have acquired life eternal, I busied myself with vanities." If one reaches more advanced age, he should regret very much that his days passed without the proper service of the Lord, May He be praised.

Master this great principle. Examine in your heart everything you have done and every commandment of which you were not heedful. Be remorseful for each one individually. You will think and argue out in your heart, "How is it that I did not pursue the will of my Creator? How did I abandon the teachings of the sages and their good instructions?" One finds that remorse is a great corrective for the keeping of the commandments.

Sefer ORCHOT TZADIKIM
Ways of the Righteous

Chapter Twelve

ON ANGER

Anger is a bad quality and just as scurvy is a disease of the body so is angering a disease of the soul. And our sages have said: "He who loses his temper is exposed to all the torments of hell" (Nedarim 22a) as it is said: "Therefore, remove vexation from thy heart, and put away evil from thy flesh" (Eccl. 11:10), and by "evil" they mean Gehenna, as it is said: "The Lord hath made everything for His own purpose, Yes, even the wicked for the day of evil" (Prov. 16:4). And not only this but an angry man is afflicted with piles as it is said: "The Lord will give you there an anguished heart and eyes that pine, and a despondent spirit" (Deut. 28:65). What ill is it that dims the eyes and pains the soul— Surely you will say "Piles".

Our Sages said further: "He who loses his temper, even the Divine Presence, is unimportant in His eyes (Nedarim 22b), as it is written "The wicked in the pride of his countenance (saith) 'He will not require', All his thoughts are 'There is no God' " (Ps. 10:4). And it (anger) also causes him to forget his studies of

Torah and increases his folly as it is said: "For anger resteth in the bosom of fools" (Eccl. 7:9) and "A fool will not understand" (Ps. 92:7), and, "But a fool unfoldeth folly" (Prov. 13:16). You may be sure that his sins are more plentiful than his merits, as it is said: "An angry man stirith up strife" (Ibid. 29:22) and his punishment is very great as it is said: "A man of great wrath shall suffer punishment" (Ibid. 19:19).

And you often see people who when they are angry and persist in their wrath, are not conscious of what they are doing and do many things in their anger which they would not do if they were free from anger, for anger draws out the intelligence of a person from within him until his angry deeds multiply and he is plunged into strife and quarrel. Therefore, it is impossible that the wrathful person should be saved from great sins. And so, did Elijah say to Rabbi Judah: "Fall not into a passion and you will not sin" (Berakoth 29b). And the Sages said: "By three things is a man known" (Erubin 65b) and one of them is his anger, for when a man is angry his true nature can be recognized. If his wrath is stronger than his wisdom and he does things in the moment of his anger without regard to his wisdom, then you can see the character of his wrath. But if his wisdom is stronger than his anger and he de does not say or do anything when angry that he would not say or do when he is free from anger, then you can see the extent of his wisdom. And the Wise Man said: "Three, the Holy One Blessed be He loves and one of them is he who does not anger" (Pesahim 113b). And our Sages said: "Nor is an impatient person fitted to teach" (Aboth 2:5), for because of his great anger, the pupils fear him too much to ask the things of which they are in doubt lest he be wrathful with them. And even when his pupils do ask the impatient teacher questions, he has neither the mind nor the patience to explain to his pupils all that is needed to make the matter clear. Then, too, he will answer questions in anger and thus the pupils will not understand the matter clearly. As for the pupils, it is their duty even when their teacher is angry with them, to ask their questions and listen carefully and not be hurt by the anger of their teacher nor quarrel with him. Concerning such pupils our Sages taught: "So the forcing of wrath bringeth forth strife" (Proverbs 30:33). Any pupil whose teacher is angry with him repeatedly but bears the teacher's wrath in silence will merit to discern between civil and criminal law. And a master said: "There is nothing more difficult than civil and criminal Law" (cf. Berakoth 63b).

The angry man does not find favor in the eyes of his fellow creatures; he is in fact hateful in their eyes. And thus, his deeds are not received favorably by his fellow creatures. Even if he possesses knowledge of the Torah and has many good deeds to his credit, people cannot learn from him.

The angry man is a burden on his household, who are always compelled to hear his wrath and his complaints, and his temper brings him very near to a calamity, for he casts too much terror on his household. As we learn in the Talmud (Gittin 7a) concerning Rabbi Hanina, the son of Gamliel; his household was brought almost to the point of feeding him a piece of meat cut from a living creature.

The wrathful man is not gracious or generous. He is constantly seeking revenge and always bears a grudge. Anger brings a man into quarrels for when he is angry with his companions, they quarrel with him and he quarrels with them. And when there is a quarrel, there is, of course resulting envy and hatred. And you already know the evils of a quarrel, as will be further explained in the chapter on quarrels.

Wrath restrains the heart of a man from all good deeds. For when a man is angry, he is insensitive and has no mercy upon the poor. Concerning the Lord, may He be Blessed, it is said "In anger, remember to have mercy" (Habakuk 3:2). But this is far from the ways of man.

Anger vitiates the intent of a man in his prayer, and the Divine Presence cannot dwell where there is anger.

The angry man cannot be very wise, for wrath causes reason to flee from the mind, so that he cannot answer as is proper, and he cannot rebuke as is proper, and all his words are not prompted by intelligence. The angry man bars from himself all corrections and rebukes, for no man feels free to reveal his errors and his shortcomings, inasmuch as every man fears him, — fears to tell him the things he does wrong, lest he be wrathful with him. And even if some person should rebuke him, the angry man will not receive correction because of his anger. In general, then, an angry man does not acquire any good quality unless he first removes his anger from his heart. Just as the angry man does not accept rebuke from others, so is he not able to administer rebuke to others, for the Torah has said, "You shall surely rebuke your neighbor, and thus not bear sin because of his wrongful conduct" (Leviticus 19:17), which means that first you must rebuke him gently, and in private, and with soft speech, pleading with him that you are thinking only of his own good. And then, if you do this, sin will not accrue to you. But if you rebuke your companion right at the beginning, with an angry voice and with wrath, and you shame him, then you are sinning for your companion will not receive correction from you. For this is human nature, if a man comes to his companion with force then his companion will be stubborn and unyielding to him, and will not listen to him. Concerning this the wise man said in Koheleth, "The words of the wise are heard gently" (Eccl. 9:17), that is to say, the wise man speaks gently.

And you already know the account of Hillel and Shammai (Shabbath 31a) that the three converts to Judaism said concerning them, "The short-temperedness of Shammai wanted to drive us out from the world, however, the modesty of Hillel brought us under the wing of the Divine Presence" As for Hillel, because of his great modesty, no man could make him angry, for he who holds himself back from anger, will acquire the qualities of modesty and compassion, while from wrath comes the quality of cruelty, as it is written : "And my anger shall blaze forth and I will put you to the sword" (Ex. 22:23). And always in the case of anger we find vengeance, "For the Lord's anger will flare up against you and He will shut up the skies" (Deut. 11:17).

Anger causes impudence in man, and because of anger, he will not yield and will not confess the truth.

And the wise man said, "If you want to choose a faithful and good companion, make him angry and if he confesses the truth to you at the moment of his anger, become his friend, but if he does not, then leave him."

Anger leads to mistakes. Who is a greater man than Moses, our teacher? Moses, upon him be peace, was angry in three places, and he made what would generally be termed "mistakes". As it is said: "And he was angry with Eleazar and with Ithamar" (Lev. 10:16), and it is written: "Why did you not eat the sin-offering in the sacred area?" (Lev. 10:17). And it is said: "Listen, you rebel" (Num. 20:10) and it is said: "And he struck the rock" (Ib.: 11). And it is said: "Moses became angry with the commanders of the army" (Num. 31:14), and it is written: "And Eleazar the priest said to the troops who had taken part in the fighting This is the ritual law' " (Num. 31:21). Which teaches that Moses forgot the law (while angry) (Leviticus Rabbah 13:1). And so, you can understand that if these things happened to Moses peace be upon him, when he was angry, what can happen to fools who are angry! And therefore, Solomon said, "Be not hasty in thy spirit to be angry" (Eccl. 7:9).

And you must be very careful not to do damage in your anger, for our Rabbis said: "He who rends his garments, breaks his utensils in his wrath and scatters his money should be in your eyes like one who worships idols" (Shabbath 105b). For this is the artful craft of the Evil Desire. Today he says to a man, "Do thus." And on the morrow, he says to him, "Go ahead and serve idols." And the man goes and serves. This is the reason it is written "There shall not be in you a strange god" (Ps. 81:10). Now which strange god can be inside of a man? You must necessarily say, "It is the Evil Desire." Look and see how the Evil Desire strengthens itself in a man in a time of anger.

Rabbi said: "There are four temperaments: Easily angered and easily pacified; his loss is cancelled out by his gain. Hard to anger and hard to pacify; his gain is cancelled out by his loss. Easily angered and hard to pacify is a wicked man. Hard to anger and easily pacified is a saintly man."

And these four qualities apply to a righteous man when he grows angry with good people, or because of worldly matters. But if a man finds it difficult to grow angry with people who do wicked deeds, and is easy with them, that is an evil quality, for he appeases the wicked. All the more wicked is the man who easily gets angry with the righteous, and finds it difficult to be angry with the wicked, — who finds it easy to appease the wicked, but finds it difficult to appease the righteous. Such a man is completely wicked.

Even though anger is a very bad quality, nevertheless, a man should conduct himself at times with the quality of anger. For example, when he rebukes the wicked, and when he desires to cause a spirit of awe and respect to dwell on the members of his household, and when he wants to obtain respect and even fear from his pupils. Even he who is angry with the wicked, must weigh the extent of his anger, for Moses, our teacher, upon whom is peace, said when he spoke wrathfully against Reuben and Gad: "A breed of sinful men" (Num. 32:14). And, Therefore, we find that his descendant (the Levite mentioned in Judges 18:30) became a priest to idols, and this even though Moses was angry because he strove for the glory of God. Everything requires a proper measure in all a man's ways. A man should speak carefully how to do the commandments, whether he rebukes out of anger or rebukes joyously.

A man who has the quality of anger, but controls that anger and wrathful manner as though he were not at all subject to temper, concerning such a one it is said: "He that is slow to anger is better than the mighty; and he that ruleth his spirit than he that taketh a city" (Prov. 16:32). And you must remember that slowness to anger, is one of the Thirteen Attributes which are ascribed to the Creator, may He be Blessed.

The Wise Man said, "He who has his anger in thought only, but restrains it, you can see dignity and glory on his countenance, but he whose anger is not only in his thought, expresses his folly in his features and in his manner.

And this too, said the Wise Man, "He whose anger and wrath are mighty is not too far away from the madness of insane ones, and he who is habitually angry, his life is no life at all" (Pesahim 113b), and he is never happy — and inasmuch as he is never happy, he does not receive the various happenings that come to man with love and with joy, and he does not declare the Justice of God, whether the happenings be good or bad, and Therefore, , he is not able to joyously serve God, may He be Blessed.

Now when a man is in the midst of a fast, or in some trouble, then anger dwells strongly in his heart. Therefore, at such times he must be particularly careful not to grow angry. Silence nullifies anger and a soft voice nullifies anger, Therefore, , a man, when he sees his anger growing strong within him, should be silent, or should speak quietly, and should not lift his voice in his anger, for the one who does lift his voice in his anger, will only arouse and stir up that anger, but a quiet voice and silence soothe anger. Another thing he should bear in mind is not to look in the face of a man that is angry with him, but should drop his eyes and speak with him without staring into his face — and thus he will cause anger to flee from his heart.

And you should know that the final sum of the intelligence of a man is his ability to govern his anger. As it is said: "It is the discretion of a man to be slow to anger" (Proverbs 19:11). Anger is very close to arrogance and no angry man can escape arrogance. You already know the evils of arrogance. It is proper for a man to be distant from anger, even on a matter where anger is proper, he should hold back his impulse and not be angry. A man who is subject to anger should do this right at the outset. When he resolves in his mind that he must not get angry, he must also determine and resolve that he should not feel any humiliation or any insult. Even though he be rebuked or cursed, he should not feel anything and should not concern himself about it.

This is clear, that he who is very impulsive, it would be better for him that he should not feel any insult or offense whatever, and that he should be silent and restrain himself completely rather than be even a little bit angry. For it is impossible for a man who is angry by nature to be angry "just a little", for he will find in the end that he is unrestrained in his anger. And he who wants to refrain from anger and cast a reasonable awe upon his children and upon his household, or if he is the leader of the community and wants to display anger towards the community in order that they should improve their conduct, what should he do? He must, in order to rebuke them, appear before them as though he were angry, but his mind must be calm just as a man does when he pretends to be angry but really is not angry. And when he does show anger, he should be very careful not to do so when there are poor guests present for, they, being very sensitive, will think that he is angry with them. Therefore, , he must show himself happy in their presence.

The wise men commanded that one must always remove himself so far from anger as to accustom himself not to feel any humiliation or hurt whatever, even at things which usually cause anger to any man until he completely roots out anger from his heart; This is the best path, and the way of the righteous : "They are shamed, but they do not shame; they hear people speak words of disgrace against them, but they do not retort, they do their deeds of goodness with love and rejoice in God's chastisements." And concerning them the Scripture says, "And those that love Him are like the sun when he goes forth in his strength" (Judges 5:31).

Sefer

ORCHOT TZADIKIM

Ways of the Righteous

Chapter Thirteen

ON GRACIOUSNESS
Graciousness is a very good quality, and is found only in the noble and precious soul. He who has the quality of graciousness is content with all that the Creator, may He be Exalted, decrees concerning him, and such a one does not question God's justice. The possessor of this quality does not seek greatness of honor, but is pleased and willing to bear whatever has to be borne. He never complains about the matters that concern him and is never angry with God, may He be Exalted, saying "Why did the Lord, may He be Blessed, do thus and thus?" And from this quality, comes the quality of being happy with his portion. And you already know the goodness and greatness of this quality.

When a righteous man likes people and people are pleased with him, then the Holy One, Blessed be He, also is pleased with him. For thus did they say: "One with whom men are pleased, God is pleased" (Aboth 3:10). And even his enemies make peace with him, as it is written: "When a man's ways please the Lord, He maketh his enemies to be at peace with him" (Prov.

16:7), as you know concerning Abimelech and Abraham ... (Genesis Rabbah 54a). And when they make peace with him it is said "In the light of the King's countenance is life, and his favour is as a cloud of the latter rain" (Prov. 16:15).

See what happened to Mordecai when Ahasheurus was pleased with him, and what happened to Joseph when Pharaoh was pleased with him. And if all of this happened to those whom people liked, then surely the ones whom the Holy One, Blessed be He, likes, will attain a lofty estate. Therefore, a person should exert himself to do the commandments of the Torah and then the Holy One, Blessed be He, will be pleased with him. And the wise man has said, "Everyone who has this quality will prosper." And from the quality of pleasantness, comes pardon and forgiveness, for when a person is gracious and generous with a person who has wronged him, and renounces his claim against him, such a person who does this — his prayer will surely be heard.

A very fine quality for man is to be filled with graciousness and to abandon his opinion in the face of the opinion of his companion (when he senses that his companion is right). And this type of conduct will cause him to be beloved, for he does what pleases every man. And such a man is very near to the paths of repentence, for if he does an evil deed, and his companion comes and rebukes him, he very quickly consents to abandon his evil way and to return to the good. The result is that he himself obtains self satisfaction in confessing his wrong and abandoning his evil ways, and his companions who associate with him are pleased.

ORCHOT TZADIKIM — Chapter Thirteen

Thus, did Solomon say, "He who listens to counsel is a wise man" (Prov. 12:15). Solomon did not mean "to listen with the ears alone," but that listening means to listen to the counsel of a wise man and to willingly do that which the wise man tells him. It is obvious, Therefore, that the whole Torah is summarized in this quality of willingness to listen and obey. And thus, it is with all the rebukes and all the blessings. What does this mean? Concerning the time that the Torah was given, it is written — "Now Therefore, if ye will surely listen unto My voice indeed, and keep My covenant, then ye shall be Mine own treasure from among all peoples" (Exodus 19:5). The meaning of "you will surely listen," is that you shall accept these commandments and receive them willingly. And the people answered "We will do" (Ibid. 19:8, 24:7) — willingly.

Concerning the curses mentioned in the Bible it is said: "But it shall come to pass, if thou wilt not hearken unto the voice of the Lord thy God, to observe to do all His commandments and His statutes" (Deut. 28:15), and it is written: "The blessing, if he shall hearken unto the commandments of the Lord your God, and the curse, if ye shall not hearken unto the commandments of the Lord your God" (Deut. 11:27-28). In all of these quotations which say: "Thou shalt surely listen" the meaning is not merely listening with the ear, but what they wanted to say was "listen with willingness to fulfill the commandments." So, we find with Jacob our father, upon him is peace, that he willingly listened to his mother and he listened to her counsel concerning the blessings. He willingly listened to his father and to his mother (when they advised him not to take a wife of the daughters of Canaan) and chose a wife as they requested. Therefore, he merited that there should come forth from him the twelve tribes. And it is written: "But whoso hearkeneth unto me shall dwell securely, and shall be quite without fear of evil" (Prov. 1:33).

There are four classifications in the matter of listening (Yalkut Shimoni — Gen. 32): There is one who hears and loses thereby, and there is one who hears and is rewarded thereby. There is one who does not listen and loses thereby, and there is one who does not listen and gains a reward thereby. One who listens and loses thereby an example of Adam, as it is said: "And unto Adam He said: "Because thou hast hearkened unto the voice of thy wife" (Gen. 3:17). And what did he lose? "For dust thou art, and unto dust shalt thou return" (Ibid.: 19).

And then there is one who listens and is rewarded. That would be Abraham, our father for it was said to him "in all that Sarah saith unto thee, hearken unto her voice" (Gen. 21:12). And what was his reward? "For in Isaac shall thy seed be called" (Gen. 21:12).

Now there is one who does not listen and is rewarded and this would be Joseph. For it is said "that he hearkened not unto her, to lie by her, or to be with her" (Gen. 39:10). And what was his reward? "And Joseph was the ruler over all the land" (Gen. 42:6).

Then there is one who does not listen and loses. That would be the children of Israel, for it is said: "Yet they hearkened not unto Me, nor inclined their ear" (Jer. 7:26). And what did they lose? "Such as are for death, to death; and such as are for the sword, to the sword"

(Jer. 15:2). And it is said in Isaiah: — "If ye be willing and obedient, Ye shall eat the good of the land" (Is. 1:19).

The stubborn and rebellious son was punished because he did not listen. As it is written: "Then shall his father and his mother lay hold on him, and bring him out unto the elders of his city. And they shall say unto the elders of his city: 'This our son is stubborn and rebellious, he doth not hearken to our voice,' " and all the men of the city shall stone him" (Deut. 21:19-20).

And concerning all Israel, it is said: "Ye have been rebellious against the Lord" (Deut. 9:7), and more is written concerning they're not being willing to listen, "For they are a stubborn and stiff-necked people" (Exod. 34:9).

And since everything depends upon the quality of graciousness, a person should incline all of his will to do the commandments of the Lord, may He be Blessed, willingly — and thus said our teachers: "Do His will as you would do your own will, so that He may do your will as He does His own will" (Aboth 2:4).

The general rule of this matter is that a man should never be stubborn and he should not "make his neck stiff" against those who rebuke him or against one who tries to teach him the upright way — but he should very willingly listen to them, and accept their words with the graciousness of his soul, for concerning stubborn people it is said: "Thorns and snares are in the way of the forward; He that keepeth his soul holdeth himself far from them" (Prov. 22:5). And it is also said "He that hath a forward heart findeth no good" (Prov. 17:20). In several instances are praised those who willingly listen to the words of the Torah, as it is written "But his delight is in the law of the Lord; And in His law doth he meditates day and night" (Ps. 1:2). And it is written "And he shall be like a tree planted by streams of water, that bringeth forth its fruit in its season" (Ps. 1:3); and it is written: "Happy is the man that feareth the Lord, that delights in his commandments" (Ps. 112:1). Notice that it says "delights" which means that a man must train himself to delight to do the commandments.

Rabbi Abahu says, "In the future, all of the people will wonder at the one who truly and willingly listened to God, and they will say, "Who is this lowly person that did not read the Torah and did not study it and yet behold he is sitting with the patriarchs and is speaking with them?" And God will say to them, "Why do you wonder? These deserve this honor because they listened to me willingly, as it is said, 'The ear that hearkeneth to the reproof of life, abideth among the wise' " (Prov. 15:31).

Now this quality — though very good — should not to be used with the wicked, and one should not be gracious to them. And he should remove his willingness from all evil things and from all things which the Torah warned him against, but he should be gracious to the one whom the Holy One, Blessed be He, desires, as it is written, "The Lord taken pleasure in them that fear Him" (Ps. 147:11).

He should direct his desire towards the commandments even though they may be very difficult for him. Yet must he train himself to willingly do them until they become beloved by Him.

ORCHOT TZADIKIM — Chapter Thirteen

Even though it was very difficult for Abraham our Father, upon him is peace to slay his only son — nevertheless he nullified his will before the will of the Creator, may He be Exalted, and arose, and with zeal, eagerness and love fulfilled God's command.

However, he who sets his desire and wish on evil deeds and is gracious to the wicked and to their deeds, and rejects the righteous ones, him will his graciousness bring to the netherworld. Concerning him it is said "Woe unto them that call evil good, and good evil" (Is. 5:20). And it is further said "He that justifieth the wicked, and he that condemneth the righteous, even they both are an abomination to the Lord" (Prov. 17:15).

Every person who wishes to enter into the very essence of piety and into the profundity of contemplating the Unity of God in order to know the Lord, may He be Blessed, cannot do so unless he is wise and understanding and has a gracious soul, free from anger. It is written "Now Therefore, ye children, hearken unto me; For happy are they that keep my ways" (Prov. 8:32). The Creator, Blessed be He, said to Israel "I want nothing else from you but that you should listen willingly and if you do listen to me, I will fulfill what the prophets prophesied "If ye be willing and obedient, ye shall eat the good of the land" (Is. 1:19). And it is written, "Happy is the man that hearkeneth to me" (Prov. 8:34).

Therefore, a man should direct his mind to the will of the Creator, may He be Blessed. And he ought not to rebel against his teachers and against his superiors in Wisdom. And so, it is said in the Torah "And thou shalt come unto the priests the Levities, and unto the

ORCHOT TZADIKIM — Chapter Thirteen

judge that shall be in those days; and thou shalt inquire; and they shall declare unto thee the sentence of judgment. And thou shalt do according to the tenor of the sentence, which they shall declare unto thee... thou shalt not turn aside from the sentence which they shall declare unto thee, to the right and, nor to the left. And the man that doeth presumptuously, in not hearkening unto the priest that standeth to minister there before the Lord thy God, or unto the judge, even that man shall die; and thou shalt exterminate the evil from Israel" (Deut. 17:9-12).

From all these we know how important the quality of graciousness is. For the whole Torah is contained in it. Even if the wise men said to you concerning the left that it is right, or about the right, that it is left, listen willingly to them (Sifre Deut. 17:11. T.P. Horayoth 1.1).

Consider well that when we pray, we say, "May the worship of Israel be accepted willingly before Thee always!" Thus, all of our deeds and all of our service depend upon the willingness of the Creator to receive them. When a man does not direct his will and his desire towards the commandments of the Lord, but rebels against Him, and chooses evil deeds, against which the Lord warned us, that we ought not to do them, why should the Lord listen willingly to this man? Why should God be gracious and desire a man who does not desire him?

A man should never be obstinate with the Creator, may He be Blessed, or with his teachers, for in this manner, one wise man praised himself. "All my days I have never transgressed the opinions of my companions. I know that I am not a priest, and yet if my companions would say to me 'Go up on the pulpit and give the priestly benediction,' I would go up" (Shabbath 118b).

It is not necessary to go any further regarding this quality, for it is contained within the quality of Love and Joy.

There is nothing as good in all the world as listening, — and thus said our Sages : "If a man fell from a roof and his limbs were broken, he needs medicated applications and bandages for every single limb and for every bone, however the one who has sinned with all of his limbs, as it is said "From the sole of the foot even unto the head, there is no soundness in it" (Is. 1:6), the Lord, may He be Blessed, heals all of his limbs with one medicated bandage. And what is this bandage? Listening carefully as it is said "Incline your ear, and come unto Me, hear, and your soul shall live" (Is. 55:3) (Exodus Rabbah 27).

Sefer ORCHOT TZADIKIM

Ways of the Righteous

Chapter Fourteen

ON ENVY

Envy is a branch of anger, and no man escapes from it completely. For we see that among men each one tries to keep-up with one's neighbor. For when he sees that his neighbor acquires food or clothes, or a home or amasses money, then he too endeavors to attain the same, thinking, "My fellow has all this; I must also have it." And concerning this matter, Solomon hinted: "Again, I considered all labour and all excelling in work, that it is a man's rivalry with his neighbor" (Eccl. 4:4).

Now any man who has this quality strongly within him, is very despicable, for jealousy brings a person to lust, for when a man does not pay attention to what his companion acquires, he does not lust. And the Torah said, "You shall not lust after the wife of your neighbor… and anything that belongs to your neighbor" (Exod. 20:14). A man who is overpowered by lust, is very close to transgressing the Ten Commandments. A parable that will illustrate this is the story of a man who had a neighbor and there was a wall that separated them and their property. Now the wicked man coveted the wife of his neighbor, and also some of his possessions. One day he overheard the man say to his wife, "I shall have to leave for a while for business," and thus he did. What did the wicked man do? On Sabbath eve, he went and broke the wall that was between them. And thus, he had already transgressed the commandment to "remember and keep the Sabbath." He then forcibly attacked the wife of his neighbor, and in that way transgressed the commandment that "You shall not covet" and he lay with her, and thus he transgressed the commandment "You shall not commit adultery." And after that when he began to plunder the possessions of his neighbor, the woman cried out, and when she cried out, he slew her — and so he transgressed the commandment "You shall not commit murder." And after he had robbed and stolen what he lusted for, he had already transgressed the commandment, "You shall not steal" as well as "You shalt not covet." Then his father and his mother stood up and rebuked him. He arose up against them and struck them, and thus he transgressed the commandment "Honor your father and your mother." And afterwards, when he was brought to court, he and his worthless companions testified that the property found in his possession had been left with him as a pledge by his neighbor and that he had permitted his neighbor to take them back in trust even though he had not paid. He had trusted his neighbor with the pledge and had never been able to obtain possession of them until now when the robbers had broken the wall which was between their properties and had slain the woman and that when he heard the commotion he had entered and taken back his pledge. Now by this testimony, he transgressed against the commandment "You shall not utter false testimony against your neighbor." Then continually, wherever he went, he swore that he had done nothing wrong, and so he transgressed against the commandment, "You shall not take the name of the Lord, your God, in vain." Finally, his crimes were revealed and his wrong became known far and wide. Because of this disgrace, he became utterly depraved, denied the living God and thus he transgressed against the First Commandment, "I am the Lord thy God." Finally, he became attached to idolatry and thus he transgressed the command "You shall have no other gods, you shall not bow down before them and you shall not serve them." And all of this was caused by his lust! Thus, we find that lust can bring one very near to transgress against all of the Torah.

There is another way to intelligently understand how jealousy and lust are very ruinous qualities, and in this vein, Solomon said: "Let not thy heart envy sinners, but be in the fear of the Lord all the day" (Prov. 23:17). When a man envies sinners seeing their wealth and prosperity and sees righteous men growing poorer and being sore afflicted, and, from all of this, his soul rejects reverence for God and His judgements, and rejects those who study the Torah and fulfill it, as it is said: "Your words have been all too strong against Me, saith the Lord. Ye have said: 'It is vain to serve God; and what profit is it that we have kept His charge, and that we have walked mournfully because of the Lord of Hosts? And how we call the proud happy, yea, they that work wickedness art built up; yea, they try God and are delivered" (Malachi 3:13-15).

This type of thinking leads to folly in the minds of people, and causes their hearts to retreat from the truth when they see the wicked prospering and the righteous suffering. Because of this they walk in the hardness of their heart and say, "So and so do thus and they are rich. We'll do the same thing and what happens to them will happen to us." All this they resolve to do because of jealousy, for such a man envies the wicked, and covets their wealth and their security. Therefore, such people cast off from themselves the yoke of the commandments. But the righteous do not envy the wicked, their money or their security, for they reflect that the wealth of the wicked is guarded only for their ultimate ruin, and their security is given them only to deprive them of the great good which is treasured up for the righteous. And they know that the poverty of the righteous and their distress purifies and cleanses them to increase their worthiness for the world to come. There is no doubt that one who thinks thus will not envy, but will on the contrary, rejoice when he sees the apparent security of the wicked, for he will say. "If those who enrage God are rewarded thus, then how much greater, will be the reward of those who do His will!" To the righteous He will give and continue to give reward.

Envy is the result of a feeling of inferiority. If one envies another's beauty, strength or wealth, then he is unhappy with what the Creator, blessed be He, has decreed for him. This is similar to a servant who

ORCHOT TZADIKIM — Chapter Fourteen

complains concerning the deeds of his master, and is not pleased with his master's matters. Such a one is not a faithful servant. All the more so, ought he not to complain against the Creator, may He be Blessed, for all His deeds are righteous and proper, and one ought never to dispute them.

Out of envy come quarrels as you see in the case of Korach, who envied the honor of Elizaphan, the son of Uzziel (Midrash Rabbah on Numbers 18), and because of this circumstance, he and all of his party were destroyed, even the tender infants. Jealousy is like a sickness of the body. It brings consumption. The wise man said to his son, "Guard yourself from jealousy, for it can easily be recognized when your facial expression changes because of the gloom in your heart and why should an enemy of yours rejoice and obtain his vengeance by seeing you in such a state?"

An envious man does violence to his own soul, for he is constantly grieving and his intelligence grows less because of the abundance of jealousy concealed within him. His heart is not free to study and to pray with earnest intent and to do good deeds.

Every man finds a certain tastiness in his food, aside from the man who is jealous, for he cannot savor his food until good fortune departs from the object of his envy.

For every hatred there is hope that it will change, for if a man hates his companion because his companion has robbed him of something, then when the companion returns the plundered object to him, his hatred will vanish, and so it is with all hatred that is caused by a specific thing. When the matter is adjusted, then the hatred vanishes. All this is true of every hatred or dislike outside of the hatred caused by envy. The wise man said to his son, "Do not envy your brother for the things which he has, for he will enjoy his life, while you, satiated with worry and pain, will not." And the wise man said, "The envious and lustful man was born only for a life of anger."

The early Sages used to pray, "May we not have any envy against others, and may others not envy us!" Now why would they pray that others should not posses this quality more than other evil qualities? But this is the explanation of the matter: — Many men cause others to envy them and covet their possessions. Therefore, the early wise men used to pray that others not envy them because of anything that they, the Sages, were responsible for. And the Torah has said, "Nor put a stumbling block before the blind" (Lev. 19:14).

Therefore, it is good for a man not to wear conspicuous or expensive garments — neither he nor his wife nor his children, and so should it be with food and other matters so that others will not envy him. Let that man who has been blessed bountifully by the Creator see to it that others get some enjoyment from his possessions whether they be rich or whether they be poor. Let him conduct himself with his companions gently and deal kindly with them. We have already dwelt at length about this matter — the matter of a man being loved by his fellow creatures — if he is loved by everyone, then they will not envy him, and they will not covet anything that belongs to him. However, it is fitting for a man, that he should attempt to excel in good qualities, so that others may envy him and long to do as he does. And he who is careful not to envy others, — his body will not wither, and no worms will rule over him. As it is written: "But envy is the rottenness of the bones" (Prov. 14:30), "Any man who has envy in his heart, his bones rot; every man who has not envy in his heart, his bones do not rot" (Shabbath 152b).

Therefore, a man should remove himself from envy and lust, and should not covet anything that belongs to others, and he should not say: "I covet some of the possessions of my companion, and I'll give him money so as to obtain those things," for if he does not want to part with these possessions, then it is prohibited to press him for he will be ashamed to turn him away empty handed. If a person does this, then he is like a robber — like one who compels another to do something against his will. All the more so if the one who covets is a respected man, for whom it is forbidden to ask anything of a companion if one does not know beforehand that he will give this gift to him with a willing heart.

A parable concerning this describes a lustful man and an envious man who were met by a certain king. The king said to them, "One of you may ask something of me, and I will give it to him, provided I give twice as much to his companion." The envious did not want to ask first for he was envious of his companion who would receive twice as much, and the lustful man wanted everything — wanted what belonged to both of them, so when the lustful man finally pressed the jealous man to ask for something, the jealous man asked the king to pluck out one of his eyes, because then his companion would have both eyes plucked out.

How many evils are dependent upon envy? The primeval serpent was envious of Adam and brought death to the world, and concerning him it was decreed. "Upon thy belly shalt thou go and dust shall you eat" (Gen. 3:14). Likewise see what happened to Cain and to Korah and to Balaam and to Doeg and to Ahithophel and to Gehazi and to Adonijah and to Absalom and to Uzziah, who hankered after that which did not belong to them! It wasn't enough that they were punished in that what they wanted was not given to them, but what was already in their hand was taken from them. From all of these instances, a man ought to learn to separate himself from jealousy and lust. If whatever a man has is not really his, for when tomorrow comes it may vanish, then what good will come to him from something that doesn't belong to him?

Great reward will come to a man who guards himself against envy and lust, for in most of the sins or transgressions which a man commits, he tries to avoid committing these transgressions because he is ashamed, he holds himself back because of fear of disgrace, and therefore, he restrains himself from robbery and theft, for he is afraid that it may become known, it may be revealed, people will publicize it, and he will be so shamed that he will lose much. But envy and lust are concealed within the heart. No man can detect that he covets or is jealous. It is a matter of the heart, and that is why it is said: "But you shall fear your God " (Lev. 25:17).

ORCHOT TZADIKIM   Chapter Fourteen

Even though jealousy is a very bad quality, there are instances where it can be a very good quality and, in fact, it can be a most noble quality, — when one envies those who revere God, as it is said: "Let not thy heart envy sinners, but those that fear the Lord all the day…" (Prov. 23:17). And in the same way our Sages said: "that the jealousy of wise men increases wisdom" (Baba Bathra 21a). When one sees another studying, it should excite his envy and he should say "This man studies all day, I shall do the same!" And similarly, in the matter of all he commandments. Everyone should envy his companion and try to emulate the good deeds of his companion. If he sees a wicked man who has even one good quality, he should envy him for that and should emulate it. But a man who envies his companion when he sees him occupying himself with Torah and with good deeds and does not envy him in order to emulate him, and does not say to himself, "This man is doing thus; I will also do thus!" but rather thinks in his heart enviously, "Because this companion has more good qualities than I, because of all this he is more honored by men," and then this envious man will plot how to confuse and take his companion away from the study the Torah and good deeds, such envy is a grievous disease, and he who deals in such envy is a sinner and one who causes others to sin. He is truly a partner of Jereboam, the son of Nebat.

A man should always honor those who revere God and occupy themselves with His commandments, and he should give them help. He should help them with his person and with his money, and then others will envy them and they will think, "If we also will do

ORCHOT TZADIKIM — Chapter Fourteen

thus, then people will honor and help us!" and from doing good "not for its sake" (but only for the sake of honor) they will eventually come to do it "for its own sake."

The Holy One, Blessed be He, said: "Be jealous for My sake, were it not for envy, the world would not stand. A man would not plant a vineyard, marry a wife or build a house (Shoher Tob 37a). For all of these matters come about because one man envies his companion. If he builds a house, then another person will have it in mind to do likewise, and thus it is concerning a wife. And since the perpetuation of the world depends upon envy, let him dedicate all these envious qualities to God. If he builds a house let him build in it room for the study of Torah, a gathering place for the wise, a place where guests are welcomed, and a place where he does kindness to men. And thus, did they say (Shohar Tov ibid). Had not Abraham been jealous he would have not acquired both worlds. And how was he envious? He asked Melchizedek 1 See Nedarim 32b, where Melchizedek is identified with Shem, the son of Noah., "How did you emerge from the Ark?" And Melchizedek answered, "Because of the charity that we did there," Abraham said to him, "What kind of charity could you do in the Ark; — were there any poor people there? There was no one there except Noah and his sons, so to whom were you doing charity?" Melchizedek answered him: "With the animals, with the beasts and with the fowl. We did not sleep but were constantly giving food to all these living creatures all night long." At that moment Abraham said, "If these people had not done charity with the animals, beasts and fowl, they would not have emerged from the Ark, but because they did justice with them, they did emerge safely, then I who will do justice with all the children of man who are in the image of the Holy One, Blessed be He, will not this be all the more favorable in God's eyes?" At that moment "And he planted a tamarisk (eshel) in Beersheba" (Gen. 21:33). (The sages take each letter of the Hebrew word Eshel and they say that the word Eshel means a place where strangers can eat, drink and lodge.) In this manner, a man ought to, indeed, increase his zeal.

One ought to be zealous against sinners and the wicked, to strive with them and to rebuke them. As our Sages said: "A man who cohabitates with a heathen woman, the zealous ones should smite him" (Sanhedrin 81b).

Moses was jealous of the Egyptian, as it is said, "And he smote the Egyptian" (Exod. 2:12). And so, we find in the case of Elijah, when he said, "I have been very jealous for the Lord, the God of hosts, for the children of Israel have forsaken Thy covenant" (I Kings 19:10). And so is it said, "In that he was very jealous for My sake among them" (Num. 25:11), and the Lord, may He be Blessed, gave him his reward for this as it is said: "Behold, I give unto him My covenant of peace!" (Num. 25:12). And it is said, "… Ye shall not be afraid of any man …" (Deut. 1:17). Now he who reveres the Lord, may He be Blessed, will gladly offer his life for the sanctification of God's name. As it is said, "Whoso is on the Lord's side, let him come unto me. And all the Levites rallied to him" (Exod. 32:26), and it is further said, "And when

Phinehas, the son of Eleazar, the son of Aaron the priest, saw it, he rose up from the midst of the congregation, and took a spear in his hand" (Num. 25:7).

It is an obligation on everyone who reveres God and who is pure of heart to arouse jealousy in himself when he sees that "the power of the princes and the nobility is used to trespass." And our Sages, their memory is for a blessing, said: "Every wild outbreak that does not begin with the great ones, cannot be called an outbreak" (Genesis Rabbah 26:5). As it is said "Yea, the hand of princes and the rulers hath been first in this faithlessness" (Ezra 9:2).

Sefer

ORCHOT TZADIKIM

Ways of the Righteous

Chapter Fifteen

ON ZEAL
Zeal for the Torah and the commandments is a great quality, and so is zeal that aims to make a better world. And it is a quality of the righteous in the service of the Creator, may He be Blessed. Our Sages, of blessed memory, said: "The zealous are early to perform their religious duties" (Pesahim 4a).

Concerning Abraham, our father, in the account of the sacrifice of Isaac, it is said: "And Abraham rose in the morning" (Gen. 22:3). Even though it was difficult for him to offer up his only son, he nevertheless did the will of the Creator with zeal, arising early in the morning. He who performs his deeds with zeal demonstrates convincingly that he loves his Creator as a servant who loves his master and hastens to do His will. For zeal depends upon the heart of a man, as when a man cleanses his heart of all other thoughts that may be in it and clings to one thought only, then he makes himself alert and will no doubt succeed. Thus, did Abraham do when he removed the love for his son from his heart and carried out the will of his Creator, nullifying his love for his son before his love for the Creator. Therefore, he made a point of rising early, for there was in his heart a great love for the Creator. Therefore, the Holy One, Blessed be He, swore to him that He would remember the binding of Isaac. For a man may do a very difficult thing for one he loves, although his heart troubles him in the doing. But Abraham and Isaac both acted out of the desire of their heart, for the degree of love that they felt for God was very great. Both of them cleaved unto the Lord in their thoughts until they were joined in a great unity. For their sole intent was to spread throughout the world the knowledge of the Unity of the Creator and to train mankind to love Him. As they lovingly performed the service of the Lord, may He be Exalted, and fulfilled His commandments, their physical nature was overcome; their minds cleaved to their love of the Creator of the world. Therefore, both of them acted with zeal.

You should know that zeal is the very beginning of all ethics. For no man can be perpetually bent over his book. He must eat, sleep and perform his bodily functions. Therefore, it requires eagerness and care to return to one's book and to study. One should not muse "the day is still long and the year is still long." Concerning this our Sages, of blessed memory, said: "Do not say, 'when I have some free time, I will study' — perhaps you will never be free" (Aboth 2:4). Nor should a man say: "It is already evening — if I start studying now, I will have to stop in a little while to pray," for it is better to spend one hour in study even if only to learn one saying, than to do any other thing in the world. Concerning this it is said, "He that turneth away his ear from hearing the law, even his prayer is an abomination" (Prov. 28:9). And thus, it is written: "The law of thy mouth is better unto me than thousands of golds and silver" (Ps. 119:72). And thus, it is also written, "For a day in Thy courts is better than a thousand" (Ps. 84:11), on which the Talmud comments: The Holy One, Blessed be He, said, "I prize one day of your studying Torah more than the thousand sacrifices which your son Solomon will offer upon the altar" (Shabbath 30a).

Rabbi Phineas, the son of Yair, said, "Zeal leads to cleanliness, cleanliness leads to continence, continence leads to purity. Purity leads to holiness, holiness leads to humility, humility leads to the fear of sin, the fear of sin leads to piety, piety leads to possession of the Holy Spirit, possession of the Holy Spirit leads to resurrection, resurrection leads to Elijah the Prophet, remembered for good" (T.P. Shekalim 3:5; see Sota 49a and Abodah Zarah 20b). Come and see how great is the power of zeal, which leads to such splendid qualities! Therefore, let a man be careful and alert to perform all the commandments and to run to study, early and late.

The quality of zeal is an ornament to all other qualities, and it corrects all other qualities.

Now, you ought to remember the things that men tend to be lazy about. If you must look up something in a book, and you do not know where to find it, you must be quick to go and to ask someone who is familiar with the subject. If a poor man comes to your house to ask for bread, do not say, "I cannot go and get the bread," but go quickly and bring it. If you are about to wash your hands (before eating) and all you have is a little water or loathsome water, or if the vessel for the washing of the hands does not quite meet the ritual specifications (e.g., there is a crack in it) and you are hungry and want to eat, let not your hunger make you look lightly upon the washing of the hands, but be quick to bring water and a proper vessel. One must be very alert when it comes to taking care of his bodily needs. He should not delay even for a moment, so as not to transgress "And ye shall not make your souls detestable" (Lev. 20:25 — see also Makkot 16b). Then, too, the one who delays performing his bodily needs brings upon himself great illnesses.

A man should be very alert and careful to guard himself in the matter of cleanliness so that his garments are clean and his body clean. He should also wash the anus after he has attended to his bodily needs, for it is impossible to wipe oneself properly without water. He must also be alert to his bodily needs at night. If he wishes to drink water, he should arise, wash his hands, go to a clean place and should make the blessing for the water before and after drinking. If he is in his bed and hears the sound of thunder or sees lightning, he should get up, wash his hands, and then make the blessing. He must also be able to rise from his bed and cause all slumber to vanish from his eyelids in order to rise early and to study the Torah. He needs zeal to remove himself from his unworthy deeds, such as envy and hatred and lustful thoughts. All these require great alertness, so that he may incline all of his thoughts to the will of the Creator, blessed be He. If he is distressed on account of the loss of his money, or the death of a loved one, or because of afflictions, he must be very alert to deepen in his thoughts his love for the Rock of Ages, to erase the distress from his heart and to make his heart pure so as to justify the ways of God in His judgments and in His laws and to receive with love God's will and to cleave to the Torah, to prayer and to good deeds, and to strengthen himself in his firm intent to serve God the Most High.

The general rule in this matter is that a man should examine himself and ask himself which sin he does customarily, and he should hasten to set up fences in order to take care to cease committing that particular transgression. He should also examine himself as to which commandment of God he is lax in. For example, an idler should understand right off that this idleness is a result of his being concerned with idle things. He who attaches himself to idle things will obviously reject Torah and prayer and all that is good. Such a man should depart from people who waste time in idle talk, and he should not be their companion; this will be a cure for his illness. Thus, should he act with respect to all bad qualities. He should understand from the start what is at the root of his unworthy conduct and destroy it, thus removing the darkness which darkness the light of his soul. And for all this zeal is required, for if he is too lazy to root out these evil qualities, then they will become fixed in his heart so firmly that he will be unable to uproot them. He should be alert to seek peace and to pursue it. As it is said: "Seek peace and pursue it" (Ps. 34:15). He should be zealous to seek knowledge of the Torah and knowledge of the Creator, as it is written. "And let us know, eagerly strive to know the Lord" (Hos. 6:3). Thus, said the Sages: "Betake thyself to a place of Torah" (Aboth 4:14). And a man should be alert to seek justice, as it is written: "Justice, justice shall you pursue" (Deut. 16:20). And it is written, "Hearken to Me, ye that follow after righteousness, Ye that seek the Lord" (Is. 51:1). It is necessary to be quick in copying out the books which one needs for one's study. When he sees or hears a new thing, he should be alert to write it down and not delay until it is forgotten from his heart.

Rabbi Judah, the son of Tema, said, "Be bold as a leopard, light as an eagle, fast as a deer, mighty as a lion to do the will of your Father in heaven" (Aboth 5:24). See how they warned that one makes himself light and strong in order to fulfill the commandments! Thus, did David say, "I made haste, and delayed not, to observe Thy commandments" (Ps. 119:60). Thus did our Rabbis expound: " 'And ye shall observe the matzot (Ex. 12:17), do not read it as matzot (unleavened bread), but read it is as mitzvot (commandments)" — meaning if an opportunity comes to you to do a good deed, do not let it grow stale but do it at once (Mekhilta de Rabbi Ishmael, vol. I., p. 74). It is very necessary to be agile and alert and strong in order to strive against the wicked — to be mighty of heart as Moses, our teacher, when he said, "Put every man his sword upon his thigh" (Ex. 32:27). And to be like Phinehas of whom it is said, "And when Phinehas, the son of Eleazar the son of Aaron the priest, saw it, he rose up from the midst of the congregation and took a spear into hand" (Num. 25:7). Therefore, take care to be quick to separate yourself from the company of the wicked, so that you will not be part of their designs and their plans. Above all it requires zeal to do repentence. One must hurry and he should not delay to follow the paths of repentence, and let him not be wicked for even one hour before God, may He be Blessed. See how alert the servants and ministers of kings are in the performance of their duties. All the more so must we be careful to be alert in our service to the King of Kings, the Holy One, Blessed be He.

Even though zeal is a very good quality, one must be careful not to work too quickly. For one who rides quickly is liable to stumble, and one who runs quickly may fall. It is not wise to attempt to repair anything in haste, but rather with deliberation. And thus, said our teachers, "Be deliberate in judgment!" (Aboth 1:1). And zeal means that one's heart must be stirred, and one's thoughts aroused and that one's limbs must be light for one's work, but one ought not to be hasty in any matter. All of these matters require great wisdom as to when to hurry and when to tarry. Even though the quality of zeal is very good nevertheless a man ought not be zealous to pursue his lusts, to busy himself in seeking pleasures, or to pursue evil deeds. For just as zeal in the matter of Torah raises a man to a very lofty height, so does alertness in the matter of transgressing bring a man down to the nether world.

Just as a man must be quick in the matter of the Torah, so should he be quick in the matters of this world and be alert in his work. Great success is in store for him who does his work with alertness. Therefore, son of man, be alert in what concerns both worlds, and be quick in your work which is needed for this world, in order that you will soon be free to do the work of Heaven.

Sefer ORCHOT TZADIKIM
Ways of the Righteous

Chapter Sixteen

ON LAZINESS

Laziness is a very bad quality. Anyone in whom this trait is strong will find his affairs spoiled in this world and in the world to come. Concerning him, King Solomon said: "I went by the field of the slothful and by the vineyard of the man void of understanding; and lo, it was all grown over with thistles, the face thereof was covered with nettles and the stone wall thereof was broken down" (Prov. 24:30-31). The wisdom of a lazy man is like the field of a lazy man. The field of a lazy man not only fails to produce, because he does not till it as he should, but it yields harmful products like thistles and thorns. Even if he were to busy himself with his field until the products grew, owing to his laziness he would lose the produce, because the stone fence is in ruin and he is too lazy to repair it, so that cattle and thieves enter and take everything. Solomon said, "... and the stone wall thereof was broken down." Even though the stone was very strong, it was still ruined because of his laziness, for he did not repair it before it fell.

ORCHOT TZADIKIM — Chapter Sixteen

Comparable is the instance of one who is too lazy to study the Torah and to observe the commandments, for the indolent love rest and as a result find God's commandments difficult for them and the study of the Torah burdensome. And so, they flee from study to rest. When they do sit in the synagogue they sleep, as it is said: "Slothfulness casteth into a deep sleep" (Prov. 19:15). For laziness creates a desire for sleep. King Solomon warned us long ago, "Yet a little sleep, a little slumber, a little folding of the hands to sleep" (Prov. 6:10).

Not only does the lazy man fail to attain knowledge of the Torah, since he does not occupy himself with the Torah as he should, but due to his laziness, false notions enter his heart. For the lazy person rationalizes his laziness: "It is good for the body to rest so that it will grow stronger, and when a man is strong, he can do more than a weak person." A lazy person also listens to vain things, but he excuses himself by maintaining that he has an open mind. Laziness, then, causes a man to seek reasons for saying that when he avoids study, he is really doing a positive good. Now even though it is true that we must rest in order to grow strong and that listening to wit helps to clear the mind, this applies specifically to the man who is zealous and occupies himself with the Torah. The strength of man is not like the strength of stones and his bones are not like brass, so that he can be busy constantly; one must rest from time to time in order to replenish one's strength. But the lazy man applies this theory to himself and embraces it so wholeheartedly that he does nothing at all. In every instance where exertion is called for, he rationalizes his laziness.

The lazy man is faint-hearted and does not make his way to a center of Torah. Of him, King Solomon said seven things. What does the lazy man say? People say to a lazy man, "There is a teacher in the metropolis — go and learn Torah from him," and he answers, "I am afraid of the lion that is in the path." As it is said. "The sluggard saith: 'There is a lion in the way' " (Prov. 26:13). They say to him, "There is a teacher in the township — get up and go to him" and he answers, "I am afraid lest there be a lion in the streets." As it is said, "Yea, a lion is in the streets" (ibid). Then they say to him, "But the teacher lives right near your house." And he answers, "The lion is somewhere outside." As it is said, "The sluggard saith: 'There is a lion without; I shall be slain in the streets.' " Then they say to him, "The teacher is right in your house," and he answers, "But if I go and find the door locked, I will only have to come back." They say to him, "The door is open." As it is said, "The door is turning upon its hinges and the sluggard is still upon his bed" (Prov. 26:14). Finally, when he does not know what to answer, he says to them, "Whether the door is open or locked, I want to sleep a bit more." As it is said, "How long wilt thou sleep, O sluggard? When wilt though arise out of thy sleep?" (Prov. 6:9). When he rises from his sleep, they place before him food to eat, but he is too lazy even to lift it to his mouth. As it is said, "The sluggard burieth his hand in the dish; It wearieth him to bring back to his mouth" (Prov. 26:15).

ORCHOT TZADIKIM

And what is the seventh trait? As it is said, "The sluggard will not plow, when winter setteth in" (Prov. 20:4). Rabbi Simon, the son of Yohai said, "This refers to one who did not study Torah in his youth and wants to study when he is old — he will be unable to do so. That is what is meant by, "He shall beg in harvest, and have nothing" (ibid.).

This is what Solomon had to say in denunciation of the sluggard, but Moses, our teacher, said the greatest thing of all. For he said: "But the word is very nigh unto thee, in thy mouth and in thy heart, that thou mayest do it" (Deut. 30:14). Only bring forth a word from your mouth (Deut. Rabbah 8:6). And he who is too lazy to do even this, to utter words from his mouth, there is no greater laziness than this!

See how removed the lazy man is from good qualities, how worthless as a messenger. He is like vinegar, which is bad for the teeth, as it is said, "As vinegar to the teeth, and as smoke to the eyes, so is the sluggard to them that send him" (Prov. 10:26). And it is said, "The desire of the slothful killeth him; for his hands refuse to labour" (Prov. 21:25). And it is said, "The sluggard is wiser in his own eyes than seven men that give wise answer" (Prov. 26:16). The meaning of this verse is as follows: There was a king who had many runners and messagers, and they all did his bidding, and they would report to the king when they returned from their errands. But one of the servants of the king was a lazy man, and he cunningly said, "I am ill!" And he rested and ate from the king's table. When he saw his companions, weary from the exertions of the journey, he considered himself wiser than all of them. But this is folly, for it is written, "Seest thou a man

ORCHOT TZADIKIM

diligent in his business? He shall stand before kings" (Prov. 22:29). Here, too, the king rewards those who did his bidding.

The principle is that the sluggard is not fit either for this world or for the world to come, for he refuses to make the slightest effort. The wise man said "The laziest of men is he who is too lazy to acquire friends who are wise and revere the Lord. But there is one that is lazier still, and that is he who had such friends but lost them."

The Holy One, Blessed be He, created a very weak creature, which gathers its food and exerts itself greatly in order to make the lazy man wise. As it is written, "Go to the ant, thou sluggard; consider her ways, and be wise" (Prov 6:6). The lazy man ought to feel shame when he sees the ant, up and about in pursuit of its affairs. He ought to learn from the ant the quality of zeal so that he may save his soul from the pit, his soul which is endangered by his idleness.

However, there is also a good type of laziness. For example, one who is too lazy to do bad things or to run after pleasure. They said this concerning a man whom the king wished to send to a dangerous place, and he did not want to go, whereupon the king abused him. Then said this man to the king, "Better that you revile me and I remain alive than that you pray for me and I die."

Concerning this matter our Sages said: "There is an alert person who receives a reward and there is an alert person who loses by his alertness. There is a lazy man who receives a reward, and there is a lazy one who loses by his laziness. The alert person who receives a reward is one who does his work all week long but does not do any work on the eve of the Sabbath. The alert person who loses by his alertness is one who does work all week long, and also works on the eve of the Sabbath. A lazy person who receives a reward is one who loes not do work all week long and does not do work on the eve of the Sabbath either. A lazy person who loses thereby is one who does not do any work all week, but does work on the eve of the Sabbath" (Pesahim 50b). Observe how the sages came up with the idea that there is an alertness that is good and an alertness that is bad. It is the same with laziness.

Therefore, you ought to think of doing good with all of your limbs and with all your thoughts and you should demand of every limb sometimes to be easy and sometimes hard, but all should be intended for the sake of Heaven. It should be easy for you to sit with companions joined together for the study of Torah and the commandments, and it should be hard for you to sit with scoffers and evil-doers. It should be easy for you to see law, justice and the commandments executed, and it should be hard for you to see frivolous deeds and to look upon idol-worship and immorality. It should be easy for you to hear words of rebuke and chastisement and the law of the Torah, and it should be hard for you to hear obscene and idle talk. It should be easy for you to be angry with the wicked, and it should be hard for you to be angry with the righteous. It should be hard for your mouth and your tongue to indulge in quarrels, falsehoods, scoffing and gossip, and it should be easy for your mouth to speak the words of the Torah and to censure when necessary and to tell people to follow the good.

ORCHOT TZADIKIM

It should be hard for you to lift a hand against your friend, and it should be easy for you to give alms and to do your work faithfully. It should be hard for your feet to walk in the paths of the wicked, to go to drinking parties and to stroll about aimlessly, and it should be easy for your feet to run to the synagogues and the houses of study, to visit the sick, to escort the dead, and to perform all the commandments of the Torah. It should be hard for you to think wicked thoughts in your mind, and it should be hard for you to indulge in envy or hatred, but it should be easy for you to think thoughts of the Torah, and to attain lofty heights of love of the Lord, Blessed be He, and a pure reverence for God. In this manner, you will be quick and alert in your heart to cleave to the light sublime.

Sefer ORCHOT TZADIKIM
Ways of the Righteous

Chapter Seventeen

ON GENEROSITY

Generosity is that trait through which man can attain great heights; when dedicated to the good it is indeed most praiseworthy. By means of this quality, one may attain many lofty heights in this world and in the world to come, as it is said, "A man's gifts maketh room for him, and bringeth him before great men" (Prov. 18:16). Because of his gifts, kings and nobles will love him and so will every man. There is nothing in the world like generosity for getting the world to love you, and even in the world to come the generous man will receive a good reward because of his gifts.

There are three kinds of generosity: generosity with money, generosity with one's body, and generosity with one's wisdom — and all three were found in Abraham, our father. He was generous with his money, as it is written, "And he planted a tamarisk" (Gen. 21:33). He was generous with his body, for he saved his nephew, Lot, and fought for his sake. He was generous in his wisdom, for he taught everyone the right path until they became converted, as it is written, "And the souls that they had gotten in Haran" (Gen. 12:5).

This quality is most praiseworthy. Through it a man is honored, as it is written, "Many will entreat the favour of the liberal man" (Prov. 19:6). His words are listened to when he reproves people and bids them to return to the service of the Creator. If he needs help, everybody helps him for all dwell in peace with him. Know, that a gift in the right circumstances, for example, alms to the poor who revere God — is a treasure which is stored up and will never be lost but will remain forever. This was the intent of King Solomon, when he said, "Cast thy bread upon the waters, for thou shalt find it after many days" (Eccl. 11:1). The verse refers literally to generosity: he who sows charity will reap its products, and he who has this quality will prosper. As it is said, "There is that scattereth, and yet increaseth" (Prov. 11:24). It is also written, "He that giveth unto the poor shall not lack" (Prov. 28:27). David said concerning generous men, "He hath given to the needy; his righteousness endureth forever" (Ps. 112:9).

This important quality really means lending to the Creator, Blessed be He, as it is said, "He that is gracious unto the poor lendeth unto the Lord" (Prov. 19:17). The wise man said, "Do kindness to him who deserves it and to him who does not deserve it, but you should be worthy to do kindness." And he said, "He who gives a large gift to one who asks for the gift is only half-generous." The truly generous man is he who gives frequently, whether much or little, before he is asked.

ORCHOT TZADIKIM — Chapter Seventeen

Our Sages, of blessed memory, said further, "The quality of generosity depends upon habit, for a man cannot be called generous unless he gives of his own free will at all times, and at all hours, according to his ability. A man who gives a thousand gold pieces to a worthy person at one time is not as generous as one who gives a thousand gold pieces on a thousand different occasions, each to a worthy cause. For the man who gave the thousand gold pieces at one time had a sudden impulse to be generous, but after that the desire left him. Also, in the matter of reward, one cannot compare a man who redeems one captive for a hundred dinars, or gives alms to one poor man in the amount of one hundred dinars (which is completely sufficient for the poor man's needs) with a man who has redeemed ten captives, or has helped to cover the needs of ten poor men, each one receiving ten dinars. Concerning this our Sages said, "Everything must be according to the multitude of the task" (Aboth 3:15); they did not say according to the greatness of the task."

One who shuts his eyes from an opportunity to give charity, it is as though he served idols (Kethuboth 68a). Such a man is called "worthless," "wicked," "merciless," and a "sinner." Worthless, as it is said, "Beware that there be not a base thought in thy heart, saying: 'The seventh year, the year of release, is at hand;' and thine eye be evil against thy needy brother, and thou give him nought" (Deut. 15:9). Merciless as it is written, "But the tender mercies of the wicked are cruel" (Prov. 12:10). And he denies his lineage; he is not of the seed of Abraham, Isaac and Jacob, for they were merciful, but he is of the seed of the heathens who are cruel, as it is said, "They are cruel and have no compassion" (Jer. 50:42). And everyone who shows mercy, Heaven has mercy upon him (Shabbath 151b). As it is said, "... and show thee mercy, and have compassion upon thee, and multiply thee" (Deut. 13:18).

He who gives alms to the poor grudgingly loses the merit of the deed, even though he gives much, and it is better that he gives only one pruta with a pleasing countenance. And it is well to give before one is asked, and it is well to give secretly, as it is written, "A gift in secret pacifieth anger" (Prov. 21:14). There were people who used to tie the money in a garment and cast it behind them and the poor would come and take, so that he who gave the alms did not know to whom he gave, and he who received the alms did not know from whom he received it, and thus the poor man was not shamed. The general rule in this matter is that as much as possible should be concealed, so that the poor man does not know who is the giver and the giver does not know who is the recipient.

When a man gives alms and the deed is accompanied by kindness for example, he buys something that the poor man needs in order to save him the trouble, or he finds something the poor man needs at a cheap price, at a time when the poor man has no money with which to buy it (and here we should make a point of giving it to the poor man without delay) — in this way does kindness with him. Concerning this, the Prophet said, "Sow to yourselves according to righteousness, reap according to mercy" (Hos. 10:12).

Now, hearken to the importance of generosity and of the men who give freely to the poor, as it is written,

"Righteousness will exalt a people" (Prov. 14:34). Come and see, how great is the power of charity, for it is described as being at the right hand of the Holy One, Blessed be He, as it is said, "Thy right hand is full of righteousness" (Ps. 48:11) (Midrash to Prov. 14).

Great is charity — it is this quality for which the Holy One, Blessed be He, will be praised when he brings salvation to Israel, as it is said, "I that speak in victory, mighty to save" (Is. 63:1). Great is charity — it brings honor and life to those who practice it, as it is said "He that followeth after righteousness and mercy, findeth life, prosperity and honour" (Prov. 21:21). Great is charity — with this quality, the Holy One, Blessed be He, will redeem Israel, as it is said, "Zion shall be redeemed with justice and they that return of her with righteousness" (Is. 1:27). Great is charity — with this quality Abraham, our father, was praised, as it is said, "And he trusted in God and He reckoned it to him for righteousness" (Gen. 15:6), and it is said further, "For I have known him, to the end that he may command his children and his household after him, that they may keep the way of the Lord, to do righteousness and justice" (Gen. 18:19). Great is charity — with this quality, David, King of Israel, was praised, as it is said, "And David executed justice and righteousness unto all his people" (II Sam. 8:15). Great is charity — with this quality King Solomon was praised, as it is said. "Blessed be the Lord thy God, who delighted in thee, to set thee on the throne of Israel; because the Lord loved Israel for ever, Therefore, made He thee king, to do justice and righteousness" (I Kings 10:9). Great is charity — it reaches up to the very Throne of Glory, as it is said, "Righteousness and justice are the foundation of Thy throne" (Ps. 89:15). Great is charity — through it Israel was praised, as it is said, "And it shall be righteousness unto us" (Deut. 6:25). Great is charity — with it, the Holy One, Blessed be He, will in future be praised on the Day of Judgment, as it is said, "But the Lord of hosts is exalted through justice, and God the Holy One, is sanctified through righteousness" (Is. 5:16). Great is charity — it accompanies those who practice it at the hour of their departure from the world, as it is said, "And thy righteousness shall go before thee, the glory of the Lord shall be thy reward" (Is. 58:8). Great is kindness — with it the world was built, as it is said, "The world on mercy is built" (Ps. 89:3). Wherefore a man should cleave to the quality of generosity which brings about all these good things (Mekhilta on Ex. 15:13).

Moreover, one should be generous with his money to purchase good deeds, as Rabban Gamliel did when he bought an etrog for a thousand zuz (Sukkah 41b). And one should be generous with one's money to adorn the commandments of the Torah (Shabbath 133b). In embellishing a commandment, one should pay up to a third more (Baba Kamma 9b).

A man should be generous with his money to copy and to purchase books and to lend them to one who has none, as it is said, "Wealth and riches are in his house; and his merit endureth for ever" (Ps. 112:3). And a man should be easygoing and not mind if the books are damaged because of their use (Kethuboth 50a). He should also be generous when it comes to his household utensils, and lend them to his neighbors and his friends.

He should be generous in loaning his money to the poor; and if he is able to do so, then he should also loan to the rich when they are in need. He should be generous in his business matters and he should never be petty in small matters. If he is measuring wine or oil, or whatever thing it may be, he ought not to hold it down narrowly to the exact measure.

He should be generous with his energy, going out of his way for people, bearing their yoke and their burden, feeling pain at their anguish, praying for their sake, rejoicing in their joy, visiting the sick, and doing kindness to the dead.

Especially should he be generous with his knowledge of the Torah, teaching every man knowledge and drawing their hearts towards Heaven. This is the greatest type of generosity of all: he who gives of himself to a person in order to lead him to eternal life in the world to come.

Even though generosity is a good quality, a person should be careful not to be a spendthrift in order to attain the desires of his heart, in all manner of food and drink or to give of his wealth to harlots, or to have expensive garments made, or to scatter his money in all sorts of schemes that do not lead to reverence of Heaven. A man who is generous should not scatter his funds for nothing or pursue desires which can only bring him all sorts of evil. But he should be very careful to be liberal with the deserving poor, to dress them, to feed them with the best, as it is written, "All the fat is the Lord's" (Lev. 3:16). His reward shall be that which is good and treasured, which "Neither hath the eye seen, save God, who worketh for him that waiteth for Him" (Is. 64:3).

Sefer ORCHOT TZADIKIM

Ways of the Righteous

Chapter Eighteen

ON MISERLINESS

Miserliness is very ugly in all of its manifestations. Concerning the miser, Solomon said, "Eat thou not the bread of him that hath an evil eye" (Prov. 23:6).

These are the traits of a miserly person: "He does not give charity, he does not have mercy upon the poor, and in business dealings he is too punctilious and does not yield on a single point. He does not feed or clothe or give pleasure to anyone but himself and he has not trust in Him who gives him his money; he is hated by all creatures. He does not take special pains to carry out the commandments, nor does he acquire a teacher or a companion in study, and thus he remains empty of Torah and good deeds.

If he is miserly with his body, he also is evil and bitter, for he does not act kindly to people. It is an evil greater than all others if he is miserly with his wisdom and with his books, for by loaning these he loses nothing at all. For wisdom is like fire, which never dims even if you light many candles or another fire from it. Of such a miser, it is said, "He that withholdeth corn, the people shall curse him" (Prov.

ORCHOT TZADIKIM — Chapter Eighteen

11:26). But of the generous man, it is said, "But blessing shall be upon the head of him that supplieth it" (Ibid.). Literally the verse speaks of charity, yet it is a parable for wisdom.

The good in this quality is that the miser does not throw away his money on foolishness and at times is restrained from committing grave sins. Then, too, because he deprives himself of good things, he does not affect the arrogance often found in the generous person who, because of the good that he does and the pleasure that he gets from it, sometimes rebels against his Creator. Therefore, a man should be careful with his wealth; he should be generous where generosity is called for, but where it is not proper for him to give, let him be miserly and niggardly. Let him weigh all this in the scales of the Torah.

Let him learn from Jacob, our father, who was miserly without parallel as it is said, "And Jacob was left alone" (Gen. 32:25), and our Rabbis, of blessed memory, said that he had forgotten some small jugs and returned to get them. This teaches us that the righteous value their money more than their bodies, because they do not get their money easily through plunder (Hullin 91a). Behold this great miserliness — that a man as rich as Jacob felt compelled to return for some little jugs. Yet we find in another place that he was genereous without parallel, as our Rabbis taught, "In my grave which I have digged for me" (Gen. 50:5). This teaches us that Jacob took all the silver and gold that he had brought from Laban's house and he made a pile and said to Esau. "Take this for your share in the cave of Machpelah" (Ex. Rabbah 31:17). Was there ever anyone else as liberal as this?

ORCHOT TZADIKIM Chapter Eighteen

From this a man can learn that he should not squander his money on useless things and to no purpose. However, when it comes to fulfilling a commandment, for example, dispensing charity and other commandments which involve expense, such as acquiring a teacher, a companion or books, he should be very liberal in order to attain lofty qualities. He thereby restores the soul to its place of purity so that it will be bound up in the bond of life, as it is written, "Yet the soul of my Lord shall be bound up in the bond of life" (I Sam. 25:29).

Sefer

ORCHOT TZADIKIM

Ways of the Righteous

Chapter Nineteen

ON REMEMBERING
Remembering is a trait without which the world could not endure, for all transactions of this world depend upon memory, and no man would trust another or loan him anything if he could not rely on the latter's memory. And all the affairs of the world involve remembering; for example, in buying and selling, if the people were to forget what they had said previously, they would not be able to do business, and they could not agree on terms if they did not possess the quality of remembering. It is not necessary to expatiate on this for it is a matter of common knowledge. Therefore, a man should employ this quality in all his affairs, for memory is a fence to truth, and it helps a man to fulfill his vows. If there is a matter between him and his companion, he must remember it and not alter his words. If someone tells him a secret and commands him not to reveal it, he must remember this and not reveal it.

If a person borrows money or household utensils from a friend, he must remember exactly what he has borrowed and take care to return everything. One who has many business interests and is very busy should be very careful not to borrow money or things from people, since he is liable to forget everything and not remember. If someone has done him a good deed, he should make a point of remembering it so that he can reciprocate. Concerning charity, one must remember the poor and constantly keep their distress in mind, and thus he will be able to help them. And if a man comes to give testimony in a court of law concerning what he has seen and what he knows, he must be very careful to remember and he must not diminish from or add to that which he saw. See how the Holy One, Blessed be He, has warned us concerning memory. As it is said, "Beware lest thou forget the Lord thy God, in not keeping His commandments and His ordinances" (Deut. 5:11). And it is very important to remember God in all of one's deeds. And thus, did David say, "I have set the Lord always before me" (Ps. 16:8).

Memory is a very lofty quality and it is an instrument that strengthens all the commandments and all the Torah. Concerning the fringes, it is said, "And remember all the commandments of the Lord and do them … that ye may remember and do all My commandments" (Num. 15:39-40). Concerning the tefillin, it is said, "And it shall be for a sign upon thee upon thy hand, and for a memorial between thine eyes, that the law of the Lord may be in thy mouth" (Ex. 13:9). And it is written, "And thou shalt remember that thou wast a bondman in Egypt; and thou shalt observe and do these statutes (Deut. 16:12). And since everything depends upon memory, I must list thirty. The idea of organizing one's wisdom into thirty precepts is based upon the kere of Proverbs 22:20. things that you ought to remember twice a day. And you should place them in the depths of your heart, and in your thoughts. Do not remember them with your mouth alone, but write them on the tablet of your heart. Then your service will be well received by God, Blessed be He, and you will obtain favor and kindnesses before Him.

The first thing to remember is how the Creator, Blessed be He, brought you forth from nothing to existence. And remember the goodness which He did for you from the time of your birth until this day, and how He has raised you and lifted you up over all creatures. And all of this He did for you, not because He was obligated to do this to you, but of His own free will and out of His great kindness He has rewarded you with all this. Because of this you are obligated to thank the Creator, Blessed be He.

The second thing that one must remember is the kindness of God for giving him a healthy body, for if he were ill in a single limb and a doctor came and healed it, how grateful he would be to that doctor. All the more so must he be thankful to God, who made him completely healthy.

The third thing to remember is the kindness of God, who has given him wisdom and knowledge. For if a man were so mad as to rip up his garments, how difficult life would be for him, and he would be reckoned as being worthless. And if a doctor were to heal him of his madness, how much would be having to praise him for this healing. All the more so, ought he to praise the Creator, Blessed be He.

The fourth thing a person ought to remember is the

good that God bestowed on him in giving him His holy Torah, thus teaching him the proper paths in which to attain the proper service of God. And he should eagerly give thanks to God, for through the Torah he will attain the light of life and to enjoy the radiance of the Divine Presence.

The fifth thing to remember is the mercy of God, who has shown mercy to him by giving him His pure Torah. Now if a king of flesh and blood had sent him a letter and he read it through and there was something in it that he did not understand, what anguish he would feel because he did not understand what the king was commanding him. And there is no doubt that if there was in the vicinity even a very insignificant person who knew how to explain that which he did not understand, he would hasten to go to him and would not be ashamed at all to inquire. How much more, then, should he be grateful for the Torah of our God (which explains everything).

The sixth matter which he should remember is to consider if there is within him any flaw which would make him transgress what his Creator had commanded him. And he should think about this, that all the things which the Creator made, obey His commandments: the donkey carries the burden, the horse and the ox plow, and not for one day do they rebel against their master. The sun each day does what God has commanded it. And if there were one day when the sun did not shine, and there was darkness, how astonishing this would be in the eyes of the world. Or if the earth did not produce its food and its fruit, then all the world would die. And now, see how all of the things that God created do his bidding. And should man not be ashamed if he does not accustom his limbs which were created in order to observe the Torah to do so, and if instead he alters their function and accustoms them to transgress the Torah?

The seventh matter he should remember is that if a slave sees that his master deals bountifully with him and provides him with all his needs, how much ought that slave take it upon himself to revere his master and to love him and submit to him and try with all his power to find favor in the eyes of his master. All the more so, should a man accept the yoke of the kingdom of Heaven, and consider himself as a servant submissive before his master and not adopt a domineering or arrogant attitude.

The eighth thing to remember is how all of the king's servants are quick and industrious in their work, and when their duties involve wisdom and counsel, they clear their minds of all other matters and concentrate all their thoughts and all their wisdom, in order to do with understanding and with wisdom and with proper intent and with all their heart the matter which the king turned over to them. And if such a man comes to praise the king, and to thank him for the good which he did to him, whether in a letter or orally, he would search his heart for pure and beautiful words with which to praise the king. All the more so should a man do so before the King of Kings, and place all of his intentions in the service of the Lord, Blessed be He, to do that which is right and fitting. Now all of the deeds in the service of the Lord are divided into three types. The first is the obligation of the heart alone: if he occupies himself in his thoughts in communion with God, he must cleanse his heart of all other thoughts so that his communion with God may be complete. The second type involves the employment of the heart and the limbs in the service of God, as in prayer. He must cleanse his heart of all other affairs and stand with great intent before the Great God, Blessed be He. The third type is that involved when he prepares a lulav or fringes or the like, which are precepts for the limbs alone and here intent does not occupy the central position it does in prayer, these precepts being addressed to the limbs rather than to the heart. Yet even here, before a man fulfills the commandments of putting on the fringes or waving the lulav, he must remember for whom he does so. And he must always embellish a commandment, even by paying up to one-third more (than the price of an ordinary religious article and buying a more expensive one) to honor the Master of the Universe. The ninth thing one should remember is that he who has a wife whom he loves as himself, or a son whom he loves with all his heart, always exerts himself to supply their every need and fulfill their every wish; and he does not do so because he fears them or because they will do good to him because he fulfills their wishes, but because of his great love for them. All the more so should he act so before God, and earnestly direct all of his deeds to His Great Name alone. He should not fulfill the Commandments out of love or fear of men or out of the hope of deriving some benefit, but he should unify all of his deeds to God's Great Name alone and not mix this with any other motives.

The tenth thing he should remember is what all his

deeds have been until the present day. If he has occupied himself with the service of his Creator, he should recall every day how he has served the Lord and in what manner he may have rebelled against Him. He should always set his mind on occupying himself more with the service of God, Blessed be He, than with his own needs. And if he has not heretofore devoted himself to the service of the Creator, then at least let him do so from now on.

The eleventh thing a man should remember is how alert he is and how he hastens in his business in order to make money and how he thinks about this night and day and he is not anxious to love any man except him who helps him accumulate gold and silver. All of his labors in the pursuit of wealth may be for nothing and there is always the possibility that he will lose all he has, or that his money will be his undoing, or that he will die before long, yet in spite of all this he exerts himself in this way. If this is the case, what should a man do for the sake of his soul which lives forever? Moreover, how obliged a man is to mend his ways and be constantly alert to remember to purify and cleanse his soul with a cleansing that lasts forever and ever. Now, see what a difference there is between the two worlds, and the excellence of one over the other is like that of light over darkness.

The twelfth thing a man should remember is that the Holy One, Blessed be He, sees the thoughts of his heart. See how a man who goes to minister before the king adorns and beautifies himself, as it is written, "For you may not enter within the king's gate clothed with sackcloth" (Esther 4:2). And as we see in the story of Joseph, "Then Pharaoh sent and called

Joseph, and they brought him hastily out of the dungeon. And he shaved himself, and changed his raiment, and came in unto Pharaoh" (Gen. 41:14). And behold and see that he who stands before the king always does not adorn himself (as lightly) as he who stands before the king for one moment. If this is so, then we who stand before the King of Kings forever — for He sees the thoughts of our hearts whether secret or revealed, and there is no escape from Him, for He is everywhere — should think always of His greatness and agree in our hearts to do His will and to adorn ourselves in our thoughts before Him.

The thirteenth thing to remember is that his deeds do not match his wisdom, that he has money but is not doing good commensurate with his wealth. And he should think: Is there a man who if another man comes along and says, "Take these hundred gold coins on condition that you give to my friends ten gold coins" — would he not accept the offer? All the more so should he do this before the Lord Blessed be, He. And he should not say, "If I had attained such and such an amount of wealth, or if I possessed more knowledge than I do, I would do what I am obligated to do in the service of God" — for all of this is a lot of nonsense on the part of him who speaks thus, for this is all at the urging of the Evil Inclination. Let a man instead do at once what he can, according to his wisdom and his wealth, in the state in which he is at present, and if he should have more at some future time, then let him do more.

The fourteenth thing a man should remember is how a person tends to love one who is friendly towards him, as it is written: "As in water face answereth to face, so the heart of man to man" (Prov. 27:19). All the more so, if a man sees that a king receives him with a friendly countenance and shows him that he loves him, how much will the man love him and praise him and extol him for this. All the more so are we obliged to love with all our hearts the Creator, Blessed be He, who has informed us that He loves us and has assured us that He will continue to love us in every generation. As it is said, "And yet for all that, when they are in the land of their enemies, I will not reject them, neither will I abhor them, to destroy them utterly, and to break My covenant with them" (Lev. 26:44).

The fifteenth thing to remember is that a man prepares his needs before he actually requires them, although he does not know if he will live to enjoy them or not. And a man who sets forth on a distant journey, how he prepares food for the journey! All the more so should we "prepare food" for the long eternity which is a long path indeed when God suddenly sends his messenger to bring man before him.

The sixteenth thing a man should remember is that his companions, better and stronger than he, enjoyed much pleasure but did not live long, and that Death does not delay coming at any moment and is not subject to the rule of man. A man should keep in mind that the soul is a pledge temporarily in his hand and that he does not know when the Owner of the pledge will come and demand the return of His pledge. Therefore, he must quickly cleanse the pledge so that he returns it as clean as it was when he got it.

ORCHOT TZADIKIM
Chapter Nineteen

The seventeenth thing to remember is that it is a very good quality to keep away from people when he can save himself from them, and sit in his room alone. For most transgressions are committed by two or more — for example, fornication, gossip, lies and flattery — and from all of these he who sits alone is saved for he will not vaunt himself over any man and he will not hear their idle talk. For when he stays with them he is obliged to rebuke them in three ways : either by striking the offender, as Phinehas did when he took the javelin in his hand (Num. 25:7); or with words, as Moses our Teacher did, when he said to the wicked man, "Wherefore smitest thou thy fellow?" (Ex. 2:13); or in one's heart, as David said, "I hate the gathering of evil-doers, and will not sit with the wicked" (Ps. 26:5). And who can constantly keep quarreling with such people, inasmuch as they constantly transgress? But when you sit alone you avoid all this guilt and you are saved from many transgressions. But pious people one should join and one should sit near them and learn from them, as it is written, "He that walketh with wise men shall be wise" (Prov. 13:20).

The eighteenth thing one must remember is the kindness of God, who saves him from the afflictions of the world. For he sees so many people dying in great pain from hunger, from thirst, from poison, from leprosy, from the sword, from drowning, and from fire, and he knows in his heart that he deserves to be visited with all sorts of afflictions because of many transgressions which he has committed, and that he has not guarded that which God has placed in his care. And even though he is a completely wicked person, God has had pity upon him and saved him from all these afflictions. He should know how fitting it is for him to be submissive before his Creator and ask Him to guard him against all the distress that takes place in the world. As it is said, "If thou wilt diligently hearken to the voice of the Lord thy God... I will put none of the diseases upon thee, which I have put upon the Egyptians; for I am the Lord that healeth thee" (Ex. 15:26). And it said, "And the Lord will take away from thee all sickness; and He will put none of the evil diseases of Egypt, which thou knowest, upon thee" (Deut. 7:15). And our Rabbis, of blessed memory, said, "It is not the lizard that slays, but it is sin that slays" (Berakoth 33a).

The nineteenth thing one should remember is that if he has money, it is a pledge in his hand, for when God wishes he can take it from his hand and entrust it to someone else. Therefore, a man ought not feel pain at paying what he owes. For example, if he has stolen something, he should be glad to return what he has stolen, and give praise to God that he was in a position to return what he had stolen. And he should be careful not to fear the cruel happenings of the times against him, but he should think that what God, Blessed be He, is pleased to do should be acceptable to him as His decree, for everything belongs to him. When He desires, He gives it into his hand, and when He desires, He takes it from him. He should not despise a poor man because of his poverty, nor should he think that it is because of his own merit that he himself has acquired his wealth, but he should think that God in His mercy gave it to him, and he should ask Him to let him so dispose of his money as to the will of the Creator, and that his wealth should not be kept by its master for its master's own evil.

The twentieth thing a man should remember is to consider the difference between what is high and what is lowly, and he should understand that he is small and lowly in comparison with the higher things and he should understand that the Holy One, Blessed be He, has apportioned to him a good portion, for He has made him to rule over all the world, over the cattle, over the animals, over the fish, over the fowl, over the fruit and over the herbs, and He has let him know the secrets of His Greatness and of His Might and of His Wonders, how much is he obligated to give thanks to Him because of all this, like a lowly slave whom his master has raised up over all of his chiefs and servants. All the more so should he do this because he has reached the stage of knowing his Creator, who is the Lord of Lords, that he is certainly obligated to humble himself before Him and praise Him with fear and awe.

The twenty-first thing a man should remember is always to be mindful of all the commandments of the King, and he should accustom himself to do what is good until it becomes a habit with him, and after that he must continue even more. He should ask God to help him and give him wisdom and to strengthen his limbs to bear the burden of His commandments and to ascend from step to step.

The twenty-second thing you should remember is always to do good to your companions, to help them with their burdens and their troubles, and you should love for them what you love for yourself and hate with respect to them that which you hate with respect to yourself. And you should try to acquire faithful brothers and friends who will help you in your study of the Torah, for if your heart is completely sincere with them, they will love you and there will be many who will seek your welfare — but reveal your secret only to one in a thousand.

The twenty-third thing a person should remember is the greatness of God, Blessed be He. And he should understand the creation of the world, the large things and the small, and revolving of the spheres, and the nature of the sun and the moon and the stars, and the falling of the rain, and the blowing of the winds, and many more wonders too numerous to relate. Inasmuch as a man sees these marvels constantly, he does not wonder in his heart about what he sees, but when there is an eclipse of the sun or the moon, then he wonders exceedingly because this is not usual and customary as the circling of the sun each day from east to west. Therefore, look upon them and let it seem as though you have never seen these wonders before, and let them appear as though you were blind heretofore and that now you have opened your eyes. Then, this will become most wonderous in your eyes. So, must you do with yourself, every day, and thus did David say, "Wonderful are thy works; and that my soul knoweth right well" (Ps. 139:14).

The twenty-fourth thing one should remember is that a man whose eyes are weak cannot see the fine engraving on gold and silver dishes. Even though he sees all these things, he cannot perceive them as clearly as one whose eyes are strong. Thus, if a man has studied Torah and wisdom in his youth and it appears to him that he understands them properly, let him not rely upon that childhood understanding, for wisdom strengthens itself as one advance in years, and he now understands more clearly than he did in his youth. Therefore, when your wisdom becomes stronger, you should begin to consider well all the matters around you, and then you will understand and increase your ability to distinguish, and you will know the matter more clearly than you did previously. And you must continue always to search out from every man what you do not know, as it is said, "From all my mentors I have learned" (Ps. 119:99). And you should not think that no one can tell you anything new that you did not know when you were young. Concerning this it is said, "Seest thou a man wise in his own eyes? There is more hope of a fool than of him" (Prov. 26:12).

The twenty-fifth thing that a person should always remember is the pleasures of the world-to-come; he should put the love of this world out of his heart and the love of the world-to-come should grow ever stronger within him. As one of the pious men has already said, "Just as water and fire cannot be united in one vessel, so can you not unite in a faithful heart love of this world and love of the world to come." And one should have some love for this world only because from this world he will take provision for the word to come.

The twenty-sixth thing one should remember is that those who stand subject to the king's command are fearful and terrified of the king's punishment. All the more so should one fear the punishment of the King of Kings, the Holy One, Blessed be He, and hasten to serve him.

ORCHOT TZADIKIM — Chapter Nineteen

The twenty-seventh thing one should keep in mind is that if someone angered the king and was sentenced to death, but the king then lightened his punishment and visited him with afflictions or loss of money in place of the death that was to have been his penalty, then surely the king has done kindness with him. Therefore, he should receive everything from God with joy and with love, and this will be a great sign that he willingly accepts the decree of the Creator.

The twenty-eighth thing a person should remember is that if someone gives his house to another man as an outright gift, and the recipient wishes to raze it and build it anew according to his own ideas, the giver of the house cannot restrain him. Thus, a man should hand over his soul, his wife, his children and all his wealth into the hands of the Holy One, Blessed be He, and let them all be given to God as an outright gift. Inasmuch as he has from the start yielded himself into the hand of God, he has placed his complete trust in Him, and Therefore, he has already resolved in his heart that he will accept with love all that the Creator decrees concerning him. And even though it turns out that God sends him no evil, not in his body, not in his money, not on his children, not on his wife, he nevertheless obtains a great reward because of his firm frame of mind, because he prepared his heart to bear all things out of the love of his Creator.

The twenty-ninth thing one should remember, in regarding people, is that one man may out-weigh a hundred, not because of physical endowment but because of his understanding, his wisdom and his righteousness. Therefore, you must always improve your soul, for all qualities stem from it. For though a man were strong and healthy and handsome he would not be worth anything if he were a simpleton. And if a man were ugly and weak, but was distinguished by his wisdom, he would rise to greatness and to importance.

The thirtieth thing a person should remember is that if a man came to a foreign land where he knew no one, and no one knew him, and the master of the country had pity upon him and gave him food every day but warned him not to rebel against him and not to transgress his commandments, and informed him that he would receive a good reward for his service, and warned him concerning his return journey, but did not let him know the time of it — in truth, this servant surely ought to be submissive, abandon haughtiness and search out how to do the king's will. He should love every stranger as himself, and he should try to work hard to serve the master of that country most diligently, for there is no compassionate one who will plead for him. Thus, in truth, man is a stranger in the world. When the time comes for him to make his entry into the world, even if the whole world should try to advance or delay his birth even by a moment, or to bind one of his limbs, they would be unable to do so. And so also after his birth, nobody could give him food except the true God. And he is like a lone person who has no friend except his master who has pity upon him, and that is his Creator.

We have completed our brief list of the things a man ought to remember always. But everyone should continue to meditate on these according to his wisdom, and he will learn from them all sorts of good and pure qualities, and these will cleanse the soul and will beautify its ugliness. Be ever alert to remember them, and this will bring out in you a superior strength you never knew before. And a man is obligated to keep all of these thoughts in mind constantly, at every hour, at every moment. And he should be careful to remember them with his every breath so that he may never lose his awe and fear and shame before God, who looks upon him at all times. Go forth and learn from what the Torah warned the king to do, as it is written, ... "that he shall write him a copy of this law in a book, out of that which is before the priests the Levites. And it shall be with him, and he shall read therein all the days of his life" (Deut. 17:18-19). And it is written, "This book of the law shall not depart out of thy mouth, but thou shalt meditate therein day and night" (Josh. 1:8). And it is written, "And these words, which I command thee this day, shall be upon thy heart; and thou shalt teach them diligently unto thy children, and shalt talk of them when thou sittest in thy house, and when thou walkest by the way, and when thou liest down, and when thou risest up. And thou shalt bind them for a sign upon thy hand, and they shall be for frontlets between thine eyes. And thou shalt write them upon the door-posts of thy house, and upon thy gates" (Deut. 6:6—9). And he has emphasized this matter in connection with the fringes, for it is written, "And it shall be unto you for a fringe, that ye may look upon it, and remember all the commandments of the Lord, and do them" (Num. 15:39—40). And according to this it is proper to remember God at every moment. And it is written, "Let thy garments be always white" (Eccl. 9:8).

See how the quality of remembering is very comprehensive, for through it one remembers all the good qualities, and if it were not for remembering, he would forget everything and would remain completely empty. Therefore, strengthen yourself in this quality which is the mightiest of all qualities. An excellent method of acquiring all the good qualities would be to go over this book at least once a week. Then he will remember all the evil qualities and repent of them. As to the references to these qualities in general that are written in the beginning of this book, these he ought to review constantly. And he should examine himself repeatedly to see whether he has fallen short of acquiring these qualities until he becomes accustomed to fulfill all the good qualities that are listed in this book.

You should know that remembering leads one to right action, as it is written, "and remember… and do" (Num. 15:39). Therefore, be very careful in exercising the quality of remembering, and with respect to every single precept remember for Whose sake you perform it, and Who is the Master of your work.

And a man should be very careful not to remember if his friend does a bad thing to him, and concerning this it is said, "Nor bear any grudge" (Lev. 19:18), but he should dismiss all hatred from his heart. But if he has done evil to another, he should remember it in order to make good what he did to him. And if he has heard idle talk, he should not remember it. He should be like a sieve which gathers the fine flour and lets the poor flour go, and not like a strainer that collects the dregs and lets the wine go.

ORCHOT TZADIKIM — Chapter Nineteen

As to the subject of remembering the Torah, we shall explain this, with God's help, in the chapter on the Torah.

Sefer ORCHOT TZADIKIM

Ways of the Righteous

Chapter Twenty

ON FORGETFULNESS

Forgetfulness is a very bad quality both in matters of this world and in matters of the world to come. A person who is in the habit of forgetting should write down all matters that arise between him and his fellows so that he will remember them. If he borrows or lends, he should write down everything; even if he borrows only a prutah, he should write down and determine not to forget. And it is fitting for an esteemed person who is forgetful not to borrow from people, for they will be ashamed to ask for the return of their loan and he will forget it and not repay it, and will bear his guilt therefor. And he who knows himself that he is forgetful should guard himself exceedingly to review all of his affairs. A parable will illustrate the point. There was once a king who gave one of his servants a slip of paper and said to him, "When you see that I am wrathful, give me this slip of paper." And on this slip of paper was written, "Know that you are not God, but you are just a physical body that wears away and whose end will devour its end [meaning that worms will go forth from part of his flesh and devour the rest of his flesh] and which will soon return to vermin and worms." And the king had a servant whom he commanded to stand before him whenever he (the king) ordered that someone be scourged with whips of fire. And he would say this to him to subdue his heart.

From this we can learn several things. A forgetful person should make reminders for himself. And high fences are needed in order that one should not forget the Torah. As it is written, "Only take heed to thyself, and keep thy soul diligently, lest thou forget the things which thine eyes saw" (Deut. 4:9). And he must be very careful not to forget the good qualities.

However, a man should employ the quality of forgetfulness to forget the commandments that he has fulfilled. For if he sets his mind on remembering the precepts that he has fulfilled and the Torah that he has studied, while forgetting his bad deeds and evil schemes, then he will be a righteous man in his own eyes and will not repent. But he should remember his transgressions and write them in a book and read them, in order to remember all of them and repent of each and every one, and he should confess them. But as for the good deeds that he has done, he should not hasten to remember them, and he should always appear in his eyes as though he were empty of good deeds and filled with transgressions. He should forget the sins of his fellow man and forgive him, and he should remove from his heart all hatred, jealousy, and evil thoughts. And at the time of prayer, he should remove from his heart everything in the world, but there should be uppermost in his thoughts the kindness of God, and he should cleave to Him with great attachment. And when he performs his bodily needs, he must forget all the words of the Torah and words of holiness, but he may think about the needs of his household, at that time. He should also think that he is filled with excrement, lowering the pride of his heart. The general rule here is that with respect to every precept of the Torah he should do something that will cause him not to forget, "For the commandment is a lamp, and the teaching is light" (Prov. 6:23).

Sefer
ORCHOT TZADIKIM
Ways of the Righteous

Chapter Twenty-One

ON SILENCE

Silence is one of the virtues mentioned in Ethics of the Fathers. Rabbi Simon, the son of Gamliel, said, "All my days I grew up among the Sages, and I have found nothing better for a person than silence" (Aboth 1:17). And thus, said king Solomon, "Even a fool, when he holdeth his peace, is counted wise" (Prov. 17:28). And the wise man said, "When I speak, my speech rules over me, for when I utter something that is not worthy, that utterance rules over me and forces me at times to beg the pardon of whoever has heard me, but when I do not speak, I rule over whether I want to give expression to a thought or whether I want to conceal it." Our Sages said (Yalkut Shimoni, Beha'alotkha): Two advocates stood before Hadrian; one taught that speech was best and one taught that silence was best. The king said to the one who taught that speech is best, "Why do you say this?" And he said to him, "My Lord, if it were, not for speech how would kings be proclaimed? How would ships sail to the sea? How would kindness be done to the dead by way of eulogy? How would brides be praised? How would business be carried on in the world?" At once, King Hadrian said to him, "Well have you spoken!" Then he said to the one that taught that silence is best, "Why have you have praised silence?" Just as the man was about to answer the first advocate interrupted him. The king said to him, "Why did you interrupt him?" said he, "My Lord, I taught from what is mine concerning what is mine, for I taught by speech the value of speech, but he comes to teach by my means, speech, concerning that which he believes in, silence. Therefore, I interrupted him." Said the other advocate to him, "Solomon did not say that God would have you sit as silent as a deaf mute. But he said, 'In the multitude of words there wanteth not transgression; but he that refraineth his lips are wise" (Prov. 10:19). This means that one ought to restrain himself from speaking against his fellow man. There is no one greater than Aaron or Miriam — through Miriam's merit a well sprang up and gave drink, and clouds of glory would surround Israel through the merit of Aaron. But inasmuch as they gave permission to their mouths and they spoke against Moses, they were at once punished (Num. 12).

There are several reasons for which the Divine Presence departs from Israel. The shedding of blood, the worship of idols, and gossip. There is a story concerning Rabban Gamliel who made a feast and gave to his servant tongues to cook. The servant cooked some of them soft and some of them hard. First, he brought in to the guests the soft tongues, and then he served them the hard tongues. Rabban Gamliel called his servant and said to him, "For what reason have you done thus — some soft and some hard?" And the servant answered, "To show that everything comes from the tongue; if a man wants to, he can make it soft, or hard" (Midrash Rabbah on Lev. 33:1).

Said some people to a wise man, "Why are you so silent?" He said to them, "I have found that speech is divided into four categories. The first is altogether harmful, for example when people are accustomed to curse other people, or to speak vile words. The second involves damage on one side, for example when one praises another in order to derive some advantage from him, and with this very praise he angers the enemy of the man of whom he speaks so highly and will surely do harm to one who praises his enemy. The third type involves neither damage nor gain, for example, idle talk — how such-and-such a wall was built, and how much money was spent on it, and romances about kings and nobles. The fourth, which is altogether beneficial, for example, the Torah and things that depend upon it." But there are some men wise in the Torah who divide speech into five categories. The first, commandments of the Torah. The second, things to guard oneself against. The third, things that should be despised. The fourth, things that should be loved. The fifth, things that are permissible. Speech involving the commandments means to speak words of Torah and reverence of God. Things to guard oneself against — such as: giving false testimony, obscenity and gossip. Things to be despised are those which are neither sinful nor beneficial, as is the case with most stories in the world. For example, to speak about what has already happened, and of the habits of kings, and this and that concerning the matters of the world. Speech which should be loved is the speech which praises good deeds and denounces evil deeds. It praises the deeds of the righteous so that their ways will appear good in men's eyes and they will follow their example, and it denounces the wicked until they are scorned and detested in the eyes of people, and their memory will be blotted out and people will stay away from them, and will not follow their evil ways. Speech which is permissible is speech concerning merchandise for trade and matters concerning clothes, and the matter of food and drink and the rest of a person's needs, but he who minimizes his words in such matters is to be praised. According to the words of the wise, most of the words spoken in the world are unnecessary, not to mention those things the speaking of which is severely prohibited, for example: mockery, flattery, lies and gossip. On these four, it is our intention to write separate chapters further on in this book.

There are times when silence is good, as when divine justice strikes against a man, as in the case of Aaron, as it is written, "And Aaron held his peace" (Lev. 10:3). If a person hears people reviling him, he should be silent. And this is a great quality, to be silent in the face of one's revilers. And one should also accustom himself to be silent in the synagogue, for this is modesty and it requires great alertness properly to direct his heart in prayer. And if one is sitting among the wise, he should be silent and listen to their words, for when he is silent, he hears what he does not know, but when he speaks, he does not add anything to his knowledge. However, if he is doubtful as to the meaning of the words of the wise, he should ask them, for to be silent in such a case is very bad: King Solomon said, "A time to keep silence, and a time to speak" (Eccl. 3:7) — there are times when speaking is good and there are times when silence is good. And the wise man said, "When you do not find a man who can teach you morality, then cleave to silence lest you speak folly." And since the tongue is very facile, one must take care to make it heavy, to guard it so that it does not speak. An abundance of words is like a heavy burden, and the weight of many words is more difficult to bear than the weight of much silence. And if a man hears his neighbor speaking, he should be silent until he finishes, "He that giveth answer before he heareth, it is folly and confusion unto him" (Prov. 18:13).

He who is accustomed to be silent, is saved from many transgressions: from flattery, from mockery, from gossip, from lies, and blasphemies. For when a man shames and reviles him, if he answers him, then the offender will double his reviling and his insults. And thus, said the wise man, "I hear a bad word, but I am silent." And they said to him, "Why?" And he said to them, "If I respond or answer my revilers, I fear that I will hear other insults much worse than the first." And he said, "Where a fool takes issue with a wise man, and the wise man is silent, this in itself is a great answer to the fool." And he said, "A fool has greater anguish in the silence of the wise man, than if the wise man would respond to him." And on this it is said, "Answer not a fool according to his folly, lest thou also be like unto him" (Prov. 26:4).

Then too, if a person is silent, others can reveal secrets to him, for inasmuch as he is not accustomed to speak much, he will not reveal the secret. Moreover, it is not his habit to indulge in gossip, and concerning this it is said, "Death and life are in the power of the tongue" (Prov. 18:21), for a man can do more harm with his tongue than he can with a sword. For a man can stand here and yet betray his companion, who is a long distance from him, and cause his death (by his word), while the sword can only slay someone who is near it. Therefore, man was created with two eyes, two ears, two nostrils and one mouth to say to him that he ought to speak less. Silence is fitting for the wise, and thus all the more so for fools. "A fence around wisdom is silence" (Aboth 3:13). "There is no better medicine than silence" (Megillah 18a).

But there are times when silence can be evil, as it is written, "Answer a fool according to his folly, lest he be wise in his own eyes" (Prov. 26:5). With respect to words of the Torah, if a person sees that the fools are scorning the words of the wise, he should answer in order to turn them back from their errors so that they do not imagine themselves wise in their eyes. If a man sees another man committing a transgression, he should protest and reprove him. And long-ago Solomon said, "A soft answer turneth away wrath" (Prov. 15:1), "and a soft tongue breaketh the bone" (Prov. 25:15). Therefore, a man should accustom himself to speak gently and not harshly. And be careful to guard your tongue like the apple of your eye, for "A fool's mouth is his ruin, and his lips are the snare of his soul" (Prov. 18:7). And it is further written, "Whoso keepeth his mouth and his tongue keepeth his soul from troubles" (Prov. 21:23). And it is said, "Oh, that ye would altogether hold your peace! And it would be your wisdom" (Job 13:5). And if you are sitting in a group, it is better that they should say to you, "Speak, why are you so silent?" than that you should speak and your words become such a burden to them that they finally say to you, "Be silent!"

One should be very careful not to shame any man, and not to cause any man anguish by his words. If one is sitting near a man who has a physical defect of which he is ashamed, or if there is some flaw in his family pedigree, then one must be careful not to speak about that type of defect or flaw. Even if one does not speak specifically about his neighbor but about such a defect or flaw in another person, his neighbor will think that the speaker is really referring to him and will be ashamed.

If a man did a shameful thing and later did repentance for it, one must take care not to speak about that act in front of him. And he must not even say to him in jest, "How could you do such a thing and not guard against it? You should have undertaken a different matter!" Or if a man tells you something that you already know, be silent until he finishes for perhaps, he will add something that you did not know before. Then too, he derives pleasure from the telling and even if you know that he is not going to add anything, be silent until he finishes.

If two men had a quarrel and afterwards, they were reconciled, neither should say to the other, "You did such and such to me, and Therefore, I did such and such to you." And this is true even if he has no intention of resuming the quarrel. For when he says to the other, "You did to me such and such!" then his companion is bound to say, "On the contrary, the fault was yours!" with the result that the quarrel is stirred up once again. And even if you do not stir up the quarrel, this comment will shame him with the knowledge that he did wrong.

There is one who sits before a wise man and is silent and derives a reward for this, for example, one who intently sets himself to listen. And there is one who is silent, and derives a sin from his silence, for example, one who thinks, "Why should I speak before him, inasmuch as he does not know enough to answer me suitably; he does not know as much as I by a long way." And he should be very careful not to think thus, as our Sages said, "There are seven marks of an uncultured man, and seven of a wise man : the wise man does not speak before him who is greater than he in wisdom; and does not break in upon the words of his fellow; he is not hasty to answer; he asks in accordance with the subject matter, and he answers to the point; he speaks of the first thing first and of the last, last; concerning that which he has not heard, he says ; 'I have not heard'; and he acknowledges the truth — and the reverse of these are to be found in an uncultured man" (Aboth 5:7).

The wise man said, "He who speaks with wisdom and intelligence, it is like salt to a cooked dish." And there is charm in the words of the wise like a ruby in a setting of gold. But "the poor man's wisdom is despised, and his words are not heard" (Eccl. 9:16). This being the case, let him put his words in the mouth of a wise man or a rich man in order that they may be heard, while he himself is silent.

ORCHOT TZADIKIM — Chapter Twenty-One

The general rule here is this: When a man makes a door for the entrance to his house, there is a time to open it and a time to close it. So, should he close the doors of his mouth, for there are actually two doors, the lips and the teeth. And be very careful as to when you open your mouth, and guard your tongue as you would silver and gold and pearls in your room and in your jewel case, and make a lock for the lock. Observe how the Sages of old guarded themselves from idle talk all their days. And in this way, you will acquire the great virtue of praying with complete devotion for most of the interference with devotion in prayer comes from frivolous things that are stuck in one's mind. Silence is also a great fence for the reverence of God, for it is impossible to have reverence of God in one that speaks too much.

Now we must explain to you in four chapters four classes of people that do not receive the Divine Presence (Sotah 42a). A company of scoffers, as it is written, "He stretcheth out his hand with scorners" (Hos. 7:8). A company of liars, as it is written, "He that speaketh falsehood shall not be established before mine eyes" (Ps. 101:7). A company of flatterers, as it is written, "That a hypocrite cannot come before Him" (Job 13:16). A company of gossipers, as it is written, "For Thou are not a God that hath pleasure in wickedness; Evil shall not sojourn with Thee" (Ps. 5:5). And now it is important to acquaint you with their ways and to divide the matter into proper divisions, for there is great advantage in understanding this matter thoroughly.

Scoffing, or mocking, may be divided into five types. The first is the man who slanders people, as it is said,

"Thou sittest and speaketh against thy brother; thou slanderest thine own mother's son" (Ps. 50:20). And he who does this is called a scoffer, as it is written, "A proud and haughty man, scorner is his name, even he that dealeth in overbearing pride" (Prov. 21:24). The meaning of the verse is that scoffer possesses two evil qualities in him. The first is that he is malicious and commits his sin deliberately, and that he plots against his fellow in a matter from which he himself derives no profit, yet he causes great damages to his fellow. For when he slanders this person and causes people to loath and to hate him, this is the height of malice, worse than the robber or the thief. For when a man steals or robs, there is no malice in his heart, but he is only bent on his own profit, to increase his wealth, but he who slanders people derives no profit from it, and it is in fact an inferiority of the mind. The scoffer is also arrogant and exceedingly proud and therefore, he slanders people. But the wise man is modest and lowly. He is aware of his own shortcomings and therefore, will never find fault with other as do the scoffers who sit and say, "So and so did thus and thus" and they jeer at him.

The second type is the one who mocks the words of people because he holds them in contempt because they too did not prosper in money matters and in the attainment of honor, and he makes fun of the poor. Not that he accuses them of any defect; they are simply despicable in his eyes. And this comes about because of arrogance or, at times, because the scoffer has ease and too much pleasure, as it is said, "Our soul is full sated with the scorning of those that are at ease, and with the contempt of the proud oppressors" (Ps.

123:4). This is proof that those who live at ease are often scoffers, and at times because of their great security they mock the righteous, as it is said, "Every one mocketh me" (Jer. 20:7). And it is said, "Whoso mocketh the poor blasphemeth his Maker" (Prov. 17:5). The explanation is that he who laughs at the poor man because he is poor, does so because it seems to him that the man is poor because of his lack of wisdom while he himself is rich because of his wisdom, as it is said, "My power and the might of my hand hath gotten me this wealth" (Deut. 8:17). Thus, he who scoffs at a poor man reviles the Creator. For he (the poor man) is the work of God, as it is written, "The rich and the poor meet together — The Lord is the maker of them all" (Prov. 22:2). And therefore, he is really scoffing at the word of God, Blessed be He.

The third type is the one who scoffs at things, although he has no intention to humiliate those who do them. Yet by his scoffing he hinders work that has hope of success and might be achieved. This type of scoffer is wise in his own eyes, and everything that he himself has not begun he considers folly and mocks it. This trait can even lead him to heresy, mocking the Commandments themselves, as it is written, "The proud have had me greatly in derision; yet have I not turned aside from Thy law" (Ps. 119:51). And this type of a scoffer does not accept rebuke, as it is said, "Reprove not a scorner, lest he hate thee" (Prov. 9:8). And it is said, "He that correcteth a scorner getteth to himself shame" (Prov. 9:7). And inasmuch as he is wise in his own eyes, he mocks the work of another man, and this is a trait for which there is no hope, as it is said, "Seest thou a man wise in his own eyes?

There is more hope of a fool than of him" (Prov. 26:12).

The fourth type is the man who attaches himself always to idle conversation and to empty matters, like those who sit at the corner of the road and look forth with all their power to find an occasion for mockery, for they have nothing else to do but to sit and jeer at people and scoff at their deeds. And there are two evils in this matter. One is that everyone who speaks too much is sure to bring about sin. The second is that he is thus kept idle from studying the words of the Torah, and this is a fatal path for it does not occur to him that in the time that he sits and scoffs he could study or do good deeds, thus acquiring life in the world-to-come.

The fifth type is he who scoffs at things, not because he scorns the deed that he jeers at, but rather that he laughs in the way of entertainers by way of amusement. There are times when too much drinking of wine causes this, as it is said, "Wine is a mocker, strong drink is riotous" (Prov. 20:1).

And know that the habits of scoffing does not become fixed in a man unless he removes the yoke of Heaven from upon him. Therefore, he must be prepared to accept afflictions with which he may be punished, measure for measure. As it is said, "Now Therefore, be ye not scoffers, lest your bands be made strong" (Is. 28:22). And the Sages would caution their pupils not to scoff, even thouth it might be by chance, without any previous intent. And on this subject, they were required to warn their pupils, for many stumbles into this fault of scoffing by chance (Abodah Zarah 18b). Scoffing at those who fulfill the commandments is a thing that comes very close to heresy, and he who does so indicates that he does not believe in the commandments. For if someone should mock at the commands of a king, is his life worth anything? Moreover, one who scoffs also causes others to sin in that they will not observe the commandments for fear of his mockery. But one may mock idolatry (Sanhedrin 63:2), and he also may scoff at those who commit transgressions, in order to withhold them from sin. Then, too, others will not commit sins if people scoff a them for so doing.

Sefer ORCHOT TZADIKIM

Ways of the Righteous

Chapter Twenty-Two

ON FALSEHOOD
Concerning falsehood, you must know that just as a man weighs silver and gold on the scales and distinguishes between the light and the heavy, so should a wise man weigh utterances on scales until he is able to distinguish between truth and falsehood. And there is a great distinction between one lie and another. How is that? One who says of wood that it is gold, that lie is easily apparent. But one who says of shining copper that it is gold, that lie needs investigation, for these metals have the same appearance, and there are counterfeiters who make copper look like gold, so that even the experts can distinguish between the two only with great difficulty. So, it is with the realm of thought and its expression. There is one who is very clever and proclaims all sorts of theories to establish a lie until it appears that is the truth. But the wise man knows how to distinguish between truth and falsehood. And this is a thing known to all, that truth and falsehood are often joined together in one heart. There is the man so false that even though he knows for a certainty that

a thing is false, yet he is attracted to it, and all the more so if there some evidence on both sides, so that the lie resembles the truth — then he is certainly attracted to his lie. But there is the honest man who will never deal in falsehood, except when there are many opinions to support that falsehood — then only is he drawn after the falsehood. But the wise man with his wisdom is able to refute those theories that are false. And you should know that every man is influenced in his opinions by his qualities: The lazy man will form all of his opinions in support of laziness, and the angry man will find rational support for his anger, and the arrogant person will find support for his arrogance. And thus, it is with all the qualities that we have explained. According to the quality that is within him will a man act: the spendthrift, according to his extravagance; the miser, according to his greed; the lover, according to his love; the hater, according to his hate. Therefore, a person who wishes to be an honest man of God must, first of all, divest himself of all the inferior qualities, in order that the quality that is imbedded in him more strongly should not attract him, and then he will be able to attain the truth.

And there are nine categories in the matter of falsehood. The first is he who denies his friend's assertion that he gave him a pledge or a loan, or he who testifies falsely, and there are many instances of these. And for this type of falsehood there are two punishments. The first, because of the lie, for falsehood, even if it causes no damage, is an abomination to the Lord, as it is said, "There are six things which the Lord hateth… Haughty eyes, a lying

ORCHOT TZADIKIM — Chapter Twenty-Two

tongue ... a false witness that breatheth out lies, and he that soweth discord among brethren" (Prov. 6:16—19). And it is said, "And the froward mouth, do I hate" (Prov. 8:13). The second punishment is given because he has injured his companion.

The second category is where there is no present damage to his fellow in the lie itself, but where the liar intends to deceive his fellow into believing in him and trusting him, so that he will not be on guard against him — and then he will be able to do evil to him, as it is said, "One speaketh peaceably to his neighbour with his mouth, but in his heart he layeth wait for him" (Jer. 9:7). Even in the eyes of people, falsehood is repulsive, as it is said, "It is an abomination to kings to commit wickedness ... Righteous lips are the delight of kings" (Prov. 16:12—13).

The third category is where one lies to his fellow not to rob him of anything he possesses, but he learns that a certain good thing is going to come to his fellow in the future, and so with falsehood and with cunning he praises this good fortune that is coming, and makes it appear that he has a share in it. Or he lies to his fellow until he gives him a gift, for example, he brings him good tidings — false tidings — in order to get a gift because of this. And there are many similar cases. And our Sages, of blessed memory, said, "Whoever dissembles in his speech is as though he had practiced idolatry" (Sanh. 92a). As it is said, "My father peradventure will feel me, and I shall seem to him as a mocker" (Gen. 27:12). And it is said, concerning idolatry, "They are vanity, a work of delusion" (Jer. 10:15). Now this does not mean that one who lies is actually like one who worships idols, but the resemblance is there, for he conceals himself in falsehood and is helped by empty things.

The fourth category of falsehood is he who lies in recounting things he has heard. He changes part of the story, and does so intentionally, although there is no profit to him in that falsehood, neither will it cause any harm. And there are times when he tells things that he has invented entirely in his heart. He is punished for loving falsehood, even though it serves no purpose, and concerning this, King Solomon said, "A false witness that breatheth out lies" (Prov. 6:19). You should know that his quality will lead him to testify falsely against his brother, because he comes to love falsehood. There are also those who change part of what they have heard without intent to do so, because they did not pay attention at the time that they heard the words and did not search out to see whether they were true. This quality is also evil, and concerning this, King Solomon said, "But the man that obeyeth shall speak out unchallenged" (Prov. 21:28). This means that he who sets his mind to listen and understand the essence of a matter, and the things that are said, because he does not want his mouth to speak a falsehood (because of his inattentiveness), that man will speak forever, for people will want to hear his words, and they will not scold him because of his words.

The fifth category of falsehood is he who promises another that he will do good to him, or that he will give him a gift, or that he will help him, but he does not say this to him with certainty, on which the other can rely. And while he is saying all this, the thought in his heart is that he will not give. Concerning this, our Sages said "that he should not say one thing with his mouth and another with his heart" (Baba Mezi'a 49a).

The sixth category of falsehood is he who assures his companion that he will do him a favor, and he assures him so much that the heart of his companion trusts in him. Then he certainly must not profane his promise. And if he lies in this, then he bears a great guilt — more than in the previous case — for there it was merely general talk. And the one who tells his fellow that he will give him a small gift, even though he does not put it in the form of a promise, nevertheless we say concerning anyone who goes back on his word, that there is something of a lack of trust in him (see ibid.).

For the heart of his fellow relies upon him and trusts in him, inasmuch as the gift in question is so small. And if it is a poor man to whom he made the promise, even though the gift mentioned was a large one (for which reason the poor man should have doubted the promise) and he goes back on his word, then his evil is very great, for he has made a vow and transgressed the commandment, "He shall not break his word" (Num. 30:3). And thus, it is with one who boasts before many that he will give a gift to a certain man, this is very much like a promise, for he boasts of his generosity, and therefore, it is not right that he should go back on his word after he has honored and praised himself in this matter.

The seventh category of falsehood is one who deceitfully tells his friend that he has done a favor for him, or that he has spoken well of him, but has not done so. Concerning this our Sages, of blessed memory, said, "It is forbidden to deceive your fellow creatures, even a heathen, for there is in this a sin, inasmuch as we are obliged to speak words of truth, for this is one of the foundations of the soul" (see Hullin 94a).

The eighth category of falsehood is he who boasts of qualities that he does not possess. And this is a great sin. And even if he really possesses these qualities when he praises himself it appears from his words that he did not do his charitable or generous acts for the sake of Heaven, but for his own sake, for his own praise. And our Sages, of blessed memory, said, "He whom others honor because they believe that he knows two tractates of the Talmud, and he knows only one tractate, is obligated to say, 'I know only one tractate' " (T.P. Shebi'ith 10:5). All the more so is it forbidden to lie and to boast about qualities that one does not possess at all.

The ninth category is he who tells a story that he has heard, but he changes some of the narrative as he likes. Now there is no loss to any man in this, but he receives a bit of pleasure out of his lying, even though he does not gain any money out of it. For example (Yebamoth 63a), Rav would say to his wife, "Make me lentils," and she would make him peas — and whenever he would say to her, "Make me peas!" she would make lentils. Hiya, his son, went and reversed the matter. Whenever his father wanted peas, he would tell his mother, "Make lentils!" and she would make peas, and this the son did out of honor for his father, in order that there should be prepared for him the food that he wanted. Even so, Rav restrained him and persuaded him not to do this any more, because, "They have taught their tongue to speak lies" (Jer. 9:4). But the guilt in such a falsehood is not like the guilt of those who lie for no reason at all as we have mentioned in the fourth category.

Thus far we have discussed the nine categories of falsehood. But a man should be careful in the following matter too. If his friend comes to him and asks to borrow something that he has, he should not say, "I haven't got it." But he may refuse him in a manner that does not call for lying. And in the Book of the Pious, there is a ruling that even if a heathen should come to the house of a Jew and ask him to loan him money, and the Jew has the money but he does not wish to loan it to this heathen, he must not say, "I have no money," but he should refuse him in any way he can without lying (Sefer Hasidim, 426). But it may well be that if the heathen were to learn that the Jew did have money, then he would not be able to take his leave of the heathen without causing hatred. Therefore, it might be better for him to say, "I don't have money" — for the sake of good relations. It all depends on the circumstances and on how he sizes up the situation. If he thinks he will cause no ill will by saying, "I have money, but I need it for something else," let him do so.

Great is a liar's punishment. For even when he speaks the truth, no one believes him (Sanh. 89b). "And falehood cannot stand for long."

No man should cause others to lie for his sake. What is meant by this? If a man sees two people speaking together about a secret matter, he should not go and ask one of them to reveal the matter to him. For he may not want to reveal it, and consequently he will put him off by telling him something else, the result being that he has lied (see Sefer Hasidim, 1201). Similarly, he should be scrupulous in all of his affairs, not lying in business matters, and not causing others to lie. And he should be careful not to associate with a liar, and he should speak to such a one as little as possible. It requires great wisdom to avoid lying, for the evil inclination is always lying in ambush for a man, to cause him to fall into his net.

But there are times when the Sages permitted one to lie, for example, in order to make peace between one man and another (Yebamoth 65b). Similarly, one may praise a bride in the presence of the bridegroom and say that she is lovely and charming, even though she really is not (Kethuboth 17a). A guest (Arakin 16a) who has been well treated by the master of the house should not to say in front of many people, "How good that man is in whose house I was a guest, how much honor he paid me," lest many come to that host who are not worthy to be his guests, and concerning this it is said, "He that blesseth his friend with a loud voice, rising early in the morning, it shall be counted as a curse to him" (Prov. 27:14).

And concerning a tractate of the Talmud, if they ask him if the lesson is fluent in his mouth, modesty demands that he should say, "No." And if he should be late to the synagogue because of marital relations, and they asked him why he delayed, let him ascribe it to something else (Baba Bezi'a 23b). And in all these cases where the Sages permitted one to alter the truth, if he can manage not to lie, that is preferable to lying. For example, if he is asked, "Do you know this particular tractate of the Talmud?" he might answer, "Do you think I know it?" And if he can put off the questioner in some way so as not to lie, that would be very good.

Sefer
ORCHOT TZADIKIM
Ways of the Righteous

Chapter Twenty-Three

ON TRUTH

The soul is created from the place of the Holy Spirit, as it is said, "And breathed into his nostrils the breath of life" (Gen. 2:7). And it is hewn out from a place of purity, and it is created from the supernal radiance, from the Throne of Glory. And in the realm above, in the place of the Holy of Holies, there is no falsehood. There everything is truth, as it is said, "But the Lord God is the true God" (Jer. 10:10). I have found written, "I am that I am" Hebrew: Eheyeh asher Eheyeh. (Ex. 3:14). And it is also written, "And the Lord God is the true Hebrew: emet. God, He is the living God and everlasting king" (Jer. 10:10).

And now it is important to make it known to you that the Holy One, Blessed be He, is the God of Truth. For you will find twenty-one times the word EHEYEH which is, by computation of letters, the numerical equivalent of Emet (Truth). And you will also note that EHEYEH (the Name of the Eternal) is by computation of letters, also twenty-one (the numerical value of Emet being 441 or 21 times 21).

TZADIKIM ORCHOT — Chapter Twenty-Three

God made man to be upright (see Eccl. 7:29), and the seal of the Holy One, Blessed be He, is Truth (Shabbath 55a and see T.P. Sanh. 1:5). And it is written, "He that speaketh falsehood shall not be established before mine eyes" (Ps. 101:7). When a man occupies himself with falsehood, then the falsehood does not cleave to the truth. And where there is Truth is as though one were able to describe it as the place of His dwelling in the heavens and directed towards mankind, for where there is Truth among mankind, then everyone concedes that He made heaven and earth and the sea and all they contain. And this is what is said, "Who made heaven and earth, the sea and all that in them is" (Ps. 146:6). And this is followed by, "Who keepeth truth for ever" (ibid.). But where there is treachery and falsehood, it would appear that the place of the dwelling of the Eternal One is not in the heaven and the earth. And he who is worthy to consider these things, how the souls are hewn out from the source of Truth, will conduct all of his affairs with Truth, and he will not permit falsehood to enter into the place of the holiness of truth. And therefore, the verse says, "The Lord is nigh unto all them that call upon Him in truth" (Ps. 145:18). For the Holy One, Blessed be He, who is Truth, draws near to him who calls upon Him in truth. And what is meant by, "Who call upon Him in truth?" This refers to the one who cleanses his heart of everything in the world, and draws near to the Holy One, Blessed be He, alone; and whose mind continually strengthens itself to cleave to the supernal light; and who directs his thought in that desire always. And this is what a man can attain when he sits

TZADIKIM ORCHOT   Chapter Twenty-Three

alone in his room and studies, and for this reason every pious person should often separate himself and sit alone, and should not associate with people, except for a great need. But if he prays with only the movement of his lips, facing the wall, and thinks about the affairs of the world, and he calls to God with his tongue, while his mind is on some thing else, or if he expects to be honored because of the sweetness of his voice, and he tries to find favor in the eyes of people, in order to receive praise from them, then his service is not true. And he is one of those of whom it is said, "Thou art near in their mouth, and far from their reins" (Jer. 12:2).

Therefore, we pray and purify our hearts to serve Thee in truth, that we should do all of our service in truth, and we should believe with a complete heart and with a soul that desires, and our faith should not be something that we demonstrate only before people, or because of money matters or because we are in distress. And that is what is said, "If thou return to the Almighty, thou shalt be built up" (Job 22:23). For when no thought divides you from the Almighty, then you will build with a mighty building in the radiant light of the Divine Presence. Therefore, David said, "Lord, who shall sojourn in Thy tabernacle? Who shall dwell upon Thy holy mountain? He that walketh uprightly, and worketh righteousness, and speaketh truth in his heart" (Ps. 15:1—2). And he did not say, "He who speaks the truth in his mouth," for what he meant was that the truth should be deeply rooted and established in the heart of man. Therefore, , when the pious men of old had some object to sell, they would sell it to the purchaser for the price they had already determined in their mind, and even if the purchaser wanted to pay more, they did not want anything except what their heart had already decided to accept. If an esteemed person who follows this path of speaking the truth in his heart, makes up his mind to do a certain thing, he should write down that thought in order not to forget it, and he should not break the promise made in his thought. And if he is unable to fulfill it, let him go to a Sage, who will absolve him of the promise made in his thoughts. And he may vow that nothing in his thoughts shall be considered binding so long as he does not utter it with his mouth.

Everyone who speaks the truth in his heart and does not want even to think falsely, even without meaning to do so, his words and his thoughts will be fulfilled, as it is said, "Thou shalt also decree a thing, and it shall be established unto thee" (Job 22:28). And he who is a man of truth, in every transaction of his, whether it be in buying or selling, or in loaning, should express his full intention at the outset, and he should accustom all those who do business with him to know that he will not alter, that he will not add to or diminish from the terms agreed on. The wise man said, "Always place the truth before you." By this he meant that a man ought to make certain signs for himself, for example, in business matters that he remembers not to speak falsehood. And he should put this down in writing, and he should bring this writing with him and he should look at it before he begins his transaction. He should write something when he sits in his study, and at his table, that he should remember not to speak falsehood, and that he may not forget to speak the truth. And so, did one person do. He wrote on the walls of his house, and in his study on the upper part of all the walls: "Remember the day of death, and you will not sin." And he who does not speak anything but the truth will live, and live long, and be free.

In support of this statement is the verse, "But the Lord God is the true God, He is the living God, and the everlasting King" (Jer. 10:10). And if a man does not speak anything but the truth, he will be free all the days of his life, as it is written, "The law of truth was in his mouth, and unrighteousness was not found in his lips... "For he is the messenger of the Lord of hosts" (Malachi 2:6—7). The angels above are in the form of truth, and they are not in physical form. The souls of men give light like the light that goes from the sun. Now the souls are in bodies, Therefore, they know only a little of the secret things and then only in the visions of the night. For the souls do not occupy themselves with the needs of the body, and he who knows the secret of the soul will testify to this. Now dreams are very much like thoughts, as it is written, "Thy thoughts came (into thy mind) upon thy bed" (Dan. 2:29). And dreams come about through an angel who accompanies man, and just as all thoughts are not true, so all dreams are not true. And he who accustoms himself that all of his thoughts are true, then even in the night he will see visions of truth, and he will know future things, just as the angels do.

As for him who speaks the truth, there is no quality like it. Therefore, "The beginning of thy word is truth" (Ps. 119:160). And it is said, "Keep thee far from a false matter" (Ex. 23:7).

TZADIKIM ORCHOT   Chapter Twenty-Three

Even the gestures of a man should be true, for the reward of truth is very great. Therefore, a person should accustom himself to walk in truth, and he should study the Torah and know the truth, so that he will fulfill the commandments truthfully as the law requires. And he should always confess the truth. Even the Aggadah [the non-legal parts of the Talmud], which does not involve the observance of the commandments of the Torah, even this he must study in order that his heart shall believe the truth. Do not be ashamed to receive the truth from any man whatever — even from the smallest of the small and the most despised, even from him should you receive the truth. For a precious pearl, even in the hands of the small and the despised, is still a precious pearl.

Now that our exile has lasted so long because of our many sins it is more important than ever that Israel should separate themselves from the vain things of the world and take hold of the Seal of the Holy One, Blessed be He, which is Truth — and sanctify themselves even in things that are permitted to them (Yebamoth 20a), and not to lie — not to a Jew and not to a heathen, and not to deceive them in any matter, as it is said, "The remnant of Israel shall not do iniquity, nor speak lies, neither shall a deceitful tongue be found in their mouth" (Zeph. 3:13). And it is further written, "And I will sow her unto Me in the land" (Hos. 2:25). Surely a man sows a seah in order to harvest many kurim, thus, the Holy One, Blessed be He, exiled Israel among the nations only so that proselytes might join them (Pesahim 87b). And so long as they conduct themselves among the heathens without guile, the latter will cleave to them. And

TZADIKIM ORCHOT   Chapter Twenty-Three

behold the Holy One, Blessed be He, was furious with the wicked for their robbery, as it is said, "For the earth is filled with violence" (Gen. 6:11).

A parable will illustrate this (Deut. Rabbah 3:3). There is a story about Rabbi Simon, the son of Shetah, who purchased a donkey from an Ishmaelite. His pupils went and found a precious stone hanging from the donkey's neck. They said to him, "Rabbi, 'The blessing of the Lord, it maketh rich' " (Prov. 10:22). He said to them, "I purchased a donkey; — a precious stone I did not purchase." So, he went and returned the gem to that Ishmaelite. And the Ishmaelite called out concerning him, "Blessed is the Lord the God of Simon, the son of Shetah." There is a similar instance in the Jerusalem Talmud (Baba Mezi'a 2:5). Some mise men of old purchased wheat from heathens, and found in this wheat a bundle of money, and they returned the money to them, and the heathens said, "Blessed is the God of the Jews." And similarly, there are many stories of people who restored an object to sanctify the name of God.

When there is truth below, God looks down with justice upon the earth, as it is said, "Truth springeth out of the earth, and righteousness hath looked down from heaven" (Ps. 85:12). Therefore, see that all your matters shall be done in truth, and rely upon "The faithful God who keepeth covenant and mercy with them that love Him and keep His commandments" (Deut. 7:9).

What is this faithfulness of God? It is that He keeps His covenant. If a righteous man commits a small sin, God exacts retribution in this world. And clearly, it is much better for the righteous person to be sentenced even with afflictions like Job's, all his days in his body, which is a valueless thing, and in this world where he has but a short time to live, and to have God give a good reward to his soul, which is honored in the upper world and never dies away, and is never finished, to the end of time. And this is surely better for the righteous person than if God did not exact retribution from him in this world, and then would have to sentence him in the world of souls to the punishments of Gehennah, and then if, because of his sins, God should lessen the lofty place of his soul in the world of souls, where otherwise he would cleave to the radiance of the Highest, to which light there is no estimate or likeness. As for the wicked, He has given them their reward in a little pleasure, which soon ceases, in the brief world that is this world, while their sins are kept for the long world-to-come, and the great torment that is Gehennah, and which is too great to be calculated.

May the Merciful One guide us with His Truth, and may He bring us to His chambers, so that we may reach the Supernal Light, where is the secret place of his strength and the beauty of His glory.

Sefer

ORCHOT TZADIKIM

Ways of the Righteous

Chapter Twenty-Four

ON FLATTERY

Flattery may be divided into nine categories. The first is where a man knows that his friend is a wicked man and a deceiver, that he spreads evil reports about the innocent, that he robs the money of others, and yet this man who knows all this comes and flatters him — not that he actually flatters or praises him, but rather he speaks smoothly to him saying, "You did no wrong in what you did."

In this case there are many transgressions and much punishment. First of all, he should have reproved the offender for his sins, yet not only does he fail to do this, but he says to him, "You have not sinned," thus strengthening the bonds of evil-doers. This flatterer will be punished because he was not zealous for the truth. Not only this, but the flatterer places a stumbling block before the sinner by saying, "You have not sinned," for then the offender will not repent of his evil deeds and will continue to sin. This is apart from the guilt that the flatterer incurs because of the injury and pain of the people whom the sinner has injured and given pain, and whom the sinner will not reimburse for the damage nor conciliate his victims because of the flattery of the flatterer. For the flatterer justifies the wickedness, it is said, "He that justifieth the wicked and he that condemneth the righteous, even they both are an abomination to the Lord" (Prov. 117:15). All the more is this true if the wrong of the sinner is known to many, and the flatterer flatters the sinner publicly and says, "Pure and upright are you," then the flatterer has profaned the Name of God, he has shown contempt for law and judgment.

A man should undergo danger rather than be guilty of this sin. And our Sages, of blessed memory, said, concerning Agrippas, that when he was reading the Torah and came to the verse, "Thou mayest not put a foreigner over thee, who is not thy brother" (Deut. 17:15), his eyes shed tears. Those who were near him said, "Do not fear Agrippas. You are our brother." In that hour the "enemies of Israel" [a euphemism for the "Chidren of Israel" where anything dire is said concerning them] became liable to destruction for they flattered Agrippas (Sotah 41a-b).

Nor should one who sits in judgement fear any man, as it is said, "Ye shall not be afraid of the face of any man" (Deut. 1:17). More over, such flattery entails the guilt of falsehood.

The second category is where the flatterer praises a wicked man before people, whether in his presence or not, even though the flatterer does not justify him in his evil deeds but makes a general statement, "He is a good man." Concerning this it is said, "They that forsake the law, praise the wicked" (Prov. 28:4). For if the one who praises the wicked man had not abandoned the Torah, he would not praise the wicked man who transgresses the Torah and its words. Nor should he defend the wicked man before people and say "He did a good act (on another occasion), Therefore, have pity on him (in this case)." He who does this is very evil, for those who hear him will think that he is really a righteous man and will honor him. And there are many stumbling blocks caused by paying honor to the wicked. For when honor is given to the righteous sages and they are held in the highest regard, then all the people listen to their counsel. Then, too, others will envy them their good deeds and will continue to seek instruction and knowledge will increase, and from studying Torah not for its own sake they will be led to studying Torah for its own sake.

Moreover, there are many people who, when they see the glory and beauty of the Torah will recognize its excellence and the thought will enter their heart to study it for the sake of the Holy One, Blessed be He. Thus, everyone will come to honor the righteous, and he who honors the righteous, so to speak, fulfills the intention of the Holy One, Blessed be He, in creating the world. And he who shames the righteous man and him who reveres God nullifies the intention of the Holy One, Blessed be He, as if to say, "To serve God is not the principal end of man." Therefore, pay honor to those who serve the Holy One, Blessed be He, in order to honor the Holy One, Blessed be He, to make it known that serving Him is alone the principal duty of man.

But in honoring the wicked there is a profanation of the Torah and of God's service, and this is a transgression that wears away flesh and bone. Then again, many may be drawn to do similarly and they receive retribution, and in this vein the Sages said, "Woe to the wicked, woe to his neighbour" (Nega'im 2:6). Moreover, in honoring the wicked the honor of the righteous is brought low, and there is no honor to the righteous except after the degradation of the wicked. And since there is a stumbling block to the world in the honoring of the wicked one should guard himself against speaking good of the wicked, nor should one mention them for good, as it is said, "But the name of the wicked shall rot" (Prov. 10:7). And it is written, "An unjust man is an abomination to the righteous" (Prov. 29:26). And if a man does not want to speak of the wickedness of a wicked man let him not speak of his goodness.

The third category is he who flatters a wicked man to his face and says to him, "What a charming and good man you are." Now even though this flatterer does not praise the wicked man in public, so that the wicked man will not become a stumbling block to the multitude, still this type of flatterer is guilty of a great sin as it is written, "With his mouth the impious man destroyeth his neighbour; but through knowledge shall the righteous be delivered" (Prov. 11:9). For when he praises him, the wicked man believes him and considers himself good, and his heart will be uplifted and he will be proud and not repent. For a man who is not righteous will say in his heart when people praise him. "I always knew that this was so." And thus, the wicked man becomes more corrupt through the flatterer's flattery.

But as for the righteous man, if a man praises him, he will not be proud of this, because our Sages said,

"Even if all the world says, concerning you, that you are righteous, be in your own eyes like a wicked man" (Niddah 30b). And they said, "If you have friends, some of whom praise you, and some of whom correct and rebuke you, love the ones that rebuke you, and hate the ones that praise you, for the ones that rebuke you are conducting you to life eternal, and those who praise you will rejoice in your misfortune even though they praise you" (Abot de R. Nathan, 29). And it is said, "And a flattering (smooth) mouth worketh ruin" (Prov. 26:28). Scripture has likened a smooth mouth to a smooth (slippery) path, for just as a man will fall and be thrust down if he walks upon a slippery path — as it is said, "The angel of the Lord thrusting them, let their way be dark and slippery" (Ps. 35:5-6) — so will a man be thrust down and fall by a smooth mouth, which is a flattering mouth filled with sin. And concerning this it is said, "May the Lord cut off all flattering lips, the tongue that speaketh proud things" (Ps. 12:4). He has cursed the smooth mouth, for with it a man destroys his friends, and he has also cursed the hard tongue that carries gossip which is the opposite of the smooth tongue.

And there is a type of flattery which one pays to the mighty, so that they will like them and raise them up and make them great. Concerning this our Sages said, "Everyone who flatters his companion in order to obtain honor, the end of the matter will be that he will depart in shame" (Aboth de R. Nathan, 29).

The fourth category of flattery is he who becomes a companion to the wicked. Even though he does not flatter him and does not praise him, but since he is near to him and in his company, he will be punished.

ORCHOT TZADIKIM

Not only does he not rebuke him, but on the contrary, he brings him near to him in companionship, and puts him at a distance from his rebuke, and there is a sin in this. He adds to his sin by bringing the wicked person so close to him, as it is said, "Because thou hast joined thyself with Ahaziah, the Lord hath made a breach in thy works" (II Chron. 20:37).

The righteous people reject the wicked, and our Sages, of blessed memory said, "Not for nothing did the starling follow the raven, but because it is of the same kind" (Baba Kamma 92b). And it is said, "Every fowl dwell near its kind and man near his equal" (Ben Sira 13:5). And they said, "It is forbidden to look at the form of a wicked man" (Megillah 28a), as it is said, "Were it not that I regard the presence of Jehoshaphat the king of Judah, I would not look toward thee, nor see thee" (II Kings 3:14). And everyone who looks at the form of a wicked man, his eyes grow dim in his old age, like Isaac, our father, whose eyes grew dim because he looked upon Esau, even though he did not know of Esau's evil deeds.

There are many and great stumbling blocks in the companionship of the wicked. The first is that he loves the enemy of the Creator of all, and a servant faithful to his master does not become companion of him who hates his master. The second is that he may learn from his deeds to do evil. The third is that others too may join with the wicked man, and trust him, and he will rob them, and they too may learn from his deeds. And even if they do not learn from him, they see him do things that are forbidden for them to see. And neither will be repent, although if they were to rebuke him and separate themselves from him, then he would repent of his evil way. And he who joins in companionship with the wicked man, the end of the matter is that the wicked man will rule over him, and this is the worst evil of all, for inasmuch as the wicked man rules over him, he will not allow him to do good. The fourth stumbling block is that a good man, out of fear of the wicked man, will have to lay aside several good things that he should have done. Therefore, , a man should not join in companionship with any one except one who reveres God. In the case of Resh Lakish, whenever he would stop to speak with anyone in the market place, everybody would trust the person to whom he spoke, and trust him to the extent of selling him merchandise without witnesses (Yoma 9b), for they were certain that if Resh Lakish spoke with a man in the market place, he must be trustworthy. This shows that merely to speak with a person may be like flattery.

The fifth category is a man who is trustworthy in the eyes of all the people, and to whom everybody listens, and who appoints his relative as synagogue warden or as Rabbi, saying, "I have appointed him because he is wise," when the fact of the matter is not so, all the people rely upon him. And the same is true of one who says about someone whom he does not know that he is trustworthy, with the result that the people put their pledges into his hand and he deceives them, and the Sages, of blessed memory, said: "Anyone who sets up a judge that is not worthy, it is as though he planted an idolatrous grove in Israel, and if he did so in a place where there are scholars, then it is as though he had planted this pagan grove near the altar itself. And the Holy One, Blessed be He, will surely exact retribution in the future from those who set up this type of judge" (Sanh. 7b).

The sixth category of flattery is he who is in a position to protest against an evil and does not protest, nor does he pay any attention to the deeds of the sinners. This thing comes close to flattery, for then the sinners think, "As long as they do not protest and do not reproach us, all of our deeds must be good." But we have been commanded to root out the evil from our midst, as it is said, "So shalt thou put away the evil from the midst of thee" (Deut. 13:6).

And our Sages said, "Everyone for whom it is possible to protest against the sinful things of the people of his household, and he does not protest, is considered guilty of the wrongs of the men of his household. If it is possible for him to protest against the deeds of the people of his city and he does not do so he is held responsible for the wrongs of the people of the city. If it is possible for him to protest against the wrongs of the whole world and he does not do so, then he is considered guilty of the wrongs of all the world" (Shabbath 54b). And it is said, "And they shall stumble one upon another" (Lev. 26:37). And our Rabbis, of blessed memory, explained it as meaning, "Each man for the sin of his brother," which teaches us that all Israel are responsible, one for another (Sanh. 27b).

The seventh category of flattery is he who sees that the people of his place are very suborn and he says in his heart, "Perhaps they will not pay any attention if I rebuke them," and therefore, he refrains from reproving them. This, too, is a sin and he will bear his iniquity, for he did not attempt to warn and rebuke them; if he had done so, perhaps they would have repented. And it was for this that the otherwise completely righteous persons were punished with the destruction of the First Temple (see Shabbath 55a).

However, if it is a thing known to everybody and it has been searched out and tested and established that the sinner hates correction and will not listen to those who rebuke him, concerning this it is said, "Reprove not a scorner, lest he hate thee" (Prov. 9:8).

And they said: Just as it is a commandment to say a thing that will be heard, so is it a commandment not to say a thing that will not be heard (Yebamoth 65b). And our Sages said, "Better that they (the sinners) should commit a wrong not knowing that it is a wrong, than that they should commit that wrong intentionally" (Shabbath 148b).

The eighth category is he who hears gossip or vile words, or who associates with scoffers and those who shame the Torah and the commandments, and he knows that they are stubborn and that they will not accept rebuke, and therefore, is silent. He, too, will be punished, for it is up to him to answer them so they connot say that he is like them and that by his silence he admits the truth of their words. He must scold them in order to ascribe greatness to the Torah and to the commandments and to be zealous for the honor of the righteous man whom they have condemned. And this is one of the circumstances where a man must leave the companionship of the wicked, for he will be punished if he hears their evil words constantly and he cannot answer them. And this matter is explained in the words of Solomon, "Be not thou envious of evil men, neither desire to be with them; for their heart studieth destruction, and their lips talk of mischief" (Prov. 24:1—2). His meaning was that you will bear their sin if you hear their evil words always and hold your peace.

The ninth category of flattery is he who honors the wicked because he wants to preserve peace. It is true that he does not speak good of the wicked and he does not conduct himself in any way that would cause people to think that the wicked person is honored in his eyes, for he does not show him any honor except in the way that people honor the rich, because their path has been prosperous, and not because of their own merit. Yet even in this there is sin and guilt, for it has never been permitted to honor the wicked, except for terror, that is to say, if one is afraid that the wicked man will injure him or cause him a loss at a time when the hand of the wicked is mighty. Therefore, it was permitted to honor the wicked man as people respect all men who are mighty, but he should not praise him and should not speak good of him to people. And so, said our Sages, of blessed memory, "It is permissable to flatter the wicked in this world" (Sotah 41b). But there are wicked whom we may not flatter. Whence do we derive this? From Mordecai, who was advised to flatter Haman, to which he retorted, "Thou shalt not seek their peace nor their prosperity" (Deut. 23:7). And they would say to him "Our Rabbis taught that we must flatter them for the sake of peace," but even then, Mordecai did not want to flatter such a wicked man as this.

And a man may flatter his wife for the sake of peace in his home, and he may flatter his creditor so that he does not oppress him, and his teacher so that he will teach him Torah. And it is a very good deed to flatter one's pupils or companions so that that they will study and hearken to his words, accepting his reproof to observe the commandments. Likewise, one may flatter any man where he thinks that he will thereby draw him to him, so that he will listen to him, and perform the commandments. If he were to come to him with anger, the man would not listen to him, but if he comes to him with flattery, the man will accept his rebuke. In such a case, it is a very good deed to flatter him in order to bring forth the precious from the vile. For there is a man that will not accept a rebuke when it is delivered with scolding, but will when it is done gently, as it is said, "The words of the wise spoken in quiet" (Eccl. 9. 17). There are times, however, when scolding is necessary, as it is said, "A rebuke entereth deeper into a man of understanding" (Prov. 17:10). And there are times when even a lashing is proper, as it is said, "And stripes for the back of fools" (Prov. 19:29). And there are times when even a lashing will do no good, as it is said, "Than a hundred stripes unto a fool" (Prov. 17:10). If so, what shall we do to him? There is no way of correcting him, Therefore, you must drive him away. There is a flattery that is very evil, for example, where a man flatters his companion and speaks to him sweet words, in order that his companion should rely upon him and trust him, and after he trusts him and relies upon him, then this man deceives him, and this is like the matter of which it is said, "For in vain the net is spread in the eyes of any bird; and these lie in wait for their own blood, they lurk for their own lives" (Prov. 1:17—18). The meaning of the verse is that those who trap birds throw wheat upon the trap, and when the birds come to eat the wheat that is spread upon the net, they are captured. And this type of flattery is like such a hunter. The Sages have forbidden us to flatter, and they said (Hullin 94a), A man should not send a gift to his companion when he knows that his companion will not accept it, and he should not invite his companion to eat with him when he knows that he will not eat with him. And if a man wants to open a barrel of wine in order to sell it, and his companion comes to buy wine, he should not say to him, "I want to open a new cask just for you." All these and the like are called "theft of the mind." And our Sages forbade us to flatter or to "steal people's minds" (ibid.).

Rabbi Simon, the son of Halafta said, "From the date that the power of flattery grew strong, laws have been twisted and deeds have been perverted, and no man was able to say honestly to his companion, 'My deeds are greater than your deeds.' " Said Rabbi Elazar, "Every man that has flattery in his nature, brings wrath upon the world," as it is said, "But they that are godless in heart lay up anger" (Job 36:13). Not only this, but his prayer is not heard, as it is said, "They cry not for help when He bindeth them" (ibid). And even the unborn children, still in the wombs of their mothers, curse him, and he falls into Gehennah. And everyone who flatters a wicked man falls into his hand. And if he does not fall into his hand, then he falls into the hand of the son of the wicked man, and if he does not fall into the hand of his son, then he falls in the hand of his grandson (Sotah 41b). Every congregation that has within it the trait of flattery is as loathsome as a woman in her impurity, and in the end will be exiled (Sotah 42a).

Therefore, a man should keep himself far from flattery and should never flatter a man so as to cause him to cling to his wickedness, even though he could thereby receive great favors from him. He should not flatter his relative, or his children, when they do not walk in a good path. For how many people remain with their wickedness because they see that no shame comes to them because of their ugly ways, and because they see that people flatter them and there is nothing in the world that locks the gates of repentance to a person as does flattery.

There is a story about a good man who had a daughter to marry off and there were at his side two men, both of whom wished to marry his daughter. And so, this good man went and asked another man to pick a quarrel with him. And he then called upon the two young men to judge the matter between him and the one with whom he quarrelled. And this is the way they did it. One of them flattered this good man so that he would give him his daughter, and he found in his favor on every point. But the second suitor said, "You are not right; the other man is." Then the father of the girl gave his daughter to the man who had found him guilty, for he said, "This man must certainly be a good man, for he did not flatter me, nor did he show prejudice in my favor" (Sefer Hasidim, 1142).

Therefore, a community leader, or a judge, or a charity official must not be a flatterer. For if the community leader flatters any man and he does not reprove him to do good and turn aside from evil, then the whole congregation will be spoiled, for everyone will say, "The community leader flatters so and so," and that man does not receive the rebuke he deserves. Similarly, if a judge flatter one of the parties to a suit, then the words of the other one become stopped up and he is unable to present his case properly, with the result that the judgment will not be a true judgment. And so is it with charity officials who are flatterers and distribute charity to one who flatters them, or they flatter him and give him charity even though he is not deserving of it. Therefore, a righteous person should keep himself very far from flattery, neither flattering nor accepting flattery from others. And he should be very careful that when he does good deeds, he does not intend by them to flatter others, but only for the sake of Heaven.

Now the worst of all forms of flattery is he who flatters another in order to cause him to sin. For example, if he has a quarrel with people and the law is not with him, and he flatters certain people into helping him and strengthening his error. Or if a certain person constantly pursues sins, such as fornication and other bad deeds, and he flatters his companion in order to persuade him to do as he does. For example: Jeroboam, the son of Nebat, merited the kingdom because he did not flatter Solomon, but rebuked him in the matter of Solomon's building Millo (Sanh. 101b).

Now he who wishes to be free from the vice of flattery should take care to remove himself from seeking honor, for one who does not care about being honored will have no need to flatter. And he should also be very careful not to derive benefit from others, for most flatterers flatter a man when they think they will obtain some benefit from him. Therefore, , he who keeps away from these two things, benefit and honor, is saved from many transgressions. For many people do good deeds in order to receive honor from others, and this spoils all of a person's good work. For many people do good deeds and lead the congregation in prayer, but, knowing that they have a pleasant voice, they think in their heart during the service "How pleasant my voice is and how much pleasure people get when they hear me!" This is the way of the Evil Inclination. It does this with all the precepts of the Torah, to cause man to fall into his net so that his deeds shall not be for the sake of God. And so, it is with one who derives benefit from another, even though he sees him commit all the transgressions in the world, he will not feel it proper to rebuke him, for he is afraid that he will no longer derive the benefit from him. This matter is a stumbling block for some of our wise men in this generation; they seek to gain some benefit from the people and so they flatter them in order that the people will maintain them strongly in their high positions. And as if it were not bad enough, they do not rebuke the people for the things they do, but, because they flatter the people, they themselves imitate their deeds and are drawn after them.

It is in the nature of man to be influenced in his ideas and his deeds by his friends and his companions, and he usually conducts himself as the people of his country do, and what they do, he does also. Therefore, a man ought to associate with righeous men and always sit among the wise so that he may learn from their deeds, and he should separate himself from the wicked, who walk in the darkness, so that he will not learn from their deeds. This is what King Solomon says, "He that walketh with wise men shall be wise, but the companion of fools shall smart for it" (Prov. 13:20). And he says, "Happy is the man that hath not walked in the counsel of the wicked" (Ps. 1:1).

If he is in a country whose leaders are bad, and whose people do not walk in the righteous path, he should go to a place whose people are righteous and follow good ways. And if all the countries of which he knows and hears conduct themselves in a way that is not good, or if he cannot go to a country whose leaders are good, because of mobilization of troops or because of illness, then let him sit by himself alone, as it is said, "Let him sit alone and keep silence" (Lam. 3:28). And if the people among whom he dwells are so evil and such sinners that they do not permit him to dwell in that country unless he mingles with them and conducts himself in their evil way, then he should go forth to caves, ravines and deserts, but let him not conduct himself in the way of the sinners. As it is said, "Oh that I was in the wilderness, in a lodging-place of wayfaring men" (Jer. 9:1).

Sefer
ORCHOT TZADIKIM
Ways of the Righteous

Chapter Twenty-Five

ON GOSSIP

The term "gossip" applies to anyone who tells anything that defames his companion, even though he speaks the truth, while one who speaks falsehood is called "one who brings forth an evil repute." A gossip who sits and says, "Thus and thus did so and so do? and thus and thus were his ancestors, and thus and thus did I hear concerning him," and he says shameful things — of him the Scriptures say, "May the Lord cut off all flattering lips, the tongue that speaketh proud things" (Ps. 12:4).

Our Rabbis, of blessed memory, said, "If one speaks gossip, it is as though he denied God" (Arakin 15b, and see T.P. Peah, 1:1). As it is said (Ps. 12:15), "Who have said: 'Our tongue will we make mighty: our lips are with us: who is lord over us?'" (Arakin 16b, and see T.P. Peah, 1:1). And therefore, our Sages considered him as though he denied God, for he does a great evil to his companion, by making him odious in the eyes of the people and causing him other losses, though he himself derives no profit out of this. There is no doubt that one who makes a habit of speaking gossip has thrown off the yoke of Heaven from upon him, for he sins without any benefit to himself, and he is worse than a thief or an adulterer, for they pursue after their pleasure (Shohar Tov, 120:3). And there is no throwing off the yoke of Heaven as bad as when one deals in gossip. Our Sages further said, "The sin of gossip is weighed equally with the sin of idolatry and sexual immorality and bloodshed" (Arakin 15b). Now it is very astonishing that gossip should be equated with these sins, which are those to avoid which a man must rather let himself be killed than transgress (Sanh. 74a). And they said, "The sin of idolatry is so great that anyone who confesses to it, it is as though he denied the whole Torah" (Hullin 5a). And they said, "One who lusts after any form of idolatry, is a rebel against the whole Torah" (Hullin 4b).

And it is important to give the full meaning in this matter, for a gossip repeats his folly; ten times or more every day he humiliates and shames people, aside from the damage that he does to the one that he speaks against. And even a small transgression, when done many times, becomes great, just as although a single hair is soft and very weak, if you gather many hairs together, you can make of them a strong rope. And when they said that gossip is on a scale with those three mortal sins, they referred to one who commits any of these sins once, because of great temptation, but not to one who is such a complete apostate that he has excluded himself from the people of Israel, in order to commit these sins repeatedly. Moreover, a gossip finds it difficult to repent, because he is used to this habit and has taught his tongue to speak evil. Furthermore, this sin appears very light in his eyes, for he says, "I did not do anything — it was just talk." He does not consider the great damage he does, and therefore, he does not repent. And even if he should repent, his repentance is not complete, for he does not realize the enormity of the sin which he has committed. Moreover, he must first obtain forgiveness from those against whom he has spoken, and he cannot remember whom they all are. And it may happen that he spoke against a man, and did him evil, and caused him harm and forgot what it was that he said about that man, for gossip is always covered up; it is a blow struck in secret. The gossiper is here and smites with his tongue a person who is far away from him (Arakin 15b, Gen. Rabbah 98:19). And this type of sinner is ashamed to let his victim know that he has done him evil. Sometimes he speaks about a defect in the family of the object of his gossip, thus injuring the generations that come after him, and there is no forgiveness for this, for our Sages said, "For one who speaks about a flaw in a family, there is no forgiveness eternally" (T.P. Baba Kamma 8:10). Moreover, one who is accustomed to speak gossip will sometimes speak words against God, as it is written, "They have set their mouth against the heavens, and their tongue walketh through the earth" (Ps. 73:9). And there is no greater guilt in all of the sins than the guilt of him who blasphemes God. And our Sages, of blessed memory, said, "With ten trials were our ancestors tried, and in all them their fate was not sealed except for the sin of gossip" (Arakin 15a, Shohar Tov, 39a). As it is said, "As ye have spoken in mine ears, so will I do to you" (Num. 14:28). And it says, "And the Lord heard the voice of your words and was wroth" (Deut. 1:34). And the Torah itself does not protect gossipers. Doeg the Edomite, as soon as he had spoken gossip, his wisdom did not avail him and all of his knowledge of the Torah did not protect him (Sotah 21a, Sanh. 106b).

As to that which our Sages said, that "One sin quenches a commandment, but one sin does not quench the whole Torah" (Sotah 21a), as it is said, "For the commandment is a lamp, and the teaching is a light" (Prov. 6:23) — this applies to one who commits a sin by chance, but not to one who completely throws off the yoke of warning against a sin. And our Sages, of blessed memory, said, "The congregation of Israel is beloved for its voice" (Shohar Tov, 39a), as it is said, "Let me hear thy voice; for sweet is thy voice" (Cant. 2:14). And it is also hated for its voice, as it is said, "She hath uttered her voice against Me, Therefore, have I hated her" (Jer. 12:8). From this we can conclude that "life and death are in the power of the tongue" (Prov. 18:21). And it is said, "And those who love her will eat her fruit" (ibid.). This means that one who loves the tongue, that is to say a man who loves to speak constantly, it is worthy and true counsel to him that he should eat of its fruit. In other words, he should not speak idle talk, but should speak words of the Torah, or words that will bring peace, or words that will teach many to do good, and he should teach them the good and keep them far from evil, and to be zealous for the truth, for there is no end to the good deeds that a man may do with his tongue. And this is the meaning of "life and death are in the power of the tongue."

Gossips may be divided into six categories. The first is he who speaks evil of people and says, "Thus did they do," when in fact they did not do so, and at times he will slander an honorable and innocent person — in which case he is both a liar and a gossip. And we have been warned by the Torah not to accept gossip because it may be false, as it is said, "Thou shalt not utter a false report" (Ex. 23:1). And one who speaks gossip, will also be quick to accept gossip. And you should know that if one who hears gossip endorses what he has heard, then he is just as guilty as the gossiper. For all who hear that he agreed, will say, "Since he endorses it, it must be true." And even if he does not agree, but simply listens intently to the words, and appears to believe them, in the presence of people, he causes others to believe them too, and thus he helps the gossiper. For if he were to scold the gossiper, then he might restrain him from telling more, but since he pays attention and shows that he is interested, he causes him to speak even more gossip. And, behold, we have been warned by the verse, "Thou shalt not utter a false report" that we should not believe a gossip story in our hearts, for this would leave a strong imprint in our thoughts that the words are true and cause us to despise the object of the gossip.

The second category; he who speaks gossip that is true Even if he should remind another in private of some evil deed of his ancestors, he transgresses what is written in the Torah, "And ye shall not wrong one another" (Lev. 25:17); it is concerning wrongs done with words that the Scripture speaks (Baba Mezi'a

58b).

The third category of gossip is he who, in the presence of others, shames another because of something which his ancestors did. Concerning this our Sages, of blessed memory, said, "Everyone who causes the face of his companion to whiten (through shame) in public has no share in the world to come" (Aboth, 3:11).

The fourth category of gossip is this. If one publicly makes known the abominations of someone's ancestors, although not in the presence of the victim of the gossip, in order to shame him in the eyes of people — concerning this they said, "A group which speaks gossip cannot receive the Divine Presence" (Sotah 42a).

The fifth category is this. If the object of the gossip is a former sinner who has repented, and someone tells about the sins that he committed before he repented, in this there is great guilt (Baba Mezi'a 58b). "For one who repents of his wrongdoing, his sins now become merit" (T.P. Peah 1:1). And this gosiper shames him with sins that, through repentance, have become his merit. Moreover, he places a stumbling block before him for the victim may think in his heart, "Just as he shamed me so shall I shame him," and enter into a quarrel with him, with the result that he perverts his repentance and returns to his former state. Moreover, others who hear of this one's shame may be restrained from repenting their evil deeds, and thus the gossiper has locked the doors of repentance. And know, that if a man sees that his companion transgressed a commandment in secret and he reveals it in public, he is guilty of a sin, for perhaps the transgressor has repented of his evil way and did not want to admit it except to an understanding Sage who would not shame him, so that he could repent of his evil deed. But one should keep away from one who has done evil until he knows that his companion has repented of his evil way. And if the sinner is a scholar and a man who fears to commit a sin, it is proper to take it for granted that he has done repentance, and that if his evil inclination overcame him once he surely must have had remorse afterwards.

He who speaks gossip is punished not only for the injury he did to his fellow man but also for rejoicing in his shame, as it is written, "And you shall love your neighbour as yourself" (Lev. 19:18). Just as he loves his own honor, so should he love the honor of his companion, and it is written, "And he that is glad at calamity shall not be unpunished" (Prov. 17:5).

In a sense, the sin of one who gossips about something that is true is greater than that of one who tells false gossip. For when a man tells true things about another, people believe him and the victim remains contemptible in their eyes even after he has shown remorse and repented his sin; but as for false gossip, most people will understand that it is a lie and will not believe it. But, in general, falsehood carries a greater guilt than the truth.

The sixth category is he who gossips about community officials who are worthy and who collect funds honestly and apportion alms to those who revere God. He who slanders them, saying that they steal from the charity funds and show bias in favor of some recipients as against others, and distribute the alms to those they favor and to their own relatives —

this is gossip in which the guilt is incalculable. For it causes officials to quit their posts and others, who are evil, to be chosen in their place with the result that the gossiper deprives the charity givers of an opportunity to do good and he robs the deserving poor, for the other collectors who are evil will have no mercy on the good. The consequence is that this gossiper has nullified the service of the Holy One, Blessed be He, and shamed the servants of the Holy One, Blessed be He, and their children and their relatives. For instead of fulfilling his duty to honor the officials, not only did he not honor them but he did evil to them. And he thus restrains other God-fearing people from being officials, for they think, "Why should we engage in an activity where people will suspect us, just as they suspected these others, who are God-fearing men?"

And our Sages, of blessed memory, said, "Gossip slays three people — the one who speaks gossip, the one who listens to it and the one about whom the gossip is said" (Arakin 15b, and see T.P. Peah 1:1). And he who listens to the gossip is guiltier than he who speaks it. It is forbidden to dwell in the neighborhood of gossips, all the more so is it forbidden to sit with them and listen to their words.

There is another evil in gossip and that is that the one who speaks gossip against his companion feels proud and appears in his own eyes as a righteous person, for he thinks, "So and so did thus and thus, but I did not do anything like it." So, we find that the gossip vaunts himself and claims merit for himself. Now if he did a good deed and claimed merit for it, that would be very bad, all the more so when he commits a great sin through gossip and claims merit for himself. And if a man speaks gossip against orphans or widows then his guilt is even greater — for they suffer affliction to begin with, and he causes them to suffer still more.

Come and see, how careful a man ought to be to guard himself against gossip. If a man says to his companion, "Where can I obtain fire?" And his companion answers, "Why in the house of so and so; he always has plenty of meat and fish." Even this is gossip! (Arakin 15b).

And there is another wrong which smack of gossip — for example, where a person says, "Oh, better be silent about so and so; I don't want to say what I know about him!" — and so in all similar cases. And our Sages further said, "Let no man ever talk in praise of his neighbor, for through his praise he will come to disparage him" (Arakin 16a, and see Baba Bathra 164b). The meaning of this is: if you praise a man to his enemy, he will retort, "How can you praise him so much when he does this and this." And concerning this it is said, "He that blesseth his friend with a loud voice, rising early in the morning, it shall be counted a curse to him" (Prov. 27:14). But to praise a man before his friends is permitted, as we have learned, "Rabban Johanan the son of Zakkai had five (outstanding) disciples, and he used to recount their praises" (Aboth 2:8). Then, there is the one who speaks gossip by way of a joke or by way of frivolity (that is, he is not speaking out of hatred), and that is what Solomon said in his wisdom, "As a madman who casteth firebrands, arrows and death; so is the man that deceiveth his neighbour and saith: "Am not I in sport?" (Prov. 26:18—19).

Then there is he who speaks gossip by way of deceit:

he tells it with seeming innocence, as though he does not know that he is indulging in gossip, and when others rebuke him, he says, "I really don't know whether so and so is guilty of these things." Or he says, "This may be merely gossip." One who speaks words that cause harm to his fellow man, whether it be to his body or to his money, even though it be to distress him or to frighten him, it is gossip. If a man says something to his companion, he is forbidden to reveal it without his permission (Yoma 4b). But anything which a man says in front of three people it is as though he intended it to be common knowledge and if one of the three who heard it told about it, we cannot say that this is gossip (Arakin 15b). But if the teller intends to reveal more than he heard, then there is something of gossip in it. And if the speaker warns those who heard him not to reveal it, even though he speaks in the presence of many people, still if one of those who were warned does reveal it, it is a sort of gossip. There is a story about a certain pupil who revealed a thing that had been said in the house of study twenty-two years earlier and they drove him out of the house of study and they said, "This one is a revealer of secrets" (Sanh. 31a).

And there is another sin which is called tale-bearing. Now, who is a tale bearer? One who loads himself with stories about others and goes from one to another and says, "Thus did so and so say," and "Thus and thus did I hear about that one." Even though what he tells is true, this kind of thing destroys the world. And we have been warned about this, as it is written, "Thou shall not go up and down as a tale-bearer among thy people" (Lev. 19:16). And what is tale-bearing? One who reveals to other things that were said about him in secret, and we have learned (Sanh. 31a): "Whence do we know that when a judge comes out, he must not say, 'I was for acquittal, while my colleagues were for condemnation; but what could I do, seeing that they were in the majority?'" Scripture states, "Thou shall not go up and down as a tale-bearer among thy people" (Lev. 19:16), and further, "He that goeth about as a tale-bearer revealeth secrets" (Prov. 11:13).

Be very careful concerning gossip for with this you shame yourself. For he who finds others unworthy is himself unworthy, and he does not speak in praise of anyone, and his way is to find people unworthy with the fault that he himself possesses (Kiddushin 70a). For this fault of his is constantly on his mind and when he gossips he expresses it with his mouth. For every man can be tested and recognized by his deeds. How? When you see a man, who is accustomed to praise women and to speak of them always, know that he loves women. And if he praises good food and wine and does so constantly, know that he is a glutton and a drunkard and so is it with everything. And proof of this you may find in the verse, "Oh how love I thy law! It is my meditation all the day" (Ps. 119:97). Because I love the Torah, I always speak of it — since whatever a person loves in his heart, he lends to speak about always.

A gossip always seeks out the faults of people; he is like the flies who always rest on the dirty spot. If a man has boils, the flies will let the rest of the body go and sit on the boil. And thus, it is with a gossip. He overlooks all the good in a man and speaks only of the evil. There is a story about a certain man who went with a wise man in the field, and they saw a corpse. The man said, "How putrid this corpse is." And the wise man said, "How white are its teeth." Thus, the wise man rebuked his companion and said in effect, "Why must you speak about its blemish; speak of its excellence, for one should always speak in commendation of the world."

If you see a man who speaks a word or does a deed which can be interpreted either favorably or unfavorably, then if he is a man who reveres God you are obliged to give him the benefit of the doubt, even if the unfavorable interpretation appears more likely. And if he is an ordinary person who guards himself from sin, but occasionally stumbles, it is still your duty to put doubt aside and decide his favor. And our Sages, of blessed memory, said: "He who judges his neighbor in the scale of merit is himself judged favorably" (Shabbath 127b). And this is a positive commandment in the Torah, as it is said, "But in righteousness shalt thou judge thy neighbor" (Lev. 19:15). And if the matter inclines to the unfavorable interpretation, let it be with you as though there were a doubt and do not judge the man unfavorably. But if the man's deeds for the most part are evil, and you know that he is not one who reveres God in his heart, then you should put the unfavorable interpretation on his deeds and words.

If a man revealed your sin, do not say, "Just as he revealed my sin, I will now reveal his sin," As it is said, "Thou shalt not take vengeance, nor bear any grudge" (Lev. 19:18). Neither may you boast and say, "Even though he has revealed my sin, I will not reveal his," for by so speaking you have already revealed the half of it. And this matter is a very great principle in the whole concept of reverence of God. But if the one who sins does not fear God then he is as one who throws off the yoke of the kingdom of Heaven from upon him, and if he does not guard himself against a single transgression which all the people of the city know to be a sin, then one does well to speak evil of him and to reveal his sins and to cause the sinner, to be odious in the eyes of the people, in order that the people may hear and despise him and set themselves apart from transgressions, as it is said, "An unjust man is an abomination to the righteous" (Prov. 29:27). And it is said, "The fear of the Lord is to hate evil" (Prov. 8:13). And they said, a wicked man who is the son of a righteous man may be called "a wicked man, son of the wicked," while a righteous man who is the son of a wicked man may be called "a righteous man, son of the righteous" — and precisely in this way is it permitted to shame him for the sake of Heaven. But a man who quarrels with another and intends to shame him for his own satisfaction and not for the sake of Heaven, may not reveal his sin (Sanh. 52a). And similarly, if the one who reveals the transgression of his companion is himself a sinner, he should not reveal the wrong of another sinner, for he certainly is not revealing the secrets of the sinner for a good purpose. "But the talk of the lips tendeth only to penury" (Prov. 14:23).

There are a few instances where it is commendable to engage in gossip. For example, in the case of two wicked men who have taken counsel to do evil, it is permitted, by gossip, to make them hate each other and do evil to one another, in order that they do not do evil to good people. And so is it with an adulterer who is pursuing an adultress, it is a good deed to gossip about them so that they should not commit the transgression. And there are times when even though the sinner is a completely wicked person it still is not proper to shame him in public — when there is the danger that this will cause him to become an unbeliever. It is permissible to use gossip against people who are always starting quarrels, as it is said, "I also will come in after thee, and confirm thy words" (I Kings 1:14) (See T.P. Peah 1:1).

Because so many things depend upon the tongue, it is necessary to guard the tongue very much. And therefore, David said, "Keep thy tongue from evil" (Ps. 34:14). And our Sages, of blessed memory, recounted a story about a certain man who cried out in the streets, "Who wants to purchase the elixir of life?" Everybody came to buy. He then took out the Book of Psalms and showed them what was written in it: "Who is the man that desireth life and loveth days, that he may see good therein? Keep thy tongue from evil" (Ps. 34:13—14). And when Rabbi Yannai saw this, he took this man into his house and he fed him and he gave him drink and money. The pupils of Rabbi Yannai came to him and said to him, "Did you not know this verse before?" And he said to them, "I did know it — but I never put it in my heart to be careful concerning this. When I used to read this verse, I would go over it hastily and did not realize its full meaning. And now this man came and made it mean something to me, and from now on I shall be more careful with my tongue" (Lev. Rabbah 16:2; Shohar Tov, 52b).

Therefore, a man whose tongue is accustomed to flatter, to scoff, to gossip, to lie, to indulge in idle talk — and who now wishes to subdue this impulse and put up a strong fence against this vice — such a man should make a fence by keeping apart from his original companions with whom he used to indulge in scoffing and flattery and gossip and lies. For if he should again draw close to them, he will not be able to restrain himself from this sin, for they will begin to speak with him as they were accustomed to do and then he will not be able to restrain himself from speaking with them as he was accustomed to do. And such a man should accustom himself severely to silence in order to develop the habit of opening his mouth very little, and he often should sit by himself in a room and occupy himself with Torah and he should join the company of the pious who speak only of the Torah and of reverence of God. And in this manner, he should accustom himself to do for a long time and then he will find healing for his wound.

It is written, "Death and life are in the power of the tongue; and they that indulge it shall eat the fruit thereof" (Prov. 18:21). There is a story about a king of Persia who became ill, and the doctors said to him, "You cannot be healed until they bring you the milk of a lioness and then we will make you a medicine that will heal you." One of the men present said, "I will bring you the milk of a lioness if you wish, but give me ten goats." The king told his servants to give them to him, and they did so. He went to a pit of lions and there was a lioness there who was giving suck to

ORCHOT TZADIKIM — Chapter Twenty-Five

her young. The first day he stood far off and threw one goat to the lioness and she ate it. The second day he came closer to her a bit and threw her another goat, and thus did he do until he was able to play with the lioness, and he took some of her milk and started back. As he was travelling along the way, he saw in a dream that his limbs were quarrelling with one another. The leg said, "There are no limbs like us, for if we had not gone our master would not have been able to bring the milk." Then the hand said, "There is no one like us, for if we had not done our part, nothing would have happened." The brain said, "There is no one like me! If I had not given counsel, of what use would any of you have been?" Then the tongue said, "There is nobody like me. For if I had not said that we would do this thing, who would have done it?" All the limbs answered, "How dare you compare yourself with us? You are in a place of darkness, and you possess no bone like the rest of the limbs." And the tongue replied to them, "This day will you say that I rule over all of you."

The man kept the dream in mind. He went to the king and he said to him, "My lord, the king, here is the milk of a bitch." The king got very angry and ordered that the man be hanged. As he was about to be hanged, all the limbs began to weep. Whereupon the tongue said to them, "Did I not tell you that you are not worth anything? If I save you, will you confess that I am king over all of you?" And they said to her, "Yes!" Then the man said to the executioners, "Take me back to the king, perhaps I can be saved." So, they returned the man to the king, and the man asked, "Why did you order that I be hanged?" And the king said, "Because you brought me the milk of a bitch." The man said, "What difference does it make as long as you are healed? And moreover, a lioness is often called a bitch. They took the milk from him and tested it and it was found to be the milk of a lioness. Then all of the limbs said to the tongue, "Now we confess to you that you are king." And this is the meaning of the saying, "Death and life are in the power of the tongue." Therefore, David said (Ps. 39:2), "I will take heed to my ways, that I sin not with my tongue" (Shohar Tov, 39:2—3, and Yalkut Tehillim, item 721).

See how the tongue is better than sacrifices, for it is said, "I will praise the name of God with a song, and will magnify Him with thanksgiving. And it shall please the Lord better than a bullock that hath horns and hoofs" (Ps. 69:31—32).

You must consider well and distinguish clearly this matter of the tongue, because all the affairs of a man, whether for evil or for good, depend upon it. With his tongue, a man can commit great and mighty transgressions without number, such as informing, tale-bearing, scoffing, flattery, lies, and the like. And all of these great transgressions bring no profit to the owner of the tongue. And with his tongue a man can also do precepts without limit. And there are many people who say, "How can we do a good deed? We do not have money which we can give to the poor." They do not know that the source of the precepts is very near to them — the source of life in this world and in the world-to-come, and that is the tongue. And thus, did David say, "Who wishes to acquire the life of this world and of the world to come?" And they said to them, "No one can stay in both worlds." Then he said to them, "It is very cheap," as it is written, "Who is the man that desireth life" (Ps. 34:13). They said to him, "Who is the one that can acquire life?" And he said to them (Ps. 34:14), "Keep thy tongue from evil" (Shohar Tov, 39:4; and see Abodah Zarah 19b).

A man should accustom himself to speak words of Torah and of reverence of God and to reprove people, and to command his sons ofter him to observe and to do (the commandments) — to comfort the mourners, to comfort the poor, to speak to their hearts good words of consolation, to speak the truth, and to accustom oneself to pray with songs and praises — and then he will be beloved below and dearly beloved above, and his reward will be in the great good which is treasured up for the righteous.

Sefer ORCHOT TZADIKIM
Ways of the Righteous

Chapter Twenty-Six

ON REPENTANCE

Said Rabbi Levi, "Great is repentance for it reaches to the very Throne of Glory," as it is said (Hos. 14:2) "Return, O Israel, unto the Lord thy God" (Yoma 86a). And our Sages, of blessed memory, said, "When Moses went up to the first firmament, he found groups of angels. They opened before him the Book of the Torah and read of God's work on the first day of Creation. And then they paused and began to tell the praises of the Torah. Then Moses ascended to the second firmament and he found bands of angels who were reading of the work of the second day of creation and then they paused and began to tell the praises of the Torah and of Israel. He then ascended to the third firmament and he found troops of angels reading of the work of the third day of Creation, and they paused and began to speak in praise of Jerusalem. He ascended to the fourth firmament where he found angels reading of the work of the fourth day of Creation and they paused and they began to tell the praises of the Messiah. Then he went up to the fifth firmament and he found companies and companies of angels reading of the work of the fifth day of Creation. And they paused and began to tell of the sadness and sorrow of Gehenna. Then he ascended to the sixth firmament and found their angels, and they were reading of the work of the sixth day of Creation and they paused and began to tell about Paradise, and they beseeched the Holy One, Blessed be He, to make Paradise the portion of Israel. Then he went up to the seventh firmament and found their heavenly creatures called Ofanim, Seraphim, and Galgalim, and angels of mercy, and angels of kindness and justice, and angels of fear and trembling. At once Moses took hold of the Throne of Glory. They began to read of the work of the seventh day, the portion beginning, "And the heaven and the earth were finished" (Gen. 2:1). And they paused and they began to tell the praise of repentance, to teach you that repentance reaches to the very Throne of Glory, as it is said, "Return, O Israel, unto the Lord thy God" (Hos. 14:2).

Rabbi Akiba said, "Seven things were created before the Universe and they are these: Torah, Repentance, Paradise, Gehennah, the Throne of Glory, the Temple, and the name of the Messiah" (Pesahim 54a). And why these seven? Know this, that the principal reason for the creation of the world is man, for there is no need for the lower world except for man, and he rules over all the lower world: over the cattle, the beasts, the fowl, the fish and the swarming things. And inasmuch as the principal reason for creation is man it was necessary first to create the Torah, which is the very existence of the world. As it is written, "If

My covenant be not with day and night, if I have not appointed the ordinances of heaven and earth" (Jer. 33:25).

And since He created the Torah first, it was logically necessary to create Repentance, for inasmuch as the Torah contains positive and negative commandments and punishments which are explained in the Torah, it was necessary to anticipate the creation of man by creating repentance, so that if a man should sin there would be time for him to repent; otherwise, the world could not exist for even one generation. "For there is not a righteous man upon earth, that doeth good and sinneth not" ((Eccl. 7:20), and immediately upon sinning this generation would deserve to be completely destroyed. It is for this reason that the story of Sodom was written in the Torah, to let the sinners know that they deserve to be destroyed — they and all that belongs to them. And that the earth too deserved to be overturned, as in the case of Sodom, but the Holy One, Blessed be He, created Repentance early and waits patiently generation after generation for man to repent.

But inasmuch as God had created the Torah and Repentance earlier than man, it was also necessary for him to create Paradise and Gehennah and the Throne of Glory before creating man, for they are the places where each man is rewarded according to his deeds.

And inasmuch as He had created all of these, it was necessary to create the Temple and the name of the Messiah before creating man. For in the days of the Messiah, the earth will be filled with knowledge and there will be no evil desire among men. And all people, great and small, will know the name of God, may He be exalted, with a great knowledge and then they will know, all of them, that the principal reason for the creation of the world was service to the Creator, may He be exalted. Therefore, He first created all of these seven before He created the world. "And saviours shall come up on mount Zion (Obad. 1:21) and "a redeemer will come to Zion, and unto them that turn from transgression in Jacob" (Is. 59:20). Amen. And thus, may it be His will.

For seven reasons should a man repent early while still in his youth when his power is strong. The first is that the labor needed to acquire Torah and reverence for God and all qualities that a man must possess is exceedingly great. And concerning this it is said, "The measure thereof is longer than the earth and broader than the sea" (Job 11:9). And, "The day is short" (Aboth 2:20). For this world is a very short day. "Like a shadow are our days upon the earth" (I Chron. 29:15). And our Sages, of blessed memory, said, "Not like the shadow of a wall and not like the shadow of a tree, but like the shadow of a bird in flight" (Gen. Rabbah 96:2). And as to the expression, "And the workers are lazy" (Aboth 2:20), this refers to a man who has within him the quality of laziness.

And now consider the case of a man who must walk a distance during the day of ten parasangs - Ancient Persian measure of length about 3-1/4 miles. and more, and his path is filled with stumbling blocks, mud and stones, and there are plunderers and murderers along that way and he must go in spite of all of this, for so has the king commanded him and he is not able to avoid it, how must this man first prepare in the morning and gird his loins with alertness and walk speedily? Therefore, how important it is to rise early and to begin early the service of the Creator, may He be exalted. And even though he does all that is in his power, he will attain only a little of the needed qualities. As our Sages expounded (Aboth de R. Nathan, chap. 16) on the verse, "For he knoweth our frame" (Ps. 103:14). They told a parable of a king who gave a field to his servants and he told them to till it and guard it and to extract from it thirty kur (of produce) every year, and they busied themselves in this matter and tilled it well, but they brought before the king only five kur. He said to them, "What is this that you have done?" They said to him, "Our lord, the king, the field you gave to us has poor soil, and though we worked it with all our might it did not produce more than this amount. Thus, man, even though he works with all his strength, his accomplishment is little and if he says, "I will wait until I have time or until I earn enough for my needs," know that the troubles and responsibilities of this world never cease. As our Sages said, "And say not, 'When I have leisure I will study'; perhaps you will never have leisure" (Aboth 2:5).

The second thing to remember is that if he delays his repentance until he accumulates wealth then he will covet and long for more wealth, as our Sages said, "No man leaves this world with even half of his desires fulfilled" (Eccl. Rabbah 1:13). If he has one hundred coins in his hand, he wants to make it two hundred. If his hand has attained two hundred, he longs to make them four hundred. And so, it is written, "He that loveth silver shall not be satisfied with silver" (Eccl. 5:9).

The third reason that a man should hasten to repent while still in his youth is that the time is so little and the work is so much — the work of studying the Torah, and the improvement of the soul, the attainment of good qualities such as love, reverence, and cleaving to God. As our Sages said, "The day is short, and the work is great" (Aboth 2:15).

The fourth reason is that if he delays improving his soul then his evil inclination will keep growing stronger and his heart will grow harder and he will get accustomed to sinning, and he will permit himself all of the sins, and then he will not be able to purify himself.

The fifth reason is that he who does not want to repent early will perhaps not have a long life and will die before he repents. Therefore, he warns, "Let thy garments be always white" (Eccl. 9:8).

The sixth reason is that if he delays in repenting, his sins will become old and he will forget the anguish they caused him and he will not worry about them as he did at first.

The seventh reason is that when he gets old, and the strength of the evil inclination weakens, he will not receive as great a reward for repentance as if he had repented in the days of his youth when he was in his full powers. And because of these things a man ought very early to reform his soul before the King, Most High.

And after a man has set his mind to do penitence, he cannot achieve complete repentance if he does not take these seven things to heart: The first is that he should be aware of his deeds and know them all. There are people who think that a man cannot be called a ba'al teshuva (a penitent) — i.e., that repentance does not apply — unless he was guilty of a mortal sin like having intercourse with a married woman or with a Gentile woman, or becoming completely corrupt, or similar cardinal sin. But as far as other sins are concerned, no one knows just how to repent for them. This is not so, because anything that our Sages warned us against is more severe than the words of the Torah itself, for anyone who transgresses the words of our Sages is liable to the penalty of death (Berakoth 4b). And anyone who transgresses either the words of the Torah or the words of the Sages must repent.

And now listen, my son, for most people do not take care to refrain from frivolous things, and from staring at women, and from speaking with them when it is not necessary. Nor do we take care to pray with sincere intent, and to refrain from speaking in the synagogue and from mockery and from disrespect. Neither in the matter of charity do we take care to give it to him who is worthy of it, and not to harden our hearts and close our hands to deeds of generosity, and not to speak harsh words to the poor. Nor have we guarded ourselves from vain oaths or from cursing our companions or ourselves with the name of God, or from mentioning the Name of God needlessly or in a unclean place or with unclean hands, or from neglect of the study of the Torah, the latter being weighed against all other commandments.

Neither have we guarded ourselves against jealousy and hatred and gossip and arrogance, and anger and all of the undesirable qualities mentioned in this book. Nor have we taken care to observe the commandments that depend upon deeds, such as the washing of the hands, and to refrain from causing injury to our fellow man, and to keep the Sabbath according to the Law.

And many people stumble in this, for it is very easy for one who is not expert in the commandments to stumble in many places. And a man commits such sins as these all of his days without being aware of it. Therefore, a man who would repent must know the sins that he has committed. And how can he know this? He must study the commandments and understand where he has fallen short in the observance of each commandment, and in what way he has transgressed. For if he does not know in what way he has transgressed, how can he have remorse? He must know his transgression and sincerely regret it, as the Scripture says, "For I know my transgressions; And my sin is ever before me" (Ps. 51:5).

The second thing a man must keep in mind if he wants to repent is that even though he knows the sins that he committed; he cannot fully regret them if he does not know clearly the evil of these transgressions. For if he thinks, "So what if I got a little pleasure from this world without a blessing!" or "So what if I took time away from Torah; that is not such a terrible thing." Anyone who thinks thus will not have any regrets, and will not repent with a complete heart. But one should think: There is nothing so bad in all the world as one who does not care about the commandments of the King who is Most Exalted. We can learn the importance of this from a king of flesh and blood.

Anyone who transgresses his commands — how bad it is for him!

Thirdly, the sinner must know and believe from the depth of his heart that severe punishment awaits him for the sins that he committed, for if he does not know this, he will be in no haste to repent. But after the punishment he may expect is clear to him, he can repent and have true remorse, and he can ask forgiveness of God, as it is said, "My flesh shuddereth for fear of thee, and I am afraid of thy judgments" (Ps. 119:120).

The fourth thing that the sinner should know is that all the transgressions that he committed all of his days, the great sins and the small, and all the evil thoughts, and all of the idle things, and all his affairs from small to large — all is written in a book and there is no forgetfulness with God, may He be Exalted, as it is written, "Is not this laid up in store with Me, sealed up in My treasuries?" (Deut. 32:34). And further, "He sealeth up the hand of every man" (Job 37:7). For if a man should think that there is forgetfulness concerning his sins, he will not have remorse and he will not ask God for forgiveness for them. For many think that because the Holy One, Blessed be He, delays in demanding retribution for sins, that these have been forgotten and that they will not come to judgment for them, as it is said, "Because sentence against an evil work is not executed speedily, Therefore, the heart of the sons of men is fully set in them to do evil" (Eccl. 8:11).

Fifthly, he must know truly that repentance is a complete healing for transgressions. For the patient who does not believe that the medicine the doctors have prepared for him will really heal him will not be quick to take it. But if he knows that the drug or the potion will surely help him, he will want to bear the bitterness of the medicine. Thus, if he is certain of the worth of repentance, he will desire to reach the high level of repentance.

Sixthly, he must think in his heart of all the good things that the Creator, Blessed be He, has done for him from the time of his birth until this day. And he must understand that he should have thanked God for these good things, but that he has not done this, but has transgressed God's commandments. And he should weigh the punishment for the sin against its sweetness and the reward for the good deed against the pain in this world (and in the world to come). As our Sages said, "Reckon the loss incurred by the fulfillment of a precept against the reward secured by its observance, and the profit of sin against its loss" (Aboth 2:1).

Finally, he should know how to strengthen himself exceedingly and to bear the great burden of restraining himself from that evil which he is accustomed to do. For this is obvious that a sin that he has been accustomed to do all his life he will regard as permissible (Yoma 86b), and it is very difficult for him to give it up. Therefore, a man needs great will power and high fences to give up what he has been accustomed to. And it requires a great accord in all his heart and soul to hold himself back from committing that sin, and he must remove this habit from his heart as though he had not been accustomed to do this. And he must become accustomed to reject in his heart all the evil things, as it is said, "And rend your heart and not your garments" (Joel 2:13). And when the sinner establishes these seven considerations firmly in his heart, he is very near to the path of repentance.

Now there are many steps in the upward path of repentance, and according to these steps a man draws nearer to God, Blessed be He. Never can a soul reach perfect purity so that the sins will be as though they had never been, except after a man has purified his heart. It is like a soiled garment — if he launders it a little, the dirt may disappear but a stain remains, and only after much laundering it becomes completely white. And thus, it is written, "Wash me thoroughly from mine iniquity" (Ps. 51:4). Therefore, you must wash away the sin from your heart, as it is said, "O Jerusalem, wash thy heart from wickedness" (Jer. 4:14).

And now, I must write down for you twenty matters that are among the principal considerations in repentance.

The first is that one should grasp the quality of remorse, and put it into his heart that there is great punishment for him who has transgressed the commandment of the Great King. As the Scriptures say, "Give glory to the Lord your God, before it grows dark" (Jer. 13:16). And when a man thinks about the dark days which will reach the one who has sinned against the God of Jacob, then he will be exceedingly afraid and he will have remorse for his deeds. And he will say in his heart, "What have I done? How is it that the fear of God was not always before my eyes? And how is it that I did not fear punishment for my wrongdoing? And how is it that I could not rule over my evil inclination when tempted by the pleasure of one moment? And how have I sullied my pure soul, the soul which was breathed into me from the Source of Holiness? And how have I changed the Great World that stands and endures forever and ever for this transitory little world? And how is it that I did not remember the day of death which will leave my soul nothing but my corpse and a bit of earth?" And he should multiply in his heart thoughts concerning this matter. And this is the subject of which Jeremiah spoke, "No man repenteth of his wickedness saying, 'What have I done' " (Jer. 8:6).

The second thing is the abandonment of sin; the sinner should leave his evil ways and determine with all his heart that he will never more walk that path. And this is the beginning of repentance: to leave his evil ways and thoughts, to agree in his heart and to undertake that he will not continue to sin, and that he will repent of his evil thought and that he will utterly put away his evil deeds.

The third principle of repentance is grief: he should sigh in the bitterness of his heart. For if a man lost one dinar, it would be difficult to bear, and if he lost all his wealth he would mourn and his heart would be bitter within him. Similarly, if he met with other misfortunes he would be in great anguish. All the more so should he be in anguish who has rebelled against the Great Lord, and has corrupted his path, though God has done him so much kindness; Therefore, should such a man feel pain at every moment. Know that the steps that lead to repentance and its ascents are achieved according to the degree of the bitterness and the pain which a person feels over the sins he has done. For the pain comes from the purity of the lofty soul. And the Holy One, Blessed be He, has mercy upon a man when his soul is steeped in pain. An illustration of this is the fact that a king will have greater mercy on those who were born in his household, those who are near to him, those that are of the nobles of the land and the most honored, than he will have on villagers. Therefore, when the soul, which had its abode above and was separated from the Holy Place, is in anguish, the Creator of all receives it quickly.

The fourth principle in repentance is the sorrow and the pain caused by the actual doing of the deeds of repentance. Thus far we have spoken about the pain and sorrow of the heart, but this concerns the pain and the sorrow of the repentant act itself, as it is said, "Yet even now, saith the Lord, turn ye unto Me with all your heart, and with fasting and with weeping, and with lamentation" (Joel 2:12). And a man must show the signs of pain and sorrow in his garments, for example, to put on sackcloth, as it is said, "For this gird you with sackcloth, lament and wail" (Jer. 4:8). And as it is said, "But let them be covered with sackcloth, both man and beast" (Jonah 3:8). And he must remove his lovely garments from him and he must reduce his pleasures, in the kinds of food he eats and, in his drink, and in strolling about. And our Sages said, "The heart and the eyes are the two agents of sin" (T.P. Berakoth 1:8). And thus, is it written, "And that ye go not about after your own heart and your own eyes" (Num. 15:39). Therefore, only in this way can the sin brought about by these agents be atoned for: the sin of the agent of the heart, by bitterness and pain, and the wrong of the agent of the eyes, by tears. As it is said, "Mine eyes run down with rivers of water, because they observe not Thy law" (Ps. 119:136). It is not said, "because I observe not," but "because they observe not." The plural form refers to the eyes, that spied out to explore sin, Therefore, have I caused rivers of water to descend from my eyes. When he weeps over his sins, he should say, "May my tears quench the wrath of your anger and may my repentant deeds turn away your anger from me, and let my table, which I have not set because of my sorrow, be considered as an altar arranged for sacrifice, and the pot which I did not place upon the coals, as fire burning upon Thy altar. And may the lack of my blood, the diminution resulting from fasting, atone as the blood which is offered on the corners of the altar. And may the lessening of my fat be as the fat which is offered from the sacrifices, and the sound of my weeping as the psalms of the poets, and the aroma of my soul's hunger as the aroma of the incense, and the weakness of my limbs as the cutting of portions for the sacrifice, and may my broken heart tear the books in which my sins are recorded. And may the change of my good garments for garments of mourning be as acceptable to you as are the garments of the priesthood, and my restraint from washing (because of my sorow) as though I had sanctified my hands and feet, and may my repentance restore me to Thee, for I am truly remorseful for the evil of my deeds that I did and I shall not return to do evil before Thee.

The fifth principle of repentance is worry. One should worry about the punishment of his sins, for there are sins where repentance holds the atonement in suspense and only afflictions cleanse away the wrong (Yoma 86a), as it is said, "For I do declare mine iniquity; I am full of care because of my sin" (Ps. 38:19). And what is the difference between sorrow and worry? Sorrow is for what has already taken place, while worry concerns the future. And a person who has sinned should always worry whether he has fallen short in the matter of repentance and has not completed the full measure of repentance. And he should worry lest his evil inclination overpower him. As our Sages, of blessed memory, said, "Do not trust in yourself until the day of your death" (Aboth 2:4).

The sixth principle of repentance is shame, as it is said, "I was ashamed, yea, even confounded, because I did bear the reproach of my youth" (Jer. 31:18). Now one who sins would be very ashamed to commit a transgression before people. Then how shall he not be ashamed before the Holy One, Blessed be He? But we have already explained the matter of shame in the chapter on that subject.

The seventh principle is submission with all one's heart and with humility. For he who knows his Creator knows how much anyone who transgresses against His words lowers himself, and he will Therefore, be humble, as it is written, "The sacrifices of God are a broken spirit; a broken and a contrite heart, O God, thou wilt not despise" (Ps. 51:19). A "broken spirit" means "a lowly spirit," and humility is one of the principles of repentance; through humility will a man draw near to God, Blessed be He. As it is said, "But on this man will I look, even on him that is poor and of a contrite spirit" (Is. 66:2). The highest step in humility which is obligatory in the path of repentance is that he should magnify and glorify the service of the Creator and should not claim any merit for himself, but everything should be small in his eyes as compared to what he must do in the service of God, Blessed be He. Therefore, he should be humble and should serve with modesty, and he should not covet honor for his good deeds.

The eighth principle is humility in deeds of repentance; he should conduct himself in a gentle manner. If a man has reviled him because of his previous deeds, let him be silent, or he should say, "I know that I have sinned." And he should not make lovely garments, and wear jewelry. As it is said, "Therefore, now put off thy ornaments from thee" (Ex. 33:5). And his eyes should always be lowered, as it is said, "For the humble person He saveth" (Job 22:29). And the signs of humility are: a soft answer, a low voice and eyes bent downward. These are the things which make the heart humble.

The ninth principle is the destruction of lust. He must lay it to his heart that lust ruins all deeds. And he should abstain from luxuries, even from things which are permitted to him. And he should conduct himself in the paths of abstinence, eating only to satisfy his hunger and to preserve his body. And the same is true in his relationship to woman. For whenever a man follows after lust he is drawn after the functions of the body and separates himself from the ways of the cultured soul. Then his evil inclination overpowers him, as it is written, "But Jeshurun waxed fat, and kicked" (Deut, 31:15). And it is written, "Lest I be full, and deny, and say: 'Who is the Lord?'" (Prov. 30:9). Now the lust that is given into the heart of a man is the root of all deeds. Therefore, he must hurry to correct that lust, and on this subject we have dwelt above. And there is a great benefit in the breaking of lust, for in this way a man reveals that his heart is good and upright, and that he rejects the character which sin has caused him to have. And one who abstains even from what is permitted erects a great fence which will keep him from touching what is forbidden. It is as if he says, "Even in that which is permitted I do not satisfy my craving; how then shall I stretch forth my hands to that which is forbidden?"

The tenth principle of repentance is to reverse one's deeds. How does one do that? If he has been guilty of looking at indecent things, then let him conduct himself with lowered eyes. If he has been guilty of gossip, let him occupy himself with Torah (Arakin 15b). And with any limb with which he has sinned let him try to fulfill commandments (see Yalkut Judges, 42). And thus, did our Sages say, "The righteous men in the very thing with which they had sinned appease God" (see Yalkut Hosca, 529). And more did our Sages say, "If you have committed bundles of transgressions, do in opposition to them bundles of good deeds. Feet which ran hastily to sin must now quickly run to do a good deed. A mouth which once spoke disobedience and rebellion now let his palate speak the truth and let him open his mouth with wisdom. Hands that spilled innocent blood, let him open his hand to the poor. Eyes that were haughty, let him be contrite and walk with lowered eyes. A heart that plotted wrongdoing, let him store up in his heart the words of the Torah" (Lev. Rabbah 21:5).

The eleventh principle of repentance is to search out one's ways, as it is said, "Let us search and try our ways, and return to the Lord" (Lam. 3:40). And searching out one's ways means that one should examine oneself with respect to all the transgressions one has done in his life. There are three advantages to this. First, he will remember all the things in which he has sinned and he will confess all of them, for confession is one of the basic elements of atonement. Secondly, he will know the amount of his transgressions and sins, and this will increase his humility. Thirdly, even though he has resolved to abandon all sin, he must know the things in which he has sinned in order to erect a fence, to guard himself against those things over which he stumbled, for a man needs more protection from those sins to which he is accustomed and which are light in his eyes when he commits them, and over which the evil inclination rules. He is like a sick person who is beginning to recover. Such a person has to be careful of a number of things, so that they will not cause him to be ill again. So, it is with one who is ill by reason of his sins; when he begins to repent, he must be very careful.

The twelfth principle of repentance is that one should search out and know the greatness of the punishment for each of one's sins: for which there is lashing, for which death by sentence of the court, and for which excommunication. And when he knows the magnitude of his sin, he will certainly cause his heart to feel bitterness in confession and will increase his humility.

The thirteenth principle of repentance is to take seriously the transgressions which one has treated lightly. For example, looking at women or speaking over-much with them, or conversing about idle things, or doing nothing, or mentioning the name of God in vain. All these and many more like them are considered trivial by many people and even by great men of the day — they must be regarded as very serious matters. And there are four reasons for this: First, one should never look at the smallness of the sin but at the greatness of Him who warned against it. A parable will illustrate this. A king commanded his two servants, the one to bring him something to drink for he was very thirsty, and the other to do something that he really did not need very much; and he warned each one, on pain of death. Certainly, if either one of them disobeyed his command he would be liable to death, for they hang a man who has stolen one dinar just as they hang one who has stolen a thousand, for each one has transgressed the command of the king. In the same way the Lord has warned us concerning all of the Torah, "Keep all the commandment which I command you this day" (Deut. 27:1). And it is written, "Cursed be he that confirmeth not the words of this law to do them" (Deut. 27:26). The second reason is that when one transgresses a little matter many times, it becames a very severe matter, because the punishments for each individual transgression are combined. Thirdly, when one is accustomed to commit sins, he comes to regard them as permissible and does not guard himself against them, and he is reckoned among those who cast off the yoke of the Torah and who are "apostates with respect to one matter." Fourthly, it is the way of the evil inclination that after he conquers in some small matter, he goes on to conquer in a serious one. Therefore, our Sages said, "Be heedful of a light precept as of a grave one" (Aboth 2:1). And they said further, "For one good deed draws another in its train, and one sin, another sin" (Aboth 4:2).

The fourteenth principle of repentance is the confession, as it is said, "That he shall confess that wherein he hath sinned" (Lev. 5:5). And a person is obliged to remember his sins, and the sins of his fathers. Now why should he confess the sins of his fathers? Because of the fact that he is considered guilty if he clings to the evil deeds of his fathers. And thus, it is written, "And they shall confess their iniquity and the iniquity of their fathers" (Lev. 26:40). And he should be very careful at the time of the confession to resolve in his heart to abandon his evil ways, for if he returns to them and does not abandon them, he is like one who immerses himself but grasps an unclean creature (Ta'anith 16a). For confession is like immersion and the sin is like the unclean worm, and it is clear that immersion is of no use when the person who immerses himself holds on to the source of his defilement.

The fifteenth principle of repentance is prayer. The sinner should pray to the Lord, Blessed be He, and beseech Him to help him in his repentance and open the gates of purity to him.

The sixteenth principle in repentance is the correction of the wrong committed; for example, if he has

ORCHOT TZADIKIM — Chapter Twenty-Six

robbed a man, he should return that which he has taken, and he should do this before the confession in order that his confession may be well received. And if he has robbed a man but has no money with which to pay, then let him pray that God give him the means that will enable him to pay.

The seventeenth principle of repentance is to pursue deeds of kindness and truth, as it is said, "By mercy and truth iniquity is expiated" (Prov. 16:6). But if the sinner does not return to the Lord, Blessed be He, then his sin will not be atoned for by kindly deeds alone, as it is said, "Who regardeth not persons, nor taketh rewards" (Deut. 10:17). And the Sages interpreted this to mean that God will not take the bribe of a good deed in order to forgive the wrongs (see Yalkut Shimoni on Proverbs, item 947). And this verse, "In mercy and truth, iniquity is expiated," applies to those who are truly repentant. For there are transgressions which repentance and the Day of Atonement hold in suspense and which are cleansed by affliction. And behold in such a case the kindness of the sinner will protect him and guard him from troubles and will also save him from death. As it is said, "But righteousness delivereth from death" (Prov. 10:2). And then there is the sin of profaning the Name of God, and in this, repentance and the Day of Atonement and even affliction hold everything in suspense, and only death cleanses a person, as it is said, "Surely this iniquity shall not be expiated by you till ye die" (Is. 22:14). And when a man tries to hold the truth in his hand and strengthens the hands of men of truth and lifts their heads and degrades the men of falsehood and causes them to reach the dust — these are ways of sanctifying the Name of God. And if a man is aroused to possess the quality of truth, then his sin of profanation will be forgiven him at the time of repentance.

The eighteenth principle of repentance is that one's sins should be before one constantly and one should not forget them, as it is said, "For I know my transgressions and my sin is ever before me" (Ps. 51:5).

The nineteenth principle of repentance is the abandonment of the sin when the sin comes again to his hands, and he is in the grip of his desire. And our Sages said, "Who is the truly repentant person whose repentance reaches the very Throne of Glory? He who is tested and emerges innocent in the same circumstance, and in the same place and with the same woman" (Yoma 86b). And the meaning of this statement is: If the temptation to do the sin should come once again to him, and he is in the grip of the evil desire and yet he conquers it because of reverence for the Lord, Blessed be He, this constitutes repentance. And if this temptation did not come to him again in this matter, then let him each day add within his soul reverence of the Lord, Blessed be He. And thus, should he do all his days, and this is even a higher step than repentance.

The twentieth principle of repentance is to cause multitudes to turn away from sin, as much as he is able, as it is said, "Return ye, and turn yourselves from all your transgressions" (Ezek. 18:30). We learn from this that this is one of the principles of true repentance. And it is said, "Thou shall not take vengeance, nor bear any grudge against the children of thy people" (Lev. 19:17). We have learned from this that if he does not rebuke him then he is guilty for the other's sin, and thus said David, "Then will I teach transgressors thy ways; and sinners shall return to thee" (Ps. 51:15).

Twenty-four things impede repentance (see Maimonides, Laws of Repentance, chap. 4, and R. Isaac Alfasi's commentary on Yoma, chap. 8). Four of these are great wrongs and he who does any one of them, the Holy One, Blessed be He, does not provide him the means to do repentance according to the magnitude of his sin. And these are they: He who causes the many to sin, and this includes he who restrains the many from doing a good deed. And he who turns his companion from a good way to an evil way, for example, one who seduces and incites people to abandon the faith of Israel. And he who sees his son falling into bad ways and does not protest, for if he had protested, he would have given up these evil ways; consequently, the father has caused him to sin. Included in this sin is anyone who was in a position to protest to others about their conduct, whether it be to an individual or to many people, and yet he does not protest but leaves them to their stumbling. And he who says, "I will sin and then I will repent." Also in this category is he who says, "I will sin and the Day of Atonement will atone for my sin." For everyone who makes such a calculation will find it very difficult to repent, for he will constantly sin, since he thinks that he will repent, and then the sin becomes light in his eyes.

Of these twenty-four things that impede repentance there are five that lock the paths of repentance before those who do them. And these are: He who separates himself from the congregation when they are doing repentance, saying, "My soul is at peace within me," and he does not share the anguish of the congregation. Therefore, he has no share in the merit which they are acquiring. And he who takes issue with the words of the Sages, for this controversy causes him to separate himself from his fellows and consequently he does not know the paths of repentance. And he mocks at the precepts. For inasmuch as they are despised in his eyes, he will not pursue the commandments to perform them, and if he does not perform the commandments, in what way will he gain merit? And he who despises his teachers, for this confuses and drives a man away from the world — as it did to "that man." And at a time when he is so troubled and confused, he will not find a teacher who will teach him the true way. And he who hates reproof, for this leaves him no path to repentance inasmuch as reproof causes repentance, for when people let a man know his sins and shame him — he will repent. As it is written, "Remember, forget thou not, how thou didst make the Lord thy God wroth in the wilderness... Ye have been rebellious against thy Lord" (Deut. 9:7); "But the Lord hath not given you a heart to know" (Deut. 29:3); "O foolish people and unwise" (Deut. 32:6). And thus, did the Prophet Isaiah rebuke Israel. And similarly did all the Prophets rebuke Israel, until they turned to repentance. Therefore, every congregation ought to appoint one of its wise men — an older man, one who has revered God from his youth and is beloved by the people — to rebuke the multitude and cause them to repent. He who hates

ORCHOT TZADIKIM — Chapter Twenty-Six

rebukes will not come to the reprover and will not hear his words and therefore, he will remain with his sins for they will appear good in his eyes.

And of the twenty-four things that impede repentance there are five that make it impossible for him who does them to repent completely, because they are wrongs between man and his fellow man in which the one who was wronged does not know that the sinner has sinned against him and must Therefore, seek forgiveness of him. And these are the cases: he who curses the many and has not cursed one particular man from whom he can seek forgiveness. And he who divides up booty with a thief, telling himself that this is not theft, because " I didn't steal." And even if this man should wish to repent and restore the stolen goods, to whom would he restore them? For he does not know from whom the thief has stolen. Moreover, he strengthens the hands of the thief and causes him to sin further. And he who finds a lost article and does not proclaim the fact in order to return it to its master. And should the finder want to do repentance he does know to whom the object belongs. And he who eats the OX of the poor and the food of orphans and widows. Such people are unfortunate; they are not well-known and they wander from city to city. And when a person eats what belongs to them, he does not know whose food he has taken so that he can return it to him. And there are those who say that instead of "AX" the word should be read "ROB" meaning "robbery" or "oppression." This would then refer to one who presses the poor for the debt they owe him until they decide to turn over to him their land, or their personal property for less than their value, and this man does not sense that there is a great sin in this, for he says, "I am only taking what belongs to me!" And he who accepts a bribe to prevent justice, and he does not know to what extent he has perverted justice and how much influence he exerted so that he should be able to restore the matter to the state where it was before he perverted justice. Moreover, he reinforces the hands of the one for whose sake he perverted justice so as to cause him to sin in this matter.

And of these twenty-four things which impede repentance, five have to do with one who has no inclination to repent, because they are things that are unimportant in the eyes of most people. Consequently, the person sins but it appears to him as though he had not sinned. And these are the things: He who eats of a meal that does not suffice for its owners. For example, a man enters the house of a poor man, and the poor man prepares very much food for his guest, not out of the willingness of his heart but because he is ashamed to invite his guest to partake of little. And the visitor does not think that he has sinned in this, because he thinks that he is eating with the permission of the master of the house, and not against his real will. And he who uses an object which has been given to him in pledge by a poor man, even if it is only an axe or a plow, and he says in his heart, "I did not take anything away from them; I did not rob." And he who looks upon indecent acts, for the one who gazes thinks in his heart that there is nothing evil in this, saying "Did I participate in this act, or did I draw near to it?" And he does not know that even looking at lewdness with the eye is a great sin, for it leads a person to violate the laws of chastity, as it is said, "That ye go not about after your own heart and your own eyes" (Num. 15:39). And he who obtains honor through the shame of his companion. He says in his heart that he has not sinned because his companion is not in his presence, and therefore, the shameful deed really did not affect his companion and that he did not in fact shame him, but that he has merely evaluated his own good deeds, his wisdom, and his keenness higher than the deeds, the wisdom and the keenness of his companion. But in the eyes of the one who hears his words, he will be the honored one, and his companion the shamed one. And he who suspects the innocent. He says in his heart that that is no sin, for he says, "What did I do to him? I did not do anything to him; it was just a mere suspicion." He does not know that this is a great sin, to picture an innocent person in his own mind as though he were a sinful man.

And of these twenty-four things that impede repentance, five of them are such that he who does them is constantly drawn after them and finds it very difficult to separate himself from them. Therefore, a man must be very careful of these, lest he cleave to them, and they are all very evil states of mind. And these are: tale-bearing, gossip, wrath, evil thoughts, and associating with a wicked man, for he will surely learn from his deeds. For when one is always with the wicked and sees these deeds, they become impressed in his heart, as Solomon said, "But the companion of fools shall smart for it" (Prov. 12:20).

All these things and similar ones, impede repentance, but they do not preclude it altogether, and if a man has truly repented of these things, then he is a penitent and has a share in the world to come.

Sins are of two kinds. There are those that are between man and God alone, Blessed be He, such as Tefillin, Fringes, the Sukkah and similar commandments. And there are sins between one man and another. As to the sins between man and God, Blessed be He, a man should do repentance in that very same matter in which he has transgressed. For example, if he has not fulfilled a particular positive precept, he should try to fulfill it. And if he has not been in the habit of giving charity, he should make a point from the time of his repentance and thereafter to give charity. And if he has transgressed the prohibitive commandments, then he should set his heart not to transgress any further.

The general rule is that he who wants to be a truly repentant person must wage a great war in his heart, and the matter is not like what most people think, that a person is not a penitent unless he has committed certain serious sins. For example, one who has had intercourse with a gentile woman, or who has committed adultery, or who has stolen, or the like. But this is not so. For there are many robbers who do not know that they are robbers. For example, if a man files suit against another, although he knows that he does not owe him anything, but he wants to provoke him and distress him and cause him loss by making him waste money in his defense. Now, the man who files this suit does not realize that this is robbery. Or there is the man who causes another to take an oath, even though he does so by right, there is guilt in this. Yet people do things like this every day, every hour

— heaps of sins like this. How is that? A man is obligated to pray with firm intent and say all the benedictions with firm intent, but there are very few in this world who do pray with all their heart. And the same is true with regard to all the commandments: there are points that even the great ones of our generation do not observe scrupulously, because they do not put their minds to it, and because they do not study the commandments and the good qualities. Therefore, he who has offered his heart in his desire to do true repentance should accustom himself to meditate in this book of the "Paths of the Righteous," and in it he will see his error and in just what manner he has erred all of his days. And he should consider every single thing that he reads and ask himself whether he has fulfilled it or not. And if he sees that he has not fulfilled it, he should strive with all his might to fulfill it. And he should also accustom himself to study the Book of the Commandments, to meditate in it and to understand every commandment properly. And he should set his heart on every precept, to fulfill it as it is explained. And this is the important highway of all the paths of repentance: to do repentance for each individual matter independently.

There are sins between a man and his fellow man that are very difficult to correct and to do repentance for, e.g., a man who has been accustomed to rob all of his days and he does not know from whom he has robbed or where his victim lives, or perhaps his victim has gone to some distant country, or perhaps the money that he should return has been lost. And there is the type of person that is so used to sins all of his life that it has become a habit with him and he is very thoroughly versed in wrongdoing, as Jeremiah said, "They have taught their tongue to speak lies, they weary themselves to commit iniquity" (Jer. 9:4).

And there is the case of a man who had intercourse with a woman who is prohibited to him and begot a son by her — this shame cannot be removed. And there is one who is accustomed to lie and to speak ill of people. And there is the one who has seduced people and misled them into doing a forbidden thing. And there is the man who sees people walking in an evil path, they having strayed from the righteous path, and he is afraid to rebuke them, or he was ashamed of them and refrained from teaching them the proper path. Of him the Scripture says, "The same wicked man shall die in his iniquity, but his blood will I require at thy hand" (Ezek. 3:18).

In all of these things and in similar cases, repentance is very difficult, but there is a great remedy which can correct everything. At first the sinner must repent in all the ways of repentance, and he must see and understand all aspects of repentance, and he must devote his soul to do this, and he must do all of this for the sake of Heaven with all his strength and with all his heart, privately and in public. And then the Holy One, Blessed be He, will make easier for him the methods of repentance and will guide him along the righteous path to repentance. For example, if he begot a son by a woman prohibited to him, the Holy One, Blessed be He, will give no perpetuity to this seed and the matter will be forgotten as though it had not been.

And if he has robbed money, the Holy One, Blessed

be He, will see to it that he gets money with which to repay his victim, and the victim will accept restitution and forgive him. And if he has done evil to another man, either to his person or to his property, the Creator, Blessed be He, will cause to enter into the heart of the victim a desire and love (so that he will forgive him). As Solomon said, "When a man's ways please the Lord, He maketh his enemies to be at peace with him" (Prov. 16:7). And if the person he has robbed is far from him, the Holy One, Blessed be He, will bring him near to him until he is placated and forgives the robber. And if the sinner does not know how much money he has stolen and does not know whom he has robbed, then the Holy One, Blessed be He, will enable him to perform some public service, for example, building a bridge, or fixing wells, or building synagogues, or other things that the people need. And thus, there will be benefit from his act to everyone; to the one whom he robbed, and also to others. And if the victim of the robbery should die, the robber must return the money to the heirs. If he has injured him physically, or slandered him, he must go to his grave in the company of ten men and ask forgiveness from God, Blessed be He, and from the dead man, and the Holy One, Blessed be He, will forgive him.

And our Sages, of blessed memory, said that repentance is not denied to the sinner unless his heart remains evil. But as for him who wants to draw nearer to God, God does not close the gates of repentance before him, but he opens the gates of repentance for him and teaches him the righteous path, as it is said, "Good and upright is the Lord, Therefore, doth He

ORCHOT TZADIKIM — Chapter Twenty-Six

instruct sinners in the way" (Ps. 25:8). And further, "But from thence ye will seek the Lord thy God; and thou shalt find Him, if thou search after Him with all thy heart and with all thy soul" (Deut. 4:29). And further, "But the word is very nigh unto thee in thy mouth, and in thy heart, that thou mayest do it" (Deut. 30:14). And further, "The Lord is nigh unto all those that call upon Him, to all who call upon Him in truth" (Ps. 145:18).

It was a great kindness that the Holy One, Blessed be He, did for mankind when he established a way for wrong-doers and sinners to flee from darkness to light, and did not close the doors of repentance to them, even if they had sinned greatly, as it is said, "Return, ye backsliding children, I will heal your backslidings" (Jer. 3:22). And repentance is accepted by God even if the sinner repents because of his great misfortunes; all the more so if he repents because of reverence and love of God. As it is said, "In thy distress, when all these things are come upon thee, in the end of days thou will return to the Lord thy God; and hearken unto His voice" (Deut. 4:30). And the Holy One, Blessed be He, helps penitents to repent even in matters which the strength of a man cannot attain, and he renews within them a pure spirit so that they may achieve the elements of repentance. As it is said, "And shalt return unto the Lord thy God, and hearken to His voice according to all that I command thee this day, thou and thy children, with all thy heart, and with all thy soul" (Deut. 30:2). And further, at the end of that passage, "And the Lord will circumcise thy heart, and the heart of thy seed, to love the Lord thy God with all thy heart" (Deut. 30:6). What this means is that in that thing which is not within your power to attain, the Holy One, Blessed be He, will circumcise your heart and give you the strength to do it.

There are four motivations in the matter of repentance.

The first is when a man repents because he has come to recognize his God. And he is like a servant who flees from his master, but when he thinks of the good which his master has done to him, he returns to him of his own free will to seek forgiveness from him, and of such as him the Scripture says, "If thou wilt return, O Israel, saith the Lord, yea return unto Me" (Jer. 4:1). And further, "Return unto Me, and I will return unto you" (Malachi 3:7).

The second motivation is when a man repents because people rebuke and shame him until he repents. And he is like a servant who has fled from his master, and a faithful servant of his master meets him and rebukes him and puts him to shame for having fled, and advises him to return, and assures him that his master will forgive him. And then the man returns and is submissive.

The third motivation is when a man sees the punishments that the Creator, Blessed be He, inflicts upon him who departs from His ways. Then he repents and returns to the Lord out of fear of his punishment. And he is like a servant who flees from his master and when he hears about the severe punishments that his master meted out to one who had run away, he returns to him.

The fourth motivation is when punishment and afflictions come upon him and he repents. And he is like a servant who has fled, and bandits came upon him and captured him, and inflicted pain upon him because of his escape, and then he returns.

He who is wise will be motivated in his repentance by the first factor, and he will return to God out of love for His Greatness.

Six things may stir the heart of a man to repent.

The first: when afflictions come upon a man, he considers this in his heart and says that this has happened because of his sins and his evil ways. And then he will return to God, and He will have mercy upon him, as it is said, "And many evils and troubles shall come upon them, so that they will say in that day: 'Are not these evils come upon us because our God is not among us?' " (Deut. 31:17). Now this type of repentance, is received by God but not by human beings. For when a man sins against another man, in time of trouble he has remorse and is submissive to him because he needs his help, this remorse is considered worthless in the eyes of the person offended. As Jephthah said, "And why are ye come unto me now when ye are in distress?" (Judges 11:7). But it is one of the great kindnesses of God that He accepts repentance even though it comes from trouble, and He is placated, as it is said, "Return O Israel, unto the Lord thy God; for thou hast stumbled in thine iniquity" (Hos. 14:2). And it is written, "For whom the Lord loveth he correcteth, even as a father the son in whom he delighteth" (Prov. 3:12).

And if a man does not repent in the time of his trouble, his punishment will be doubled. It is just as in the case of a king of flesh and blood: if a man has sinned against him, and the king punishes him, and the man does not want to receive his punishment, the king will continue to punish him and will increase the weight of his yoke. And such is the character of the Holy One, Blessed be He, as it is written, "And if, for all that, you do not obey Me, I will go on to discipline you" (Lev. 26:18). And if he does not understand that the evils which come upon him are because of his sins, but he says, "It was chance that happened to us" (see I Samuel 6:9), there will be great wrath against this man, for he does not believe that because of his sins the troubles came upon him. Therefore, you must know, and you must intelligently consider, that when God punishes a man, it is for the man's good, to favor him with two benefits: one, to atone for his sins, as it is said, "See mine affliction and my travail; and forgive all my sins" (Ps. 25:18); and the second, to rebuke him, and to cause him to return from his evil ways, as it is said, "Surely thou wilt fear Me, thou wilt receive correction" (Zeph. 3:7). And if a man does not repent because of his troubles, then woe to him who has borne troubles and has not yet atoned for his sins! And even then, his punishment will be doubled, because he does not believe that it is because of his sins that he was punished.

It is important for one who has trust in the Lord, Blessed be He, to know that the afflictions are for his own good, and in the end, it will be well with him. As it is said, "Rejoice not against me, O mine enemy; though I am fallen, I shall arise; though I sit in darkness, the Lord is a light unto me" (Micah 7:8). And our Sages, of blessed memory, said, "If I had not fallen, I would not have arisen! And, if I had not sat in the darkness, I would not have seen the light!"

(Shohar Tov 22:7). Therefore, , any man who has troubles in his body, or with his money, or with his children, should set his heart to fast in addition to doing repentance, just as the community is obligated to fast in the time of their trouble, and as our Sages have decreed (Ta'anith 10a, 12b). Therefore, , in time of trouble, a man should examine his deeds. If he has searched and has found no transgression, he should know that his afflictions have been prompted by God's love (Berakhoth 5a).

The second thing that can stir the heart to repentance is when old age comes upon a person and he sees the weakening of his strength, then he understands what must ultimately be his fate, and he will remember his end, and he will return to God, and He will have mercy upon him. And he who does not return in repentance at the time of old age, his punishment will be double, as our Sages, of blessed memory, said, "There are four kinds of men that the mind of man cannot bear, and these are they: A poor man who is arrogant, a rich man who deceives, an old man who is lecherous, and a community leader who lords it over the congregation without reason" (Pesahim 113b). And when a man sees that his days are passing, and that his constitution is growing weaker, and that this is the beginning of the journey that he is taking to his Eternal Home, and that he is travelling day and night, it would be a matter of great astonishment if such person did not set his heart upon preparing provisions for his great and distant path. This only happens if he has little faith.

And there are people who never see the light of repentance because they are innocent and pure in their own eyes, and they sin exceedingly to God, Blessed be He. And they are like a sick person who does not feel his illness and because he does not feel his illness he does not think about a remedy; so is the man who does not feel his sins, and does not consider his end, and therefore, he does not hasten to correct his affairs. And there are people whose every desire, and every thought and every deed are centered upon matters concerning their bodies, and they occupy themselves all day with the vanities of the world, and they do not devote even a portion of their day to Torah, and to reverence of the Lord, Blessed be He. How have they sunk to the very lowest state! Therefore, , he who in his youth has walked in the hardness of his heart should in his old age set his heart to driving out from within him the affairs of this world, and he should arrange to be alone and to mediate on the reverence of the Lord, and he should seek to study the Torah and to perform good deeds.

The third thing that can stir the heart to repentance is when he hears the chastisement of the wise and of those who reprove him, and this arouses his heart to repent, and he receives upon himself all the words of these rebukes. From the time that he accepts them, this man earns great merit, and in a short space of time he has gone forth from darkness to light, and he has gained reward and merit for all of the commandments and all of the chastisements, inasmuch as he has resolved to receive them upon himself. And happy is he who receives this upon himself, for he has won merit in a brief moment. And thus, did our Sages, of blessed memory, say "And the children of Israel went and did." Now had they already done this (i.e., prepared the Passover)? Surely, they did not do so until the fourteenth day of the month! But when they took it upon themselves to do it, Scripture ascribes it to them as though they had already done it" (Mechilta on Exodus 12:28). And thus, did our Sages say, "All whose deeds are greater than his wisdom, his wisdom will endure" (Aboth 3:12). As it is said, "We will do and we will hear!" (Ex. 24:7).

The meaning of the matter is that a man who has taken upon himself, with a faithful heart, to keep and do all the words of the Torah and to do as the Sages will tell him, and then, after having undertaken this obligation to fulfill everything, he seeks and searches and asks the Sages what to do, then he receives a reward even for those commandments and instructions that he does not know, inasmuch as he has received them upon himself and resolved in his heart to do them, just as Israel said at Mount Sinai, "We will do and we will hear!" They put the "doing" before the word "hearing" (Shabbath 88a). Not always, however, is it true that a man's deeds should be greater than his wisdom. But (returning to this matter) it is said about Daniel, that greatly beloved man, "Then said he unto me: 'Fear not, Daniel, for from the first day that thou didst set thy heart to understand and to humble thyself before thy God thy words were heard' " (Dan. 10:12). Consequently, when a man sets his heart upon doing good, then his resolve is at once willingly received by God, Blessed be He. But he who does not arouse himself to repent after he is rebuked will find his punishment doubled. The fourth means to stir up repentance is when a man meditates on the commandments of God, and he reads the Prophets and the Scriptures, and the words of the Sages of the Talmud, and he sees the warnings and the punishments, and he understands the pleasant chastisement, then he arouses himself in his heart and he thinks, "How can I read the contents of the Torah as though they were merely a parable? No. I will instead set my heart on the words of the Torah, to keep them and to do them, in every particular as I read them," as it is written concerning Josiah, "And it came to pass, when the king had heard the words of the book of the Law, that he rent his clothes" (II Kings 22:11). And concerning Ezra it is said, "For all thy people wept, when they heard the words of the Law" (Neh. 8:9). And the man who does not set his heart on the words of God, Blessed be He, this too will be added to his wrongs. As it is said, "Yet they were not afraid, nor rent their garments" (Jer. 36:24). And our Sages, of blessed memory, said, "He who studies but does not fulfill (the commandments), it would have been better for him to have died at birth (T.P. Berakoth 1:5). And it is said, "Though I write for him ever so many things of My Law, they are accounted as a stranger's" (Hos. 8:12). And it is said, "How do ye say: 'We are wise, and the Law of the Lord is with us?' Lo, certainly in vain hath wrought the vain pen of the scribes" (Jer. 8:8).

The fifth way in which repentance can be aroused is when the Ten Days of Repentance draw near, then every man should arouse his heart and tremble as he goes to meet the Day of Judgment, for he should ponder that all of his deeds are written in a book, and that at this time God will bring to judgment every deed and every hidden thing, whether it be good or bad. For a man is judged on Rosh Hashanah, and his decree is sealed on the Day of Atonement (Rosh Hashana 16a). Now, if a man were to be brought for judgment before a king of flesh and blood would he not tremble with a great trembling, and would he not take counsel with his soul? And it would not occur to him to do any other thing, than to find some merit that might save him from that judgment. Therefore, how foolish and stupid are those who do not know what their judgment will be, and yet they occupy themselves with idle things other than the repentance that would find favor before the Great Judge!

Therefore, , it is proper that everyone who reveres God should lessen his usual occupations and let his thoughts be calm, and let him fix hours, during the day and a night, when he can sit alone in his rooms and examine his ways and search them out, and arise even before the watches of the morning to occupy himself with the paths of repentance. And let him not do as in most cases where people fast, or rise early to pray, but they do not actually wage war against the sins in order to remove from themselves every ugly thing. For if a man prays and fasts, and confesses, and still clings to his former ways — this is not the path of repentance. But a man should arouse himself to do complete repentance during the Ten Days of Repentance, for this is a time when God accepts his plea and his prayer is heard, as it is said, "In an acceptable time have I answered thee, and in a day of salvation have I helped thee" (Is. 49:8). And our Sages, of blessed memory, said, "Seek the Lord while He may be found" (Is. 55:6) — these are the ten days that are between Rosh Hashana and Yom Kippur

ORCHOT TZADIKIM — Chapter Twenty-Six

(Rosh Hashana 18a). And they also said that the Day of Atonement, together with repentance, atones. Therefore, Scripture has warned us that we should repent and make ourselves pure before God, Blessed be He, in our ways of repentance. As it is said, "From all your sins shall ye be clean before the Lord" (Lev. 16:30). And then he will atone for us with this day, to purify us (Yoma 85b).

The sixth means of arousing the heart to repentance is this, for a man should always regard himself as though he were about to die. And he should not say, "When I grow old, I will repent," lest he die before he grows old. Thus, at all times he must be prepared to meet his God, for no man knows when his time will come. Therefore, , he should arouse his soul to be pure, to return his spirit in purity to God who gave it within him. And he should examine his deeds at every moment, in accordance with the saying of Rabbi Eliezer, "Repent one day before your death" (Shabbath 153a and Eccl. Rabbah 9:8, letter 6). His pupils said to him, "Oh, our teacher, does a man know on what day he will die?" And he said to them, "All the more so! Let him return today, lest he die tomorrow, and if he does so, then all of his days will be spent in repentance, and let him adorn himself at every hour, as though at this very moment he will come before the Great King" (See Eccl. Rabbah, ad. loc.).

Therefore, a man should always worry, even when he is secure and at ease, and he should tremble on account of the day of death, for then he will have to render an account. And he should confess at all times, with a broken and a contrite heart, as though he were now about to die, and the fear of Heaven should be upon him. And a man should renew another precept each day, for perhaps the time of his death has come, and if he does so, he will not be lacking even one of all the commandments. For our Sages said, "Everyone who fulfills one commandment near the time of his death, it is as though he fulfilled the whole Torah" (Eccl. Rabbah 3:18, letter 24). Therefore, should a man awaken from his deep slumber and arouse himself to understand his final end, to adorn himself with the ornaments of the precepts and to be before God at every moment.

There are four kinds of repentance: repentance by conquering a temptation that comes towards him; repentance by building of a fence between himself and temptation; repentance by the weighing of values, and repentance by following what is written.

Repentance by conquering a temptation that comes towards him — what is meant by this? If he sinned with a woman, or through the commission of a theft, and this woman comes, or that opportunity to steal comes once again to his hand, and he might have sinned like the previous time, for he is still in the strength of his lust and in the full eagerness of his desire, and his heart burns after her, and she is willing, but he withholds his spirit from committing the sin, and tears away his lust because of his reverence for God alone — this is a complete repentance.

What do we mean by repentance in which one builds a fence between himself and his temptation? A man should not look at the laughing amusements of matrons and virgins and he should not look directly in the face of a woman or between her breasts, and not even at his own wife before she has immersed herself after the period of prohibition. And thus, should he make a fence around all the commandments. And our teacher, Abraham ben David, of blessed memory, wrote: "And we have seen in connection with our Sages that they were completely pious men and they used to build many fences to protect themselves from temptation. And there was among them even one who separated himself from his wife after he had fulfilled the commandment of "Be fruitful and multiply!" And each of them would fence himself off from temptation according to the manner of man he knew himself to be. For there is a man who has a lust to commit one sin but not another. For example, one may have a desire to commit fornication but not to steal, and another may have the lust to steal but not to commit the sin of fornication. Therefore, every one must make fences according to what he sees in himself, against those temptations wherein his evil inclination is gaining strength. If his mind is drawn to theft, let him refrain from receiving pledges in trust or from managing the property of others. And thus, must one make fences for everything wherein he is tempted. And thus, our Sages said concerning Abraham, that his desire made peace with him (Gen. Rabbah 54a). And concerning this it is said, "When a man's ways please the Lord, He maketh even his enemies to be at peace with him" (Prov. 16:7). And King David waged war against his desire, and when he saw that his desire was not mild and his nature gentle, and when he realized that he could not overcome it, he stood up and slew it, as it is said, "And my heart is wounded within me" (Ps. 109:22). And the meaning of it is that Abraham had a desire that was gentle, and his nature was easy and pleasant, and it was not necessary for him to wage war against it. As they said (Nedarim 32b): At first, the Holy One, Blessed be He, caused Abraham to rule over two hundred and forty-three limbs. But later God caused him to rule over two hundred and forty-eight limbs, by giving him dominion over his two eyes, his two ears, and his membrum (i.e., because of his willingness to undergo circumcision, he achieved complete control over any sex impluse). But as for David, his desire was always hard and strong, and he had to wage war against it every day, and when he saw that he could not withstand it, he arose up against his evil desire and slew it. There are those who say that David slew his desire by fasting, and there are those who say he kept away from women altogether, for he feared lest that which was permitted might seduce him into doing something that was forbidden. Whichever version is correct (they both agree that) after David saw that his desire was gaining mastery over him, he set himself to make it yield, to fight against it, until he succeeded in subduing it.

The best fence with which to subdue the evil inclination is to learn to bear physical hunger — that is, to lessen the pleasures and the delights of eating and drinking, but not to refrain from enjoying the pleasure of aromatic odors and from washing with warm water for he gets pleasure from its warmth. And the little food that he eats should be well seasoned and well prepared so that it will be pleasing to him and so that his soul will accept it and be appeased with a little of it. And a man should always take a little less food than he needs and that would satisfy his desire. And he should not drink wine unless it is diluted, in order that he should not become drunk. And concerning this, our Sages, of blessed memory, said, "Do not indulge too freely in a meal which you enjoy" (Gittin 70a). There are two advantages in this. First, his eating will have no harmful effects. And, secondly, there is the subduing of the evil inclination and the breaking of lust.

And just as I have explained concerning the meal, so should this be the way of treating all the pleasures and delights of the world: a man should never satisfy his desire completely. And, needless to say, a man should guard himself against foods that he knows are harmful to him, for a man who eats things that harm him, even though he can get other food, commits a crime against his own body, because he goes after his lust and does not care about the loss of his body. And this is the way of the evil inclination and its counsel: it seduces him from the way of life, to the way of death.

Every living being should know that there is no way that the evil inclination can triumph except through seduction. At first, it seduces him to do what is permitted in order to satisfy his desire, and after he has become accustomed to satisfying his desire with what is permitted and has accustomed his soul always to hunger after the satisfaction of his desire, then the evil inclination seduces him to violate a minor prohibition. And then from the minor prohibition to the major. Therefore, be very careful in what is

ORCHOT TZADIKIM — Chapter Twenty-Six

permitted, to erect a fence which will lessen the desire even for what is permitted. And then if it should come to your mind to partake of what is forbidden, you yourself will apply Kal va-homer (an inference "from minor to major"), i.e., if you refrain even from what is permitted, you will surely put out of your mind any thought of violating a clear prohibition, not to mention committing the deed itself.

A person should not make a practice of fasting, lest his heart grow weak and his mind become befuddled, and his loss will be greater than his gain, for he will neglect the study of the Torah on account of his weakness. And even when he does study the Torah, he will not be able to distinguish every point as clearly as he should or to understand the matters fully, because the Torah can be acquired only in a spirit of joy.

Nor should a man hold himself back from any joy arising out of the performance of a percept of the Torah, so that his eyes may be open against (desires stimulated by) the evil inclination. And he should always be on guard not to satisfy all of his desire. And if his heart grows weak because of the small amount of food he eats, it is better that he eats a little bit twice a day and not fill his stomach at one time. And if he does not have an opportunity to eat twice, he should keep at hand some jam that makes the heart rejoice, and eat a little of that, and his heart will be strengthened. Also, if he sees clearly that he must fast one or two days of the week, let him fast according to the requirement of such a fast, for he who sits fasting when he needs it is called "holy," provided however, that he does not neglect the Torah and the commandments on this account.

Every man is in a position to know for himself, just what kind of a fence he should build, in accordance with his own requirement. But the best of all fences is that he should guard his eyes from longing for what does not belong to him. And if he lessens his eyeing of things that are not his, he will be called modest, and bashful. As was said concerning the woman who had one arm amputated and yet her husband was not aware of this until the day of her death. And they said of him, "How modest is this man that he was not aware of this in his wife!" (Shabbath 53b). And if he guards his eyes, his heart will also be well-guarded. And since his eyes and his heart are well-guarded, he will be well-guarded through and through.

Repentance through the weighing of values — what is meant by that? This means that he should suffer pain in proportion to the pleasure that he derived from the sin. He should afflict himself by fasting and by the lessening of food and drink, and in cohabitation and in all manner of pleasures, he should reduce the amount.

Repentance by following what is written — what is meant by that? If he had intercourse with his wife during her unclean period, for which transgression the penalty is that he be cut off from his people, or if he committed any of the sins for which he must be sentenced to death by a court of law, or to be lashed, let him accept it upon himself to suffer pain and let him inflict pain upon himself, as it is written in the Torah. Now, the Rokeah Eleazar of Worms (died 1238). has written how one may inflict pain upon himself for various sins. And we also find in the Talmud that they were accustomed to fast even for a very minor sin, even for mere talk. As in the case of the Sage who said, "I am ashamed of your words, oh House of Shammai." And because of this remark he sat fasting until his teeth became black (Hagigah 22b). And there is also a story concerning Rabbi Hisda who said to Rabbi Huna on the question of respect due to another, "What of a disciple whom his teacher needs (because the disciple possesses traditions received from other scholars and which the teacher does not know), does this disciple have to stand in honor of the teacher?" Rabbi Huna retorted to Rabbi Hisda, "I do not need you." And for this apparent slight each one sat fasting many times (Baba Mezi'a 33a). And so have we found, concerning David, that the Divine Presence and the Holy Spirit departed from him for twenty-two years and every day he would shed tears and eat his morsel of food dipped in ashes. As it is said (Ps. 102:10), "For I have eaten ashes like bread, and mingled my drink with weeping." David said to God, "Master of the Universe, receive me as completely repentant before Thee, in order that I may purify the wicked in the world, as it is said (Ps. 51:15), "Then will I teach transgressors Thy ways, and sinners shall return unto Thee" (Tana Debé Eliahu, chap. 2).

Every man can learn from David in the matter of repentance. And so do we find with Adam. When Adam saw that the world was punished with death because of his deed he sat fasting one hundred and thirty years, and separated himself from his wife and covered his body with garlands of figs (to remind him constantly of his sin in eating the fruit of the forbidden tree) (Erubin 18b).

If a man has repented and then returned to his former wrongdoing, even if he has repeated this many times, he can nevertheless still repent. But it is necessary to make repentance more severe the second and third time than it was the first time. We have learned in the Jerusalem Talmud: he who has been wicked all his days and has repented, the Holy One, Blessed be He, receives him. Rabbi Johanan said, "Not only this, but all his transgressions, now that he has overcome them, are considered as merit" (T.P. Peah 1:1). And in the chapter (of the Babylonian Talmud) entitled, "Yom Kippur Atones" we read (Yoma 86b) that if he repented out of love of God, the intentional sins that he committed become merit; if he repented out of fear of God, then his intentional sins become as sins committed unknowingly. And as for all those that have no portion in the world to come and are condemned to Gehenna for generations — they are the ones who died in their wickedness. But if they repented, nothing can stand in the face of repentance. And a man should not think, "Since I sinned and caused others to sin, I cannot repent," for he thereby weakens his hand from doing repentance. God forbid that he should do this, for the Sages said in the chapter entitled, "A share in the World to Come" (Sanh. 102a), even Jeroboam who sinnned and caused others to sin — even to him the Holy One, Blessed be He, said, "Now you must repent." And he did not want to (Pirke de-Rabbi Eliezer, chap. 43; Menorat Hamaor, item 254; and see T.P. Sanh. 10:2).

Go forth and learn from the example of Ahab, king of

Israel, who robbed and coveted and murdered. And he called for Jehoshaphat, the king of Judea who lashed him three times each day. And Ahab would pray and fast early and late before the Holy One, Blessed be He, and he never returned to his past evil deeds, and his repentance was accepted as it is said, "Seest thou how Ahab humbleth himself before Me? Because he humbleth himself before Me I will not bring the evil in his days" (I Kings 21:29).

And they said in the Pesikta (of Rab Chana, Piska Deshuva Cant. Rabbah 1:5, letter 36. Yerushalmi ibid. And see Ta'anith 28b and Rashi ad. loc.) : If he was accustomed to eating after three hours let him eat after six, and if he used to eat after six hours let him eat after nine. And what is meant by, "And went softly" (I Kings 21:27)? Rabbi Joshua, the son of Levi, said that he walked barefoot, and from him (Ahab) every man should learn. Moreover (Pirke de-Rabbi Eliezer, chap. 43), go forth and learn from Manasseh, the son of Hezekiah, who did all the evil abominations in the world, yet the Holy One, Blessed be He, received him when he repented. Moreover (Sanh. 103a), Rabbi Johanan said, "Anyone who says that Manasseh has no share in the world to come weakens the hands of those who would repent. As a Tanna taught before Rabbi Johanan," Manasseh repented for thirty-three years and the Holy One, Blessed be He, received him.

And now in these generations, when men are physically very weak and they have not the strength of the earlier generations, what should man do who has sinned all his days through gossip, flattery, and all other bad qualities, and he was not careful all his life about the precepts themselves for he never saw a man fulfill the commandments so that he might learn from him. And he did not hasten all his days to pray or say the benedictions, and so he did with all the commandments — how such a one can bear the pain according to his transgressions, for there is no reckoning the multitude of sins which are committed by a man who is not careful about his deeds.

Therefore, it is important to make a path before the people who are eager to repent. And there is a difference between people. How so? If the one who sinned is well-versed in the Torah and if the anguish and the fasting are too difficult for him, he will not be able to correct his evil qualities, and so it is best to lighten the burden of the various pains and fasting that have been laid upon him, and he should be instructed to occupy himself with great effort in the study of Torah. And thus, did they say (Lev. Rabbah 25:1): "If a man went astray and sinned and is deserving of death at the hands of Heaven, what can he do and live? If he was accustomed to read one page in the Talmud let him read two, if he was accustomed to study one chapter of the Mishnah let him study two, since there is atonement in much study. And let this man do kindness and truth, and through these means his sins will be atoned for, as it is said, "By mercy and truth, iniquity is expiated" (Prov. 16:6). And he should exert himself to perform every single precept as it is set forth, and he should trouble himself to cause the many to have merit, to do kind deeds to people, to pray with serious intent and with submission to God and with a rending of the heart, and he should ask forgiveness from the Lord for all his sins. And he should avoid frivolous laughter and aimless strolling about and idle things, and from hearing "the latest news." Similarly, he should avoid all the things that are only for this world, and he should set a definite plan of what he can do and what he can bear in the way of repentance together with his occupying himself with Torah and the commandments. And he must always try to be submissive to God, and he should fast at least one day a week and on that day, he should free himself of everything in the world and sit by himself and arrange thoughts in his heart towards God — to cleave to Him and to be sad of spirit because he has raised himself in rebellion against the Great King. And he should weep and mourn with broken heart and multiply pleadings and multiply praises of God and should receive a lashing three times on that day and when they lash him, he should say, "But he, being full of compassion forgiveth iniquity and destroyeth not; yea, many a time doth He turn His anger away" (Ps. 78:38). And so, must he say three times at every lashing and so should he continue to do until he finds favor before the King, Most High.

And if the sinner who comes to do penance is a man who cannot study, or is burdened with a large family, or is an ignorant man, or he is learned but cannot constrain himself to follow everything in this book — all such as these must increase their ability to bear difficult afflictions. And these afflictions are not the same for every man, for one man is very healthy and another is weak. When there was a court of law in Jerusalem in the Chamber of Hewn Stone and when they sat in judgment in capital cases or those punishable by lashing; they would, in the case of lashing, estimate the number of lashes the condemned man should receive according to his strength to endure it. And so, we should do now: everything according to the condition of the man. There is a man who, if we make his pain too severe, will abandon the matter altogether and will not do penance. Therefore, the wise man should search out the condition of the man and decide as he sees fit.

And now we must write down the details of how one should afflict oneself to atone for particular transgressions. A man who had intercourse with a gentile woman should fast and be lashed, and he should not eat meat or drink wine for at least forty days, or he should fast three days, night and day, in three successive years. And, if after the repentance, he returns to his evil conduct, he must place a heavier burden upon himself. In the summer, he should go to a place where there are many ants, and he should sit among them naked, and in the winter, he should break the ice on top of the water and sit in the water up to his nose, and if he reverts to his evil ways, then he should make the anguish more and more severe.

He who pours out his seed for nothing (i.e. masturbates), should fast for forty days, though they need not be consecutive and he should sit in water in the days of winter for as long as it takes to roast an egg and swallow it, all those forty days, and he should not eat meat and should not drink wine or any warm thing, except on Sabbaths and festivals, and he should wash his head a little with water two or three times during all those forty days.

If he embraced or kissed his wife during her unclean

period, he should fast forty days, and if he had marital relations with his wife during the time of her separation, he should fast for forty consecutive days and should receive a lashing each day, and should not eat meat or drink wine, nor eat any warm food, except on Sabbaths and festivals, and he should not wash himself all those days, and he must confess his sin every day. One who has kissed or embraced a woman other than his wife should fast each Monday and Thursday, and should keep away from the doorway of her house. One who has copulated with an animal or a bird should fast and not wash himself for forty days, and should not look at an animal or a bird when it is in heat.

A murderer should wander in exile for three years, and he should be lashed in every city, and he should say, "I am a murderer," and he should not eat meat and he should not drink wine and he should shave the hair of his head and his beard only once a month. And he should bind the hand with which he committed the murder to his upper arm and neck (in the fashion of a sling,) and he should walk barefoot and he should weep because of his sin, and he should fast every day until he completes his fast and his exile. And afterwards he should fast on Mondays and Thursdays for one year. If people revile him, he should be silent, and during those three years, he should not go strolling or engage in laughter. And when he wanders in exile, he should lie down before the doorway of the synagogue and all those who come and go should pass over him, they should not step upon him.

An apostate should remove his nice clothes, and he should mourn and weep and afflict himself all the days of his life, and he should lower his spirit and his pride and he should confess three times a day, and he should not eat meat or drink wine, except on Sabbaths and holidays, and he should wash but little, and he should not wash his head more than once or twice a month, and he should not go to any place of entertainment or to a wedding (but he may be present when the marriage blessings are recited), and he should keep away from idolatry and from those who serve it, and he should not sit with priests or church officials, and he should not sit in a place where people speak heresy, and he should stay far from the entrance to their houses, and he should derive no profit from them. Immediately upon repentance he must immerse himself, and he must bear the pain and the afflictions that are prescribed for one who has committed his sin, for he has denied God, and he has profaned the Sabbaths, and he has had intercourse with heathen women, and he has committed transgressions that are punishable by being cut off from his people, or by capital punishment at the hands of a court of law. Therefore, he requires great affliction and great repentance.

If a man has had intercourse with another man's wife or with a betrothed maiden, this, of course, prohibits her to her husband or to her betrothed, inasmuch as she consented, and for this sin he is liable to death at the hands of a court. Therefore, he must bear a pain which is as difficult as death. In the winter, he should sit in snow or ice, every day once or twice or three times, and in the summertime, he should sit in front of flies or bees, or he should endure other sufferings which are as difficult as death. And he should confess all that he has done with weeping and sighing, and for a whole year he should not eat any warm food, and he should not wash except a little on the eve of the Sabbaths, and festivals. And he should not see any kind of amusement, except to hear the blessings of bridegroom, and he should not adorn himself with anything, and he should be lashed every day, and he should lie down upon the earth or upon one board without a pillow or cushion (and only on Sabbaths and festivals may he lie down upon straw and hay with a pillow under his head), until he removes the vulgar spirit and the lust that is within him. He should live a life of anguish and he should wear sackcloth on his flesh, and he should not speak of the desire for women and he should not look at women or their ornaments even when the ornaments are not upon the women. He should not listen to the sound of their song — and he should not be with women at all, not even to converse with them through gestures and not for any reason, and even as regards his own wife he should not be alone with her during her unclean period, he should not be close to her with any sort of nearness.

One who has sworn falsely or has trespassed against a consecrated object must be lashed several times all the days of his life, and he should confess for many days. And after this he should be very careful not to swear even to a truth — not by the Torah, and not by the soul of his ancestors — but he may make a vow by the life of his own head, and he may swear to observe the commandments. He must be very careful not to utter the name of God in vain, and his limbs should tremble when he mentions the Name of God,

ORCHOT TZADIKIM — Chapter Twenty-Six

Blessed be He, and he should be careful not to utter any blessing without purpose. And if he has made an error and did utter a blessing for nothing, then he must say after it at once, "Blessed is the glorious name of His Kingdom forever and ever." And as for those who accustom their mouths and the mouths of their children to mention the Name of God for nothing, woe to their souls and to their children that they have so taught their tongues. Therefore, he should guard and set up a fence for himself and for his children and for his companions who listen to him, so that he will not mention the Name of God in vain. And if the penitent is compelled to make an oath to his creditor, even though it is a true oath, he must fast that day every year.

If he has got in the habit of talking in the synagogue and engaging in jocularity and frivolity, from the time he becomes a penitent he should take care not to speak in the synagogue about any secular thing, even when the congregation is not engaged in prayer, and he should sit in great fear, and he should pray with great humility. And he should fast for forty days, either consecutively or intermittently, and he should be lashed in private every day.

If he has stolen or taken usury, he must ask forgiveness from the man he has injured, and he must fast for forty days, and he must be very careful not to receive any pledges, and he should not get in the habit of going to the money of his companion, and he should do kindly deeds with his person and with his money, and he should be liberal with what belongs to him for the benefit of those who labor in the Torah and revere God, Blessed be He. And as for the One who has taken usurious interest, if he can manage not to take interest, even from a heathen, it would be good.

He who informs on a fellow man thereby makes him hateful in the eyes of the ruler, causes him ill and deprives him of his money, and enslaves him and his wife and his sons. Such a man should reimburse the other for all that he has lost, and should beg forgiveness of him, and he should be lashed, and he should fast more than two years, and he should confess all the days of his life, for it is reckoned as if he had slain his companion and his wife and his children. How many sins he has committed by his act! Therefore, , he should break down his spirit. And if he has nothing with which to pay, he should send intercessors and beg his companion's forgiveness, and he should live very frugally so that he will be able to reimburse his companion or his heirs.

He who goes about tale-bearing has a similar penance to fulfill, and there is no remedy for him unless he begs forgiveness of his injured companion. And he should fast for forty days or more and be lashed every day, and he should confess his sin all the days of his life. And he should spend all of his time in the fulfillment of the commandments, and in making peace between men and between man and wife.

He who smites his companion and causes him pain, whether it be in money matters or through fraudulent words, there is no atonement for him unless he can appease his companion. And the Day of Atonement atones only for sins that are between man and God. But as for sins between him and his fellow man, he must first appease him (Yoma 85b). He who lifts his hand against his companion, even though he did not smite him, is called a wicked man (Sanh. 58b), and he must ask forgiveness of him: only thus can he do atonement.

He who shames his companion should fast for forty days or more, and he should be lashed every day, and he should confess his wrong all the days of his life. He who calls his companion by a derogatory nickname must beg him for forgiveness in the presence of many, and he must fast forty days and he must confess privately every day.

He who deceives a proselyte must beg his forgiveness, and must be lashed and must confess and must fast for forty days.

He who provokes his companion must bring three groups of three people, as it is said, "He cometh before men and saith" (Job 33:27), and he must say in their presence, "I have sinned and perverted that which was right, and it profited me not." But he does not have to ask him for forgiveness more than three times. If the man whom he provoked dies, he should take ten men to his grave and say, "I have sinned to the Lord, the God of Israel and to this person, for I have provoked him" (Yoma 87a).

But to begin with, before he does these forms of penance, one who has grieved his companion should go to him and say, "I have sinned against you," and if he does not accept his apology, he should bring three people and ask for forgiveness in their presence. All this applies where he has not shamed his companion publicly, but if he did shame him publicly, it is not sufficient that he should ask of him forgiveness by appeasing him privately. But the one who is asked to forgive should not be cruel (Baba Kamma 92a). And if he provoked him by spreading an evil report concerning him, there is no forgiveness for him ever (T.P. Baba Kamma 9:10), unless he fasts and is lashed privately forty days or more.

One who profanes the Name of God — profanation of the name of God is an exceedingly great sin. And what is profanation of the name of God? Rav said, "For example, if I go to a butcher and buy meat and I haven't the money to pay for it at once." The meaning of this is that if one makes light of dishonesty or robbery, then people will learn very quickly from him and will make even lighter of such a wrong (Yoma 86a). Rabbi Johanan said, "As far as I am concerned, if I walk four cubits without speaking words of the Torah or wearing Tefillin, I am guilty of profaning God's name." And the meaning of this statement is that from his example people may learn to regard these sacred things very lightly. Isaac, of the school of Rabbi Yannai said, "Profanation of God's Name is anything which causes shame to a person's companions when they hear of it, that is to say, when it is said of him that he has done unworthy deeds, people will learn from his deeds and will think, "If he can do these things, then we certainly can" — and permit themselves to commit transgressions which otherwise they would not. Rabbi Abahu said in the name of Rabbi Haninah (Kiddushin 40a), "It is better that a man should commit a transgression secretly, so that he should not profane the Name of God publicly." And the meaning of this is that other people should not learn of his bad deeds.

ORCHOT TZADIKIM

Rabbi Ilai, the Elder, said, "If a man sees that his desire is strengthening itself over him, he should go to a place where nobody knows him, and let him put on dark clothes, and let him wrap himself in dark garments, and then let him do what his heart desires, but let him not profane the Name of God publicly." And Rabbi Hananel explained this as follows: "God forbid that a man is permitted to commit a sin! But the wise men stood firmly against the evil inclination and believed that one lusts only for that which is forbidden and in order to gratify his lust, and that if a man were to go a long distance and put on dark garments, then his heart would be broken and thus he would refrain from sin. But as far as doing something which is forbidden (even in a distant place), absolutely not. It is just that this type of conduct breaks the grip of the evil inclination and restrains one from sinning." As Rabbi Ilai said, "The weariness caused by long journeys and stopping at inns and putting on of black garments, breaks the evil inclination and restrains a man from transgression." And they said, "Whosoever takes no thought for the honor of his maker, it was a mercy if he had not come into the world" (Hagigah 11b). And in the Gemara, Rabbi Joseph said, "It refers to one who commits a transgression in secret" (Hagigah 16a). And Rabbi Issac said, "Everyone who commits a sin in secret, it is as though he restricted the Divine Presence."

Profanation of the Name of God is a transgression that bears bitter fruit, for when a man has done this evil thing, others learn from him. And a man ought to be very, very fearful of committing this sin, for profanation of the Name of God can occur in many ways and there is no limit to it. For everyone who belittles one precept or takes the glory of God lightly is called "one who profanes the Name," for others will learn from him, and they will treat the matter even more lightly. Therefore, a man must be on guard exceedingly in all his deeds, so that people will not learn from him to take lightly and despise what is sacred.

If a man has committed transgressions for which he is liable to be cut off from among his people or to be condemned to death by the court, then repentance and the Day of Atonement atone for half of his sin, while afflictions that come upon him atone for half. "But if he has been guilty of the profanation of the Name, then penitence has no power to suspend punishment, nor the day of Atonement to procure atonement, nor suffering to finish it, but all of them together suspend the punishment and only death finishes it" (Yoma 86a, and see T.P. Yoma 8:8). Therefore, , a man should guard himself exceedingly from profaning the Name of God, and he should keep away from ugly conduct and from that which resembles it. And the principal requirement in repenting for profaning the Name of God is that he should make known his sins in the presence of many, and he should say, "Do not learn from me, for in my folly I have sinned, I have perverted, I have trespassed, I have profaned the Name of God, Blessed be He." And he should keep many fasts and he should confess every day until the day of his death.

For every single sin that a man does, whether it be done unwittingly or intentionally, for example, if he touched a lamp or kindled a fire, not remembering that it was the Sabbath, or if he did this without knowing that he did it, he must confess and fast for at least two days, on Monday and on Thursday. And, similarly, for all transgressions, that a man commits, great or small, he should fast. There are two virtues in this. The first is that the fast atones for what he has already done, and the second is that he will be restrained from further transgressions, for he will think, "If I do this, I will have to fast," and so he will hold himself back from transgressing. And this is the high fence that one can place in the way of all transgressions: he should afflict himself or give alms, or cause pain to his body when he transgresses. And thus, should he do with respect to all the sins of which he is guilty, for example: hatred, envy, rejoicing at another's misfortune, idling, engaging in gossip, failure to pay attention to the blessings or to the prayers (but he merely cast the blessings from his mouth without any intention of the heart), and the like. One should examine oneself exceedingly in these matters daily and if he has transgressed in any one of them, he should hasten to cause himself anguish and to mourn and to confess the sin which he committed and to ask forgiveness from God, Blessed be He, with a broken heart.

Confession is a matter of great importance, for our Sages, of blessed memory, taught (Sanh. 43b): When a man condemned to death was a distance of ten cubits from the place of stoning, they would say to him, "Confess." For it is the way of all who are about to be slain that they do confess, and every man who confesses has a share in the world to come. For thus have we found in the case of Achan. When Joshua said to him, "My son, give, I pray thee, glory to the Lord, the God of Israel, and confess unto him, and tell to me know what thou hast done, hide nothing from me." And Achan answered Joshua, and said, "It is true, I sinned to the Lord, the God of Israel and thus and like thus have I done" (Josh. 7:19—20). And how do we know that his confession atoned for him? Because it is said, "And Joshua said, 'Why hast thou troubled us? The Lord shall trouble thee this day' " (Jos. 7:25). This day you will be troubled, but you will not be troubled in the world to come. And if he does not know how to confess, they say to him, "Say these words: 'May my death be an atonement for all my sins'."

All the commandments of the Torah, whether positive or negative commandments, if a man has transgressed one of them, either intentionally or unintentionally, when he repents and returns from his sinfulness, he must confess it before God, Blessed be He. As it is said, "When a man or woman shall commit any sin that men commit, to commit a trespass against the Lord, and that soul shall be found guilty then they shall confess their sin which they have done" (Num. 5:6). This is confession by words. And as for all men who have sinned or trespassed and all who are liable to death by the court, or to lashing, their sins are not atoned for by death or by lashing, or by sacrifice until they do repentance and confess. And anyone who injures another, or who causes him monetary loss, even though he paid him, there is no atonement for the offender until he confesses and resolves never to do a similar act. And how does he confess? He should say, "Pray, O God, I sinned, I dealt perversely, I trespassed before You, and I did thus and thus, and now, behold, I am repentant and I am ashamed of my deeds, and I shall never repeat such a thing." This is the essence of confession. And he who confesses at length and dwells upon this matter deserves praise. Also, it is an important part of confession for him to say: "But we have sinned."

It is very good to specify in his confession the sin he has committed. For example, if he has eaten carrion or flesh torn by beasts or other forbidden things, then after he says, "I have trespassed," he should say, "I ate a forbidden thing." And if he sinned in fornication, when he says, "I have rebelled," he should say, "I committed fornication," and he should specify in his confession if he had intercourse with a gentile woman or with his wife during her unclean period. And if he stole, then when he says, "I have robbed," then he should also say, "I stole from such and such a person," and if he poured out his seed for nothing (i.e., if he masturbated), then when he comes to the words, "I have dealt perversely," he should say, "I brought forth seed for nothing." And if he committed incest, when he reaches the part where he says, "I have dealt impudently," he should say, "I have fornicated." And if he has profaned the Sabbaths, where he comes to the phrase, "I have done violence," he should say, "I have profaned Sabbaths." And if he has coveted, he should say, "I have coveted." And thus, with all the letters of the alphabet which are found in the confession; for every single letter in the confession, he should declare the sort of sin he has committed. And he should say with weeping, "Let the wicked forsake his way, and the man of iniquity his thoughts;

and let him return unto the Lord, and He will have compassion upon him" (Is. 55:7), and then it will avail him.

At the end of the confession, he should say, "I have transgressed the positive commandments and the negative commandments; I have committed transgressions which make me liable to being cut off from my people or to death by order of the court. I have transgressed against the Written Torah and against the Oral Torah. I forgot Thy Great Name. I forgot the yoke of Your kingdom and the reverence due You, and You, O God, are just in everything that comes upon us." And it has been said in the Jerusalem Talmud (T.P. Yoma 8:9): How does he confess? "Master of all worlds, I have done what is evil in Thine eyes, and I have stood in evil ways, but I shall not do so again. May it be Thy will, O Lord my God and God of my fathers, that You will grant atonement to me for all my sins, and forgive me for all my wrong-doings, and pardon me for all my errors."

The general rule of the matter is that a man should repent of all bad qualities, and one who does repent his evil qualities needs very great strengthening, for when a man is already used to them it is very difficult for him to abandon them, and on this subject, it is said, "Let the wicked forsake his way and the man of iniquity his thoughts" (Is. 55:7). And let not a man who is truly repentant think that he is far away from the status of the righteous because of the sins and the wrongs which he has committed. It is not so, for he is as beloved and dear before the Creator, Blessed be He, as though he had never sinned. Not only this, but his reward is great, for he has tasted the taste of sin, and yet abandoned it and conquered his evil inclination. Our Sages said, "In the place where penitents stand, even the wholly righteous cannot stand" (Berakoth 34b), that is to say, their status is even higher than that of those who never sinned, for they subdue the evil inclination more than the others. All of the prophets without exception commanded us concerning repentance (ibid.), and it is only through repentance that Israel is redeemed (see Yoma 86b, Sanh. 97b). And the Torah has already assured us that Israel will ultimately repent at the end of their exile, and they will immediately be redeemed. As it is said, "And it shall come to pass, when all these things are come upon thee, the blessings and the curse which I have set before thee and thou shalt bethink thyself... and shalt return unto the Lord thy God... that then the Lord thy God will turn thy captivity, and have compassion upon thee, and will return and gather thee from all the peoples" (Deut. 30:1—3).

Great is repentance, for it brings man near to the Divine Presence, as it is said, "Return, O Israel, unto the Lord thy God" (Hos. 14:2; and see Yoma 86a). And it is said, "Yet have ye not returned unto Me, saith the Lord God" (Amos 4:6). And it is said, "If thou wilt return, O Israel, saith the Lord, Yea, return unto Me" (Jer. 4:1), that is to say, "If you will return with repentance, you will cleave to me." Repentance brings near those who are far off. Last night this man was hated before God, Blessed be He, — defiled, far removed, an abomination — but today he is loved and precious and near and dear. And so you find this clearly shown in the language with which the Holy One, Blessed be He, thrusts away the sinners and the language with which He receives those who are repentant, whether it be one person or whether it be many, as it is said, "And it shall come to pass that instead of that which was said, unto them 'Ye are not my people', it shall be said unto them 'Ye are the children of the living God' (Hos. 2:1)".

Concerning Coniah in his wickedness, it is said, "Write ye this man childless, a man shall not prosper in his days" (Jer. 22:30), and, "Though Coniah, the son of Jehoiakim, King of Judah, were the signet upon My right hand, yet would I pluck thee thence" (Jer. 22:24). And inasmuch as he repented when he was in exile, it is said of Zerubbabel, his son, "In that day, saith the Lord of hosts, will I take thee, O Zerubbabel, my servant, the son of Shealtiel, saith the Lord, and I will make thee as a signet" (Hag. 2:23).

How excellent is the quality of repentance. Last night this one was separated from the Lord, the God of Israel, Blessed be He. As it is said, "But your iniquities have separated between you and your God" (Is. 59:2). He cried and he was not answered, as it is said, "Yea, when ye make many prayers, I will not hear" (Is. 1:15). And he fulfilled precepts and they were torn up before his face, as it is said, "Who hath required this at your hand, to trample my courts" (Is. 1:12), and, "Oh that there were even one among you that would shut the doors" Mal. 1:10), and, "Hold your burnt offerings unto your sacrifices and eat ye flesh" (Jer. 7:21). Yet today he is closely attached to the Divine Presence, as it is said, "But you, who hold fast to the Lord your God" (Deut. 4:4). He cries out and is answered at once, as it is said, "And it shall come to pass that, before they call, I will answer" (Is.

65:24). He fulfills the commandments and they are received with pleasure and with joy, as it is said, "For the Lord hath already accepted thy works" (Eccl. 9:7). Moreover, his commandments are desired, as it is said, "Then shall the offering of Judah and Jerusalem be pleasant unto the Lord, as in days of old and in ancient years" (Mal. 3:4).

It is the way of those who repent to be lowly and exceedingly modest, and if fools revile them because of their prior deeds and say to them, "Only last night you did so and so and only last night you said so and so," they do not feel any resentment, but they listen and they rejoice and they know that this is merit to them, that so long as they are ashamed of the sins that they committed their merit is very great and their virtue increases. And it is a great sin to say to a repentant person, "Remember your prior deeds" or to mention his sins in his presence in order to shame him. And on this subject is it said, "And ye shall not wrong one another" (Lev. 25:17).

He who is a true penitent should seek to do good deeds, and to remove himself from thoughts of this world, and to strengthen himself in the counsel of God, Blessed be He, and to take shelter in His shadow, and bear the yoke of the Torah of God, Blessed be He, and bear the revilement of fools, and to be like one who is deaf, blind, and dead against their attacks, as it is said, "Because for thy sake I have borne reproach... I make sackcloth also my garment... but as for me, let my prayer be unto thee, O Lord, in an acceptable time" (Ps. 69:8—14).

Sefer ORCHOT TZADIKIM
Ways of the Righteous

Chapter Twenty-Seven

ON TORAH

"With three crowns was Israel crowned: the crown of the Torah, the crown of the Priesthood and the crown of Kingdom" (Aboth 4:17, Yoma 72b, Eccl. Rabbah 7:1). Aaron merited the crown of the Priesthood, as it is said, "And it shall be unto him, and to his seed after him, the covenant of an everlasting priesthood" (Num. 25:13). David merited the crown of Kingdom, as it is said, "His seed shall endure for ever, and his throne as the sun before Me" (Ps. 89:37). As for the crown of the Torah — it lies there waiting for all Israel, as it is said, "Moses commanded us a law, an inheritance of the congregation of Jacob" (Deut. 33:4): anyone who wants the crown of Torah can come and take it. And should you say that the other crowns are greater than the crown of Torah, then behold he says, "By me kings reign, and princes decree justice. By me princes' rule, and nobles, even all the judges of the earth" (Prov. 8:15—16). From this you learn that the crown of the Torah is greater than the crown of Priesthood, and greater than the crown of Sovereignty. And the Sages said, "A bastard who is a scholar takes precedence over a High Priest who is ignorant" (Horayoth 13a). As it is said, "She (wisdom) is more precious than rubies" (Prov. 3:15). The Hebrew word "peninah" means both "ruby" and "inside", and the verse can Therefore, be interpreted as meaning: More precious is the Torah and he who studies it than the High Priest who enters the very inside of the Temple — into the Holy of Holies.

No other commandment is equal in value to the precept of studying the Torah, but the study of the Torah can be weighed against all of the other precepts together, because the study of the Torah leads to the performance of the deeds commanded there (Kiddushin 40b). And the statement that "the study of the Torah outweighs them all" (Peah 1:1) applies to him who studies in order to learn and to teach, to observe, to do, and to fulfill, but who, because of his constant study of the Torah, is not able to fulfill all of the commandments, and when he is not studying, he does all that he can, thus showing the state of his mind, that he wants very much to perform the commandments. It is in such a case that "the study of the Torah outweighs them all." For when he studies the precepts and wants to fulfill them, then he already is rewarded as though he had fulfilled them, inasmuch as he has been kept from fulfilling them only because of his diligent study of the Torah. And so, he finds that the reward of doing and of studying are both his. But he who frequently is idle, and is able to perform the commandments at the time that he is idle but does not hasten to do them, or when he does fulfill a commandment does not do so with great care, as is befitting, of him it is not said that the study of the Torah outweighs all the other commandments.

He whose heart has prompted him to perform this commandment (of studying the Torah) and to fulfill it as it merits and to be crowned with the crown of the Torah, should not let his mind wander off to idle things, nor should a man plan in his heart to acquire the Torah, wealth and honor all together. For this is the way of Torah: "A morsel of bread and salt shall you eat, and water in a measure shall you drink, and on the earth shall you sleep, and a life of anguish shall you live and in the Torah you shall labor" (Aboth 6:4).

And if you should say, "After I gather some money, and after I am free of my business affairs, then I will return and read and study the Torah" — if such a thought should come into your heart, then you will never acquire the crown of the Torah. But "fix a period for the study of Torah" (Aboth 1:15), and let your daily work be secondary. "And do not say, 'When I have leisure I will study' for perhaps you will have no leisure' " (Aboth 2:5).

It is written in the Torah, "It is not in heaven" (Deut. 30:12) and the meaning of this is: it is not to be found among those that are arrogant and consider themselves as high as heaven. "Neither is it beyond the sea" (Deut. 30:13), which means that it is not to be found among those who are constantly travelling on sea voyages (Erubin 55a). Therefore, our Sages, of blessed memory, said, "Nor can one who is engaged overmuch in business grow wise" (Aboth 2:6). And they said, "Engage less in business, but occupy yourself with the Torah" (Aboth 4:12).

ORCHOT TZADIKIM — Chapter Twenty-Seven

Since a man occupies himself with the Torah for its own sake, and troubles himself and exhausts himself for the sake of Heaven, his two kidneys (his very vitals) will be like two fountains, and he will bring forth meanings and new laws from within himself — truths which he never learned from another and which were not given even to Moses at Sinai. As we find in the case of Abraham, our father (Gen. Rabbah 95:3), that he never studied in the presence of any man (who served as his teacher), but he himself would sit and think about the commandments, and he learned from his own heart all of the Torah and the commandments, until Scripture testified of him, "And (he) kept My charge, My commandments, My statutes, and My Law (Gen. 26:5). And our Sages, of blessed memory, said that Abraham knew even the laws of Eruvei Tavshilin. The laws governing the preparation of food for the Sabbath on a holiday which falls on Friday. And our Sages also said, "Abraham our father learned four hundred chapters, and who was there to teach him all of this? It must Therefore, be that his two kidneys became like two fountains, and flowed forth bringing to him wisdom and Torah.

And so we find with Rabbi Eliezer, the Elder (Prike de-Rabbi Eliezer, chap. 2): because he occupied himself with much study of the Torah, our Sages testified of him, that there was revealed unto him what had not been revealed to Moses at Sinai. And so our Sages said, "From the generation of Moses, our teacher, until the generation of Joshua, and from Joshua to the Elders and to the Prophets and to the Men of the Great Synagogue and to the Tannaim (the

ORCHOT TZADIKIM   Chapter Twenty-Seven

teachers of the Mishnah) and to the Amoraim (the interpreters of the Mishnah) and to the Geonim, and to all the Sages of the generations, who occupied themselves with the Torah, and dedicated their lives to it, there were revealed the mysteries of the Torah and the secrets of wisdom, which no man can discover by himself.

And long ago our Sages, of blessed memory, numbered forty-eight qualities through which the Torah can be acquired (Aboth 6:6). And he who resolves in his mind to be deserving of the path of the Torah must exert himself to fulfill those forty-eight requirements, and then he will ascend to all goodness. He who studies must be alert and careful to study (without interruption), for the craft of the Torah is not like other crafts, because in the case of one who studies another craft, even though he should stay away from it for several years, he will not forget it, but when a man studies the Torah and does not review it, he forgets it immediately. And even though he reviews it a hundred times, if he allows himself to be distracted from it, he will forget everything. It stands to reason that no craft requires concentration except when one is first learning it, but that in the actual performance of the task one does not have to pay strict attention, for a man can do his work mechanically once he is accustomed to it, and think about this and that. But the study of the Torah can not be done in this manner, for one must concentrate continuously and can not think about any thing other than what one is studying in the Torah. Therefore, , a man who turns his heart to emptiness will immediately forget what he has labored for all of his days.

And the Sages also said, "If it were not for the fact that a man forgets the Torah if he does not study it constantly, he would learn all of the Torah and after that he would go idle, and idleness leads a person to boredom and to sin (Kethuboth 5:5; Aboth de-Rabbi Nathan chap. 11). Therefore, it was decreed that the Torah is easily forgotten, so that man would occupy himself with Torah all of his days, and thus not come to sin.

And the Torah leads one to good deeds. For when a man occupies himself with Torah, and learns what is the punishment for sins and the reward for good deeds, then he sets his heart to do good. And the effort required in studying the Torah causes him to forget and restrains him from sin, while idleness leads to sin and brings him down to the nether world. Therefore, a man should be alert to occupy himself always with the Torah — day and night — even when he walks along the road or when he lies in his bed. And if he is not able to study by heart, let him think in his heart about what he has learned and let his mind be on his study, so as not to remove the thought of it from his heart, and then he will have fulfilled "But thou shalt meditate therein day and night" (Josh. 1:8); for the Scripture does not say, "You shall speak about it day and night," but "You shall meditate about it," and meditation is in the heart. And concerning this it is said, "And shalt talk of them when thou sittest in thy house, and when thou walkest by the way, and when thou liest down, and when thou risest up" (Deut. 6:7, 11:19). And our Sages took pride in the fact that they did not walk four cubits without discussing the Torah.

ORCHOT TZADIKIM — Chapter Twenty-Seven

Either they would learn and study or they would think in their hearts about what they had heard concerning the Torah, or about their studies.

Therefore, , you must set your heart and all your mind on the Torah at all times. For in the Torah a man learns wisdom, proper conduct, humility, modesty, and all good deeds, and Heaven will provide him his necessities. And the Torah guards him and uplifts him and exalts him, as the Sages taught: Rabbi Meir said, "Everyone who occupies himself with the Torah for its own sake merits many things; and not only this, but he is worthy of all the world. He is called friend, beloved ... and it raises him and exalts him over all created things" (Aboth 6:1). And lo the fruit of the reward for this devotion to Torah is in this world, and in the world to come the reward is such that no eye has seen it but the eye of God (see Is. 64:3), and there is nothing greater than that reward in the world to come. They said in the Midrash (Ruth Rabbah 1:1 letter 2): Rabbi asked Rabbi Bezalel, "What is the meaning of what is written in Hosea 2:1, 'For their mother had played the harlot' "? And he said to him, "When do the words of the Torah become like harlots? When those who study them shame them by their conduct. How would that be? A wise man sits and learns 'you shall not incline or wrest judgment' (Deut. 16:19), but he does in fact wrest judgment. He studies, 'You shall not be prejudiced in favor of the mighty,' but he does respect the presence of a wealthy or powerful person in court. 'You shall not take a bribe,' and he does take a bribe!"

And thus, did our Rabbis interpret the text, "The poor man's wisdom is despised" (Eccl. 9:16). What wisdom of what poor man is despised? It refers to a man who is poor in good deeds; then his wisdom is despised. And if one teaches laws that instruct us to do good and he himself does not do good deeds his words are not accepted, for "not learning but doing is the chief thing" (Aboth 1:17). Wherefore it is necessary tor every man to direct his deeds for the sake of Heaven and see and understand from the example of Elisha, the son of Abuyah: because his father taught him Torah not for its own sake, the son turned to heresy. As it is said in the Jerusalem Talmud (Hagigah 2:1), and in the Midrash (Eccl. Rabbah 7:8, letter 18): When Elisha, the son of Abuyah was circumcised his father made a feast for the Sages and invited Rabbi Eiezer and Rabbi Joshua and the other Sages, and they sat at the feast and spoke words of the Torah to the extent that a fire came and encircled them. The father of Elisha came and said to them, "My good friends, did you come to burn down the house?" And they said to him, "The fire that you see is only because we are studying the words of the Torah and the Prophets and the Scriptures. And the words of our discussion joyously testify to the truth just as when they were given at Mount Sinai. From Mount Sinai where they given, and from the fire where they given!" The father of Elisha ben Abuyah then said, "Now that I see the power of the Torah, if this my son will live on, I shall give him to the study of Torah." And because the father had it in his mind that he would teach his son Torah not for its own sake but for the power it would give him, his son became a heretic. And even so, a man should study the Torah even if not for its own sake, because from studying it not for its own sake, he will ultimately come to study it for its own sake (Pesahim 50b).

And now I must write down matters pertaining to the Talmud and the commandments that are there contained.

All of the commandments that were given to Moses from Sinai were given with their interpretation, as it is said, "And I will give thee the tables of stone, and the law (the Torah) and the commandment" (Ex. 24:12). "Torah" refers to the written Torah "and the commandment" refers to the interpretation of the written Torah (Berakoth 5a). And we have been commanded to fulfill the Torah according to the commandment, and this commandment is called the Oral Law. Moses, our teacher, wrote the whole Torah with his own hand, before he died, and he gave a copy to each tribe. And one copy he placed in the Ark, as testimony, as it is said, "Take this book of the law, and put it by the side of the Ark of the covenant of thy Lord your God, that it may be there for witness against thee" (Deut. 31:26).

And the commandment, which is the interpretation of the Torah, he did not write down, but commanded it to the Elders and to Joshua and to the rest of Israel. As it is said, "All this word which I command you, that shall ye observe to do: thou shalt not add thereto, nor diminish from it" (Deut. 13:1). And because of this it is called the Oral Law. And from the days of Moses, our teacher, until our sainted Rabbi, Rabbi Judah the Prince, the Oral Law was not written in a book from which the multitude could study, but they studied everything orally, and everyone would take notes for his own use on the things he learned from

ORCHOT TZADIKIM — Chapter Twenty-Seven

his teachers, and would teach orally to the many. And so everyone would write for himself, according to his ability, the explanation of the Torah and its laws just as he heard it; and those things which were created anew in every generation, and laws that they had not learned from tradition but through the application of the "thirteen rules of interpreting the Torah," and on which the great Bet Din was in agreement. And so, did they do until the matter came before Rabbi Judah, the Prince. And when Rabbi Judah saw that in his days the situation had altered, for he saw that the pupils were growing less and less, and that new troubles were coming upon the Jews and that the dominion of Rome was spreading over the world and growing mightier, and that Israel was wandering to the borders of distant countries only to be enslaved; when he saw this state of affairs, that Israel was confused and that the Torah was being forgotten from Israel, then he compiled the Mishnayot so that they could be in the hand of every single person so that they could learn them and they would not be forgotten. And he sat all of his days, he and his colleagues, and they taught the Mishnah to the multitude. And there were in his presence the greatest of the wise men of Israel and they received the Mishnah from him, and with them were thousands and thousand of other Sages. And the pupils of Rabbi Judah, the Prince, likewise compiled their own compilations. Rav compiled the Sifra and the Sifré to explain and make known the principles of the Mishnah. And Rabbi Hiyya compiled the Tosefta to explain points of the Mishnah. And Rabbi Hosaya and Bar Kappara compiled the Baraitot to explain the words of the Mishnah. And matters developed in this manner until the Amoraic came and they had differences of opinion as to the meaning of the Mishnayot and the Toseftot and the Baraitot until Rabbi Johanan compiled the Jerusalem Talmud in the land of Israel almost three hundred years after the destruction of the Second Temple, and it was called the Jerusalem Talmud because Rabbi Johanan lived in Jerusalem. About a hundred years later, Rav Ashi, who lived in Babylonia, compiled the Babylonian Talmud. And the purpose of both of these Talmuds is to explain the words of the Mishnah and to interpret its deep meaning, and the things that were created anew with the coming of every Bet Din from the days of our sainted rabbi, Rabbi Judah Hanasi, until the compilation of the Gemara. And from the two Talmuds and the Tosefta, and from the Sifra, and the Sifré and the Baraitot, from all of them we can find the explanation of what is forbidden and what is permitted, what is clean and what is unclean, what is obligatory upon us and what we are exempt from, what is unfit according to the Torah and what is fit just as they copied it, one man from another's mouth, all the way back to the mouth of Moses, our teacher, of blessed memory, as he received it from Sinai.

These works will also make clear the rules which the Sages and Prophets of every generation decreed in order to make a fence about the Torah, as they heard explicitly from the mouth of Moses, as it is said, "Therefore, shall ye keep my charge" (Lev. 18:30), that is to say, make a guard for the laws which were to be guarded (Moed Katan 5a). One can also obtain from these works a clear interpretation of the customs, and the regulations that our Sages enacted in every generation according to the way that the Bet Din of that generation understood the matter, for it is forbidden to turn away from the words of the Sages, as it is said, "Thou shalt not turn aside from the sentence which they shall declare unto thee, to the right hand, nor to the left" (Deut. 17:11). And similarly included were all those judgments and excellent laws which our Sages did not receive from Moses, our teacher, but which the Bet Din of that generation decided according to the rules by which the Torah is interpreted, and also the decisions which the Elders made and concluded that the law was thus. Everything was included in the Gemara by Rav Ashi, from the days of Moses until his own day.

And after the Bet Din of Rav Ashi, in the days of his son, Israel was scattered in a great dispersion over all the countries and they reached the ends of the earth and the distant islands, and strife increased in the world, and the roads were mobbed with mobilizations, and the study of the Torah diminished, and Israel did not enter their yeshivot to study by the thousands and tens of thousands as had been the case earlier, but only a few would gather together, that remnant which the Lord summons in every city and in every country, and they occupy themselves with the Torah and understand all the writings of the Sages and know from them the commandments which the Lord of all, Blessed be He, has commanded.

After the Amoraim, there arose the Gaonim who knew the whole Talmud — the Babylonian and the Jerusalem Talmud — and the Sifra and the Sifré and the Tosefta. And they brought forth into the light the mysteries of the Talmud, and they explained all of its matters, for the path of the Talmud is very profound. Moreover, it is in the Aramaic language, mixed with other languages, for Aramaic was known to all of them in Babylonia at the time that the Talmud was compiled. But in other places and in the days of the Gaonim who were in Babylonia, they did not know that language unless they learned it especially. And the people of every city would put many questions to every Gaon who lived in those days, asking them to explain difficult points in the Talmud. And they would respond according to their wisdom. And the questioners would gather the responses and would make books of them in order to understand them better. The Gaonim in every generation also wrote treatises to explain the Talmud. Some of them explained individual laws, some explained individual chapters, and some explained whole tractates and complete "orders" of the Talmud. And there were others who compiled laws which had been decided in the matter of what is forbidden and what is permitted, and what one is obliged to do and what one is exempt from doing in matters that demanded a decision at that particular time in order that those who were not able to descend into the very depths of the Talmud should have the matter close to their mind.

And the following is an excerpt from the words of Maimonides, of blessed memory, in his preface to Mishneh Torah:

"And this is the work of the Lord, that the Gaonim of Israel engaged in from the day that the Gemara was compiled until this very time, which is the eleven hundreth and eighth year since the destruction of the

ORCHOT TZADIKIM — Chapter Twenty-Seven

Second Temple and it is the 4,937th year since the creation of the world (1177-78 C.E.).

"And in these times, troubles have grown mightily against us and the urgency of the hour has pushed everything else aside, and the wisdom of our Sages is lost, and the understanding of our discerning people is hidden. Therefore, those interpretations and laws and responses which the Gaonim compiled, and which they regarded as having been explained, have grown very difficult in our days, and there are very few who understand them properly. And, needless to say, the Gemara itself, both the Babylonian and the Jerusalem Talmud, and the Sifra and Sifré and Tosefta, all require a broad knowledge and a wise spirit and much time, and only then can one know the correct path concerning which things are forbidden and which permitted, and how it is with the rest of the laws of the Torah.

"Therefore, , because of all of this, I stirred up my breast and girded my loins, I, Moses, the son of Maimon, the Spanish Jew, and I leaned upon the Rock, Blessed be He, and I considered well all of these books and I saw that it was necessary to compile words that are very clear out of all of these writings, with respect to what is permitted and what is forbidden, what is unclean and what is clean, with the rest of the Laws of the Torah, all of them in lucid language and briefly, so that the entire Oral Law would be completely arranged on the lips of everyone without any difficulty and without any omissions, or with this one saying thus and this one saying so, but clear words, near to the mind and heart, true according to the judgment which has been elicited

ORCHOT TZADIKIM — Chapter Twenty-Seven

and clarified out of all of those compositions and commentaries which have been extant from the days of our holy Rabbi (R. Judah, the Prince) to now, and until all the laws would be clearly revealed to small and great according to the law of every single precept and according to the law of all the regulations which the Sages and the Prophets decreed.

"The general object of all this is that no man should require any other work in the world concerning any law of the laws of Israel, but that this compilation gathers together the whole Oral Law, together with the regulations customs and decrees that have been in force from the days of Moses, our teacher, and until the compilation of the Gemara, and as the Gaonim interpreted in all of their writings which they wrote after the Gemara. Therefore, I have called the name of this compilation Mishneh Torah or (Repetition of the Torah) because if a man reads the written Torah first and afterwards, he reads this book, he will know from it the entire Oral Law and will not have to read any other book."

And after this there arose our teacher, Moses of Coucy, and compiled another book and selected portions of Maimonides' book and joined to this work some of the views of scholars of the later generation. And so, did many rabbis make compilations of halakhic rulings. For example, the "Rokeah" and Rabbi Eliezer of Metz, and the "Avi Haezri," and the "Or Zarua". There are seven books by this name; the reference may be to the work on the Talmud written by Rabbi Isaac bar Moses of Vienna. And so did many rabbis do. Each compiled a book according to what he saw that the circumstances of his generation demanded, for they perceived that because of our great sins the knowledge of the Talmud had diminished and no man would be able to know what the law was if he did not have a book of decisions.

And also, our teacher Solomon (Rashi) who saw in his own days the lessening of minds and hearts, and that because of our great sins the generations of scholars were lessening and departing, and therefore, his heart was aroused to explain the Talmud and to teach the children of Israel knowledge. And afterwards, there arose those who came forth from his loins — Rabbenu Tam and Rabbenu Isaac and the rest of the rabbis. And they debated with great sharpness of mind until they compiled the Tosafot, in the academy of Rabbenu Issac, who was the master of the Tosafot. And there were great scholars there, such as our teacher, Samson of Sans, who also compiled Tosafot, besides the other scholars who now were very many, and were mighty in the Torah, and their minds were very great, and as open as a wide hall. And they studied with great assiduity, and gave their lives for the Torah, and without having to glance at a page they knew all of the Talmud as well as the comments of Rashi and the Tosafot.

After this, because of the greatness of our sins, troubles multiplied and our academies of study diminished. And the later Tosafot became very difficult for them to understand and they could not bear the burden. Then came other great ones and abridged those Tosafot, everyone according to his wisdom, to make this study easier for the man of his generation. And even in those days there were still men who knew all of the Talmud completely and knew the commandments from their knowledge of the Talmud, until it came about that the Jews were driven from France (1391), where they were holding strongly to the Torah and were studying it with great diligence, just as the Early Sages had done in the days of the Talmud, when the principal goal of study was to review the Talmud over and over again in order to fulfill what they said (Sifré to Deut. 6:7, Kiddushin 30a), "And ye shall teach them diligently to thy children": "May the words of the Torah be sharp in your mouth, so that if anyone should ask you a matter of law you will not stutter and give him any answer but you will give him the corect answer at once." For it is impossible that the commandments will be on the tip of a man's tongue, so that he can readily respond to a questioner, unless he has reviewed many times, as they said, "He who has repeated his chapter one hundred times is not to be compared with him who has repeated it a hundred and one times" (Hagigah 9b).

Resh Lakish would go over a law forty times before he came before Rabbi Johanan (Ta'anith 8a), and so did they all do in the days of the Sages of the Talmud, for the essence of their study was constant review. And they said (Megillah 7b): Rabbi Ashi was sitting before Rabbi Kahana; it grew late, and still the rabbis did not arrive. He said to him, "Why have the rabbis not come?" "Perhaps they are busy with the Purim feast," he said to him. "Could they not have held it last night?" He replied, "Is your honour not acquainted with the teaching of Raba? If one eats his Purim feast on the night (of the 14th of Adar) he does not thereby fulfill his obligation. What is the reason for this? For it is written (Esther 9:22), 'Days of feasting and gladness'." He said to him, "Did Raba really say so?" He replied, "Yes." He then repeated it forty times, until it was safely stored in his mind.

And now observe that this was a very simple matter and even so he would review it many times. And nowadays there is no man at all who would review a thing like this more than once or twice. And there are great and clear proofs in many places in the Talmud that all of the Sages were accustomed to review, and that every one had a set sum of chapters to review each day. And if they were too busy in the daytime then they would fulfill their set amount at night (Erubin 65a), and every thirty days they would review what they had studied. In this manner they also studied in France, until they had attained the lofty heights and possessed great knowledge and no longer needed the books of decisions, for they knew the precepts out of the Talmud and the Tosafot themselves. But, from the day that they were driven out of France, the study of the Talmud diminished greatly.

And in this generation the Torah is still being forgotten, because those who study it try to do exactly as the earlier Sages and cling to subtle argumentation, but they do not resemble the wise men of France at all. For the minds of the latter were as open as a hall, and Torah was their art, and they renounced the world for its sake, day and night, and that is why they reached new truths though their subtle argumentation. But our scholars of today do not know Torah thus, so they confuse one another and waste most of the day and occupy themselves with such study about half the day, and their study is strictly incidental, while time-wasting is the established practice. It was otherwise in the days of the Sages of the Talmud: the students would go to study for ten years or more, and their study was outstanding because of the fixed times for Torah, to the extent that if anyone should sneeze, they would not say, "Good Health!", because that would interrupt their studies in the Beth Ha-Midrash (Berakoth 53a).

From this one see how much importance they attached to their fixed time of study. And they said: R. Joseph the son of Raba was sent by his father to the academy under R. Joseph, and they arranged for him to stay there for six years. Having been there three years and the eve of the Day of Atonement approaching, he said, "I would go and see my family." When his father heard of his premature arrival, he took up a weapon and went out to meet him. "You have remembered," he said to him, "your mate!" Another version: He said to him, "You have remembered your dove!" They got involved in a quarrel and neither the one nor the other ate of the last meal before the fast (Kethuboth 63a). See and understand from this incident how devoted they were to the Torah; Therefore, they merited to have the Divine Spirit within them.

Thus, it was in the land of France that they occupied themselves with great industry and much time, and they would sit in one place to study all of the Talmud, and they would constantly review, and the Torah did not cease from their mouths. And they did according to the deeds of the earlier Sages, as they said, "Let one by all means learn, even though he is liable to forget, yea, even if he does not fully understand all of the words which he studies" (Abodah Zarah 19a). And they said, "That a man should study and subsequently understand." And all of this they do not do now, for everyone wants to study Tosafot, and new interpretations before he knows even the structure of the Talmud. This being the case, how can they make any progress? For they do the opposite of what the Sages of the Talmud said, for everything that is said in the Talmud is all true and one ought not to take issue with it or change it, nor add to it nor subtract from it.

And it is because of the difficulty of studying, and concentrating and discussing keenly that many people abandon the study of the Talmud, because of the difficulty of understanding its tradition and its grammer when taught orally, for they say, "How can we understand all of these opinions that come from outside the book itself? Would that we knew what is in the books!" Yet if they would study at fixed times, day and night, then they would learn and be completely familiar with the Talmud and they would develop a strong desire to study, for then they would have mind to understand things easily, and a man would then come to study constantly whether sleepy or awake and they would acquire through this means a complete reverence for God. And then pupils would increase and they too would occupy themselves constantly with the Torah. But now, because of the great difficulty of understanding the tradition when taught orally, the study of the Law has become a heavy burden to them, and they cannot look at the Talmud any more, and because of this they occupy themselves with madness and frivolity, and they are confused and they waste their time and they engage in all sorts of scheming plans, and they have no fear of Heaven.

And they said, in the chapter entitled "The hiring of workers" (Baba Mezi'a 85a and see Rashi): When R. Zera emigrated to Palestine he fasted forty days (some texts read 100 fasts) to forget the Babylonian Talmud, that it should not trouble him. And they said: If a man stumbled by committing a sin for which the penalty is death by the decree of Heaven, what should he do so that he may live? If he was accustomed to read one page of the Talmud let him read two pages, if he was accustomed to repeat a chapter once let him repeat it twice, if he was accustomed to study one chapter let him study two chapters (Lev. Rabbah 25:1). We thus see that study is the principal thing, for if sharp debate were the principal thing, to cry out and to raise one's voice half a day over one statement, then he should have said, "If previously he was accustomed to raise one objection let him raise two objections".

And in the chapter entitled "Man Takes unto Him a Wife" they said that when Rabbi Meir died, Rabbi Judah said, "Let not the pupils of Rabbi Meir enter here for they are argumentative" (Kiddushin 52b). All this he said because he did not want to pause in his studying. For Rabbi Meir was very sharp and his companions could not successfully debate with him (Erubin 13b and 53a). Moreover, R. Johanan said, "The hearts of the ancients were like the door of the Ulam, but those of the last generations were like the door of the Hekhal, but ours are like the eye of a fine needle". The Ulam and the Hekhal were two of the chambers in the Temple. The door of the Ulam was 20 cubits wide while that of the Hekhal was only ten. And Abaye said, "We are like a peg in a wall in respect of Gemara." And Raba said, "We are like a finger in wax as regards logical argument." "We," said R. Ashi, "are like a finger in a pit as regards forgetfulness" (Erubin 53a).

And now we are empty of understanding and we are not able to learn like a finger and we are like a block of marble with respect to the Gemara and logical argument. And this is what is said in the chapter entitled "Where with May We Kindle": Raba said, "When man is led in for judgment he is asked, 'Did you deal faithfully (i.e., with integrily) ... did you engage in the dialectics of wisdom...' " (Shabbath 31a). Does this mean that one must engage in sharp debate? Here it means the study of the Gemara, where they present difficulties as between the Baraitot and the Misnah and reconcile them; it also means that when one occupies himself with the Torah constantly and meditating on it, one sets his mind to be very particular and he will discover its true meaning. But to sit all day and just chat! —obviously, one ought not to do thus. And yet now in these times, most of the students admit themselves that they are not studying as they should, and they also know that they are not studying properly. For as the result of so much idle chatter in which they engage they waste their time completely, and they do not manage to study either the Pentateuch or the Prophets of the Hagiograph, or the Aggadot, or the Midrash, or any sort of true wisdom, because of their many clever schemes.

And the verse in Proverbs 24:30-31 — "I went by the field of the slothful, and the vineyard of the man void of understanding; and lo, it was all grown with thistles, the face thereof was covered with nettles, and the stone thereof was broken down" — was expounded by our Sages as follows (Aboth de-Rabbi Nathan, chap. 24): He who does not constantly review his Talmud will at first forget the chapter headings, then he will change the words of the Sages, and finally he will say of unclean that is clean and of clean that is unclean, and thus he destroys the world. We thus see that he who does not constantly review his studies cannot declare the Law properly, but errs because he cannot decide between the many teachings. And it is said (Midrash Prov. 10:1): Rabbi Ishmael said, "Come and see, how severe is the Day of Judgment! For the Holy One, Blessed be He, will in the future judge all the world in the Valley of Jehosephat; and when a scholar comes before him, He will say to him, 'Did you occupy yourself with Torah?' Then he will say to Him, 'Yes.' Then the Holy One, Blessed be He, will say to him, 'Since you have admitted this before Me, tell Me what you have read, what you have studied, and what you have heard in the academy?' It is on this basis that our Sages said, 'Everything that a man has read should be at his fingertips, so that shame and humiliation will not overtake him on the Day of Judgment'."

Sefer
ORCHOT TZADIKIM
Ways of the Righteous

Chapter Twenty-Eight

FEAR OF HEAVEN

It is written in the Torah, "And now, Israel, what doth the Lord thy God require of thee, but to fear the Lord thy God?" (Deut. 10:12). And it is writen, "You must revere the Lord your God" (ibid., 10:20). And it is written, "And the fear of the Lord which is His treasure" (Is. 33:6). And they said (Shabbath 31b, and see Berakoth 33b), "The Holy One has nought in His world save for the awe of Heaven," as it is written, "And unto man he said, "Behold (hen), the fear of the Lord, that is wisdom" (Job 28:28). (The fear of the Lord is unique in God's affections — Rashi, (ad. loc.) The Hebrew word hen can be interpreted to mean "one" for in Greek they pronounce the word "one" as "hen."

And Raba said, "When man is led in for judgment he is asked, 'Did you deal faithfully (i.e., with integrity) did you fix times for learning, did you engage in procreation, did you hope for salvation, did you engage in the dialectics of wisdom, did you understand one thing from another?' " (Shabbath 31a). Even then, if reverence of the Lord is his stored-up treasure, all is well; if not — nothing else avails. This can be compared to a man who said to his messenger, "Bring me up a kur of wheat to the upper floor." He went and brought it up. The man said to him, "Did you mix in with the wheat a measure of humtin, (a soil which is used to preserve the wheat)?" He answered, "No." The master said to him, "It would have been better if you had not brought it up." And Rabba, the son of Rabbi Huna said, "Every man who possesses knowledge of the Torah but has not within him fear of God is like a treasurer to whom they have delivered the key of the inside vaults, but the keys of the outer doors they did not deliver to him. What good is it?"

Rabbi Jannai proclaimed: "Woe to him who has no courtyard yet makes a gate for same!" (Shabbath 31b, Yoma 72b, and see Rashi on VTRAH). In the same manner the Torah is merely the gate by which we enter the courtyard of fear of Heaven. And Rabba said to the Sages (Yoma 72b, and see Rashi on RTTY), "I beseech you, do not inherit a double Gehinnom, to busy yourself with Torah in this world and not to keep her precepts, and you will merit Gehinom after your passing! In your lifetime you did not enjoy this world because you busied yourself with study. After your passing you will lose the world to come".

Now we see that everything depends upon Fear of Heaven, and that the whole Torah is of no use to a man unless it is accompanied by Fear of Heaven, which is the very peg upon which everything hangs. And it is Fear of Heaven alone that stands by a man forever and ever. And thus, did David testify, "The fear of the Lord is clean, enduring for ever" (Ps.

19:10). And thus, also King Solomon testified and said, "And God hath so made it, that men should fear before Him (Eccl, 3:14). And it is written, "Better a little with the fear of the Lord, than great treasure and turmoil therewith" (Prov. 15:16).

Therefore, it is important to know that there are three kinds of fear : The first is a very inferior kind, for example, a man who actually has no fear of God, but when he does a good deed he does it because of people for, if he does not do this good deed — whether it be in study or in charity or in prayer or in anything else — they will not trust him and will hold him in contempt; Therefore, whatever he does is only to find favor in their eyes. And if this man acts thus all his life, in the end he will be utterly lost, for his intention is not to serve the Holy One, Blessed be He. The second kind of fear is when a man does fear God but he does so because of the punishment of Gehenna, or because he may not enter Paradise, and it is for this reason that he strengthens himself to do a good deed. Such a man, even though he fulfills the whole Torah with this intention, and even though it is good that he should be fearful before the Holy One, Blessed be He, who will bring him to judgment, nevertheless he has not attained the essence of goodness, for his whole intention in his service is merely for his own good and not for the honor of the Holy One, Blessed be He.

But the third kind of fear of God is the precious pearl. This is when he fears the Holy One, Blessed be He, for no reason in the world, except that he trembles before Him and all of his limb's shudder with awe as he remembers His Greatness and His Might. Now this is a very profound thing for people to understand, since the way of people is that they do not do their deeds unless they hope to derive some sort of profit or to avoid some injury to themselves. And if one of these considerations does not apply, then they consider the deed worthless and empty.

And because the third stage is difficult to attain, the Sages have permitted us to perform the commandments out of fear of punishment and hope of reward. Therefore, you will find blessings and curses in the Torah, to frighten the heart of the reader in order that his heart may be aroused, as we do with a child — because he is still small in wisdom, we stir up his heart by giving him nuts and fruits as his reward. And we find that the boy does not study in honor of the Torah, because he does not know its value and sees no good in his studies, but he regards his studies as an ordeal, and the reason that he works and studies is to obtain the fruit. And this is just like one who performs a task that is not important in his eyes except for the profit that is in it.

But if we were to promise a boy, "Study, and I will give you a beautiful wife, or a house, or you will become king," he would not study because of such promises. His heart would be more aroused by the promise of one piece of fruit than by these, for it does not know the benefits to be derived from having a good wife or being king. And thus, it is the method of the Torah; to arouse the heart of man with things with which he is familiar and which he knows to be good, to draw his heart to do what is good. And all this we must do for a man, because his wisdom is small and weak, and he has not the understanding to discern the secret of the matter, and this is what is called studying the Torah not for its own sake. Therefore, do not be like that boy, but seek the truth for the honor of the truth. However, such an attitude requires great wisdom and discernment.

Therefore, it is important to inform you of the power and might of the soul, and then you will devote your intelligence to the uppermost foundation of all. And this matter is like the case of the king's son, a boy of a year or two, who was kidnapped and taken a distance of a thousand parasangs or more. And he was raised in the house of a villager and was taught the work of a villager and he did not think about or remember the time of his royal state, for he did not recognize or know anything of it. And after he had reached maturity of thought, someone came to him and informed him, "You are a king's son!" But he did not tell him what manner of prince he was. Then his heart swelled with pride but he did not pay too much attention to this information for he did not know who his father was. And after this another bearer of tidings came to him and told him which king was his father and told him his country and his land. Then his heart became even more proud and he longed to go there. Nevertheless, his heart felt suddenly cast down as he thought, "Even if I do go there, they will pay no attention to me for they will not recognize me." After this the king heard where his son was and he sent members of his household who knew certain signs on his body, and he sent with them nobles and garments of royalty with the command to bring his son to him. And when these emissaries came to him and saw him and recognized him and showed him the royal garments, then his heart became exceedingly proud.

ORCHOT TZADIKIM — Chapter Twenty-Eight

And after they had dressed him and mounted him on the horse that the king was accustomed to ride, then he knew his power and his might and there was now within him the heart of a king and he was exceedingly proud. So, it is with the soul. The soul is the daughter of the king, breathed into man from the very Throne of Glory and brought into a body that is soiled, and which has a great desire for this world and many sorts of longings. Before the soul is aware that she is the daughter of the king, she is drawn after all the longings of the body and forgets her Exalted Father. But when they show her the heavens and the stars, and the sun and the moon, how they move with even and precise motion, and they tell her that she was created by the Same One who created them, she feels herself more and more exalted. And when they teach her the secret of the Unity of the Holy One, Blessed be He, and the secret of the wisdom of the soul, then she clothes herself in her royal garments and enters into the secret of reverence. And even a man who does not know all this, but who thinks about this lofty concept from the depths of his heart, and discerns the might of God, Blessed be He, then such a one will clothe himself with awe in his heart, as it is written, "Lift up your eyes on high, and see: who hath created these? He that bringeth out their host by number, He calleth them all by name; By the greatness of His might, and for that He is strong in power, not one faileth" (Is. 40:26).

Also consider that the Holy One, Blessed be He, has given permission to no people in the world to tell His praises other than Israel, as it is said, "The people which I have formed for Myself, that they might tell of My praise" (Is. 43:21). And it is written, "For thou art a holy people unto the Lord thy God" (Deut. 7:6). And it is written, "And the Lord hath avouched thee this day to be His own treasure" (Deut. 26:18). And it is written "To make thee high above all nations" (Deut. 26:19). And the Holy One, Blessed be He, did not give any creature the ability to know the Name, Blessed be He, save to Israel, as it is written, "Unto thee it was shown, that thou mightest know that the Lord, He is God; there is none else beside Him" (Deut. 4:35). And it is written, "And what great nation is there, that hath statutes, and ordinances so righteous as all this law, which I set before you this day" (Deut. 4:8). And it is written, "Thou shalt fear the Lord thy God; and Him shalt thou serve" (Deut. 6:13).

From these verses we learn that Israel is obligated to fear God, Blessed be He, and to occupy themselves with meditation over His Torah, and to fulfill His commandments and that from their meditation over the Torah they will understand the meaning of its directives and the new interpretations that may be obtained from each verse and they will grow wise in order to know God, may He be Blessed, and His strength and His power and his greatness and His great works, awesome and wondrous, as it is written, "Say unto God : 'How tremendous is thy work!' " (Ps. 66:3). And it is written, "Come, ye children, hearken unto Me; I will teach you the fear of the Lord" (Ps. 34:12).

Nothing in the world outweighs reverence — not silver, not gold, not pearls and not all the hidden treasures; they are all as nothing when compared to

ORCHOT TZADIKIM — Chapter Twenty-Eight

reverence for the Holy One, Blessed be He. For it is said, "Fear of the Lord which is His treasure" (Is. 33:6). Therefore, a man should hasten to treasure up in his heart a thing that is the very treasure of the Holy One, Blessed be He, and a man should learn in this world that every man tries to hoard all the good that he can. And one who can store up the things that kings treasure will certainly do so. If this is the case, then where is there a man who will not treasure up that which is treasured by the King of Kings, the Holy One, Blessed be He?

And now I will cause you to know that wisdom which treats of life, the spirit, and the soul, in order that you may acquire the quality of reverence for the Holy One, Blessed be He. The seat of life is in the liver, for blood is life, and it longs to eat and drink and it loves dominion and the attainment of its desires, because the liver is filled with blood and longs for delights and pleasures. And this is "the full soul loatheth a honeycomb" (Prov. 27:7). The spirit is the heart, and it seeks power, greatness, and royalty; it is in the heart of people to chase after honor. Therefore, the pride of the heart is called arrogance, and it is this spirit which prompts the minds of people to try to obtain mastery over others and to make themselves great. The soul is wisdom, and it dwells in the mind like a king at the head of his troops. It is similar to the glory of its Creator, and it rejects the pleasures of men and the vanity of their delights. The soul imparts wisdom and intelligence, and all of its thoughts are to serve the Holy One, Blessed be He, in reverence. And it ponders, what will be the end when the body dies and withers away? How will she, the soul, return in purity to Him who Created her and caused her to enter the body?

A man has two masters, and when he dies, he is freed from both of them. As it is said, "The small and great are there alike; and the servant is free from his master" (Job 3:19). The two masters are the spirit and the life, for they think only of pleasures, of multiplying wealth, eating, drinking, and being happy, of doing according to all the thoughts of the heart and the sight of one's eyes, and of speaking vanities and of pleasing the body. But the soul turns those thoughts upside down and says, "What good is it and what profit will there be to a man in all of his work at which he labors when in one moment he ceases to be and the body withers away, and then where is his wisdom and his beauty? If so, then there is no good except to serve the Holy One, Blessed be He, and to cleave unto Him.

The spirit says one thing and the soul says another. If the life and the spirit are stronger, then the soul grows weaker, as she has not the strength to stand up against them. Therefore, one who occupies himself with eating and drinking will never grow wise. But when the soul grows stronger than the spirit and the life, then the eyes of the soul are opened to understand the highest forms of wisdom. Therefore, the soul must weaken the spirit from which come wrath and arrogance, and must weaken life, which is the mistress of lust. And when the soul strengthens itself with wisdom it leads to modesty.

Now even an animal has life and spirit, for an animal has desires and gets angry just as man does. But man has a superior soul that speaks and that can distinguish between truth and falsity. And when the body dies then the life of lust and the life of the spirit die and there is left the form of the superior soul which is wisdom and which does not die when the body dies. As it is said, "And the spirit shall return to God who gave it" (Eccl. 12:7). This means the spirit of wisdom. And when a man sins then the essence of his life and the essence of his spirit die, as it is written, "The soul that sinneth, it shall die" (Ezek. 18:4). And Moses, our teacher, the man of God, said, "That soul will I destroy from among his people" (Lev. 23:30). From this you can understand that we call by the word nefesh or "life" that which dies. After the death of the wicked man, the wise soul is hurled as though from a sling far away from salvation because it listened to the spirit and the life. But the righteous person in whom the soul was uppermost and was stronger than spirit or life — that soul is found beneath the Throne of Glory. But the fool who hearkened to the spirit and to the life, his soul will be utterly cut off. And the wise man who listened to the supernal soul that was breathed into him from the Throne of Glory — his soul will merit the great good which is treasured up.

Now incline your ear and you will understand and know that the soul dwells in the mind, and that is the seat of reverence for from there goes forth the thought. And the thought raises itself and grows within the chambers of the mind just as the waves of the sea raise themselves. The soul seeks and searches and pays close attention to all deeds. And the mind travels far in its wisdom and looks with its vision at many things. For a brief moment it thinks about this and that and it runs and returns from matter to matter.

ORCHOT TZADIKIM Chapter Twenty-Eight

The Rock of Ages has made man wise and given him intelligence and taught him wisdom and knowledge. With this wisdom man remembers all that is past and foresees coming events. And with this wisdom he makes wheels and mills that grind without labor. And with this wisdom he raises armies and maintains troops and encourages them, and prospers in his rule, and conducts his government and holds it. And with this wisdom he spreads nets in the depths of the oceans and rivers to catch fish from the depths of the deep. And with this wisdom he traps animals of the deserts, and with it he snares the birds that fly in the heights of heaven. And with it he knows how to withstand the ills of the body and how to heal it (by seeking medicines), and he can distinguish between the benefit and the harm of drugs. And he learns to recognize roots and herbs and all sorts of fruits, cold and warm, moist and dry. And with it he knows what medicines to give the body to drink in order to restore it to its strength.

And behold, your eyes see the greatness of man and his glory, whom the Holy One, Blessed be He, has made great and uplifted above all creatures and has caused him to rule over all the lower creatures. And there is no power in the mouth to tell the greatness of the works which man can do in this lower world. And even in the upper world man sends his longings, and he flies and soars on the wings of wisdom. And even though this body goes into the earth like those of the cattle and the creeping things, his soul goes on in the upper world because of the greatness of its wisdom. And this soul stands and knows the wisdom of science that is in the realms above and the wisdom of science in the firmaments, and the movement of the stars and the measure of their heights. Even though the body of man is very small, his soul is greater and wider than heaven and earth, for the soul knows their height and their extent, and the ways of the sun and the constellations and all their divisions; everything enters into the soul. And since everything is contained in it, surely it must be greater than all of them for if this were not so, then the soul would not be able to contain everything, for it is impossible to cause the waters of the ocean to enter into a small leather bottle. And now that we have seen that man rules with his wisdom in two worlds, the lower world and in the upper world, every man ought to think and consider well why the Holy One, Blessed be He, caused him to know all this. It can only be to give him the intelligence to serve Him with a complete heart, for when he understands and knows the great and awesome wonders, then it will be apparent to him why he should subdue himself and subject his body to his soul. For all these great wisdoms come from the soul and not from the body. For it is the soul that leads the body, just as a man who rides on a horse leads it and turns it in every direction that he wants. If this is so, then the horse is secondary to the man, and man is not secondary to the horse. Therefore, woe, misery, and alas to those who enslave the soul to the body and make the principal part sumit to the secondary one.

And one should be able to realize that since the upper world serves the lower world, for example, the sun and the moon and the stars, certainly it should be clear that all this is not for the pleasure of the body, that it should enjoy the pleasures of this world, for in this

ORCHOT TZADIKIM — Chapter Twenty-Eight

world there is no real substance, but it is dust and worms and vermin and constantly subject to plagues and ready to die. The sun and the moon and the stars, however, are pure and clear, and how could it be that all this great activity should minister to the body which withers away and grows constantly poorer? It is for the soul which is clear and pure and is lifted up to the heavens and even higher, and which is greater than heaven and earth, for the knowledge of heaven and earth enters into the soul and the soul contains them. In truth, this is logic and also great proof that the heaven and the earth were created for the needs of the soul and to serve her.

And it is the soul which reflects upon this and clearly distinguishes it and asks, "Who am I that heaven and earth were created for my need?" This can be only so that I shall serve the Holy One, Blessed be He, understand His wonders, praise Him, and laud Him. And were it not for the Torah which purifies and whitens the soul of man, what need would he have of this world? Can anyone then seriously believe that the world was created for the delight of the body, for darkness and for lowly values.

And now, when we see that man was chosen out of all the creatures because of his great wisdom and because of his many deeds, for all other creatures are subservient to man, and he has the strength to learn wisdom, to understand the deep secrets, the mysteries of the lower world and the upper world, this is a clear sign to man that his soul will be bound up in the bond of life if he fulfills the Torah. A parable will illustrate this. There was once a king who invited his servants into the innermost chambers of the palace and showed them his treasures and his pearls and all his precious jewels. And he caused them to govern and rule over all of this and he revealed his secrets to them, and he warned them that they should serve him faithfully and that then he would give them great goodness and he would exalt them many, many times over what they had been heretofore. And this would be to them the sign that he had revealed to them his secrets and his treasures, the fact that he had caused them to rule over his earth in truth. Thus, the Holy One, Blessed be He, showed man His greatness and His glory, and revealed to him His secrets from His highest to His lowest, and caused him to rule over everything. Certainly, in this way He demonstrates man's destined greatness in the future, if only he will be careful in the service of the Holy One, Blessed be He. There is also a great proof that the soul comes from above, for we see that no man is satisfied with what he already possesses, but he always seeks a state higher than his present one. If he has a thousand, he longs for two thousand. If he rules this country, he wants to rule over another country as well. And there is no king or nobleman that does not seek a higher state than that one in which he finds himself. And this comes from the fact that the soul is not content with these boons but is constantly longing for greater virtues. For the soul is superior to all created things. And therefore, man walks erectly because of the soul. And all the rest of the creatures go on their bellies or bent downward.

And inasmuch as the soul comes from above, from the Throne of Glory, Therefore, the body in which the soul dwells has within it the likeness of all the world.

ORCHOT TZADIKIM — Chapter Twenty-Eight

And therefore, man is called a microcosm. The soul is like its Creator and the body is like the lower and upper worlds.

And now listen to this wondrous wisdom! Just as God is the Highest and rules over man and over all the world above and below, so does man, as long as he does the will of his Creator. For at the time of the making of the golden calf, the Holy One, Blessed be He, said to Moses, "Let me alone, that I may destroy them" (Deut. 9:14). And in the affair of Korah, the earth swallowed them and all that belonged to them, by the word of his mouth (Num. 16:28—32). And in the case of Elijah, of blessed memory, he swore that there would be no dew or rain except at his word (I Kings 17:1), and he brought on fire (I Kings 18:36—38, II Kings 1:10—12), and he slew the prophets of Baal (I Kings 18:40), and he resurrected the dead (I Kings 17:17 — 24), and he decreed concerning Elisha, that Elisha should have twice his spirit (II Kings 2:9—10, and see Sanh. 47a and Hullin 7b).

Thus, all the holy men that were on the earth were able to rule over what is above and what is below through the will of the Holy One, Blessed be He, when they did His will. Therefore, , you must be careful to fulfill His laws, His judgments, and His commandments, in order that you may merit the great good which is stored up. And just as God knows and understands what is behind and what is before, so does man to whom God has given wisdom. And just as God sustains and gives bread to all flesh, so does man sustain the members of his household and his servant and his animal. And just as God repays both good and bad, so does man. And just as God creates the structure of the world and the foundations of the earth, and the spreading of the firmament and the gathering of the waters, so also is man made to build, to found, to spread aloft, to gather water, to produce seed, to cause to sprout, to plant and to do all things, but only with exertion and trouble, and everything in accordance with the Will of the Creator.

And just as no creature can see God, so no creature has the power to see the soul. And just as God knows the future, so does man, at such time as his spirit and his body rest from engaging in the labor necessary to provide for his needs, and when the spirit of life relaxes and is free from occupying itself with the needs of the body. Then he may see the future in his dreams. And he may even see the spirits of the dead, and places that he has never seen and people whom he has never seen, and great things and visions, which he is unable to perceive when he is awake. And just as there is no creature in the world that knows the secrets of God, so can no creature among men know the secrets that are in the heart of man, but only God, as it is written, "The Lord knoweth the thoughts of man" (Ps. 94:11).

In many things man appears to be a little like God, in proportion to the little strength and the brevity of life that God has given man. The Holy One, Blessed be He, has added the evil inclination for man's good or for his evil, to test and try him as to whether he will choose the good or the evil, and to give him an opportunity to improve himself, to build and to plant, or to ruin and to uproot, or to slay, to rebuke, to gather wealth, to make war, to rule, to plunder, or to be full of wrath. And if there were no evil inclination, then, out of the fear of death, he would not have children and he would not build a building and he would have no desire to buy cattle or any other article, and he would not plant or sow, for he would say in his heart: Since the decree of death has been leveled against mankind, why should I work for another's benefit? And then the whole world would be lost and ruined.

And the Holy One, Blessed be He, created the world from the day of its beginning only so that is would be built and guided, in His Great Mercy, by men. And when a man strengthens himself with his good inclination to subdue the evil inclination so that he does not sin before his Creator, but uses his evil desire to serve God, Blessed be He, with fear and without sin or transgression, then this is his good, happy is he and happy is she that bore him.

Just as man in a little way is like God, so is the structure of his body like all the world. He made the dome of his head like the expanse of the upper heavens. He made the roof of his mouth in which are planted the teeth and molars, like those heavens which are above us. And just as this lower heaven which is over us separates the upper waters from the lower waters, so does the roof of the mouth divide between the moisture of the mouth and between the moisture of the head and between the moisture of the upper crust. And just as God as caused His Divine Presence to dwell in the upper heavens which He spread over the waters, as it is written, "Who layest the beams of thine upper chambers in the waters" (Ps. 104:3), so has He caused the spirit of the soul of life and knowledge and understanding to dwell in the crust of the head which forms a crust around the brain and its moisture. And observe and understand the truth, that if the crust of the brain should be torn or pierced then the man would die at once because in it dwells the spirit of life.

And just as God, Blessed be He, has caused His Divine Presence to dwell in the west, so has he placed the brain in the back of the head, over the ears, and caused the spirit of life to dwell over the brain. And just as all the world is sustained and functions through the power of One God, so does all the body function through the power of one spirit of life which God, Blessed be He, has given it, and this spirit endures in it to give it health and remains until its end comes. And if some evil spirit should infect the body, it could not endure as at first.

And just as God has placed in the expanse of the heavens two lights and five planets so has, He created in man's head seven servants: two eyes, two ears, two nostrils and the mouth. The right eye is like the sun and the left eye is like the planet Venus; the right nostril is like Mercury and the left is like Mars; the mouth, the tongue and the lips are like Jupiter, the moon, and Saturn. And just as air was made to fill the space between the firmament and the earth so was there made in the body of man the space in the chest and the body. And just as God caused the wind to blow in the atmosphere which fills the void of the world, so does the breath of the wind of life go forth from the lungs which are in the chest and body, and fills the void of the body. And just as He spread the earth over the water so did, he solidify and spread the flesh which is on the liver and the belly and the bowels and the spleen, and the flesh that is between the lungs and between the liver, the spleen, the bowels and the belly.

And just as God, Blessed be He, made some birds, fish and animals that are too tame and loving to plunder one another, and others that are cruel and prey upon and swallow one another, so also did he make men. The good men may be compared to the good birds and cattle as it is said, "My dove, my undefiled" (Cant. 5:2). And it is said, "And ye are My sheep of My pasture" (Ezek. 34:31). And evil men may be compared to evil beasts. To a lion, as it is written, "He is like a lion that is eager to tear in pieces" (Ps. 17:12). And some are like bears and wolves, as it is said, "Her judges are wolves of the desert" (Zeph. 3:3).

In the world there are trees and herbs and good and bad fruit. Some of them have a pleasant aroma and fruit that is good for nourishment and healing. And there are herbs and roots and fruit that can slay, like the herbs which produce deadly poison or like the thorn and the thistle. The good flora may be compared to good people, as it is written, "As a lily among thorns... As an apple tree among the trees of the wood" (Cant. 2:2—3). And the evil flora to evil people, as it is written, "But the ungodly, they are as thorns thrust away" (II Sam. 23:6).

And just as below the earth God made the depths and mud and mire, so did He make in man the upper intestine and the bowels which receive food and drink. And just as from mud and mire there swarm creeping things of various kinds, so do there swarm, in the bowels of man, from the mires of the dregs of the food and drink, various creeping and worm-like things, long and short, big and small. And just as God made a gathering of waters in the world, so has he made a gathering place for the urine, namely the bladder of the urinary tract.

And just as He made the pillars of the earth below the earth, so has He made as the foundation of the structures of the body, the bones of the pelvis on this side and that, and the two thighs. And just as He made stones which are firmly set in the depths and from between which the water goes forth, so did He make the two kidneys so that from between them and from their sinews the water of the legs, that is to say the urine, goes out to the urinary tract; and also, the semen crosses and goes forth from between them to the testicles. And just as deep calls unto deep, as it is written, "Deep calleth unto deep" (Ps. 42:8), so does the upper bowel, which is the stomach, call to the intestines to receive the rest of the food and the drink. And the bowels call to the sinews of the kidneys, which are like tubes, to receive the water. The urine is pressed out and separated from the food in the intestines to go to the urinary tract. And the tubes of the kidneys call out to the sinew of the urinary tract to receive those waters, to cause them to be gathered within the bladder which may be compared to the lowest depth, for it is the lowest of all the bodily depths. Moreover, that intestine calls to the intestines leading from the stomach to receive the excrement.

And just as God made the rivers to water the world, so did God make veins in the body of man. These are the vehicles of the blood that draw forth the blood to nourish all the body. And just as there is in the world clear water and muddy water, sweet, salty and bitter water, so it is with man. From his eyes there goes forth salt water, from his nostrils cool water, from his throat warm water, from his mouth sweet water, and from his ears, bitter water. And the waters of the urine are bitter and fetid.

In the world, there are cold winds and warm winds. So is it with man. When he opens his mouth and blows, then his breath is warm. And when he closes his mouth and blows, then his breath is cool. The thunders of the world are like the voice in man; the lightning of the world is in the face of man when it shines like lightning. There are constellations in the world, and those who view the stars can tell the future from them. So are there signs in man. When a man has a rash, which does not come from a boil or a louse or a mite, experts in this matter can foretell the future. And so, it is with the lines in the palm of a man's hand and with the form of his features that people may know the future. Now this wisdom was in the possession of the wise men of old but has been forgotten by the later ones. Similarly, the wise men can tell the future by trees and herbs, and this is according to what they said concerning Rabban Johanan ben Zakkai that he knew the language of the date palms (Sukkah 28a). The meaning of this is that he was expert enough to perceive the motion of the date palms and from this he could tell the future (Aruch 68).

And just as from the south, which is the right side of the world, there go forth warmth and the dews of blessing and the rains of blessing, so from the right side of man there goes forth warmth from the gall which hangs near the liver; and likewise, the moisture of blood goes forth from the liver, which is in the right side of man. And just as evil goes forth to the world from the north, so does cold go forth from the left side of man, from the spleen and from the black bile which dwells within the spleen. And just as evil goes forth to the world from the north, so does every bad and severe illness come from the black bile which dwells in the spleen on the left side. And just as in the northern side of the world dwell all sorts of injurious and terrifying things, and winds and lightning and customary thunder, so is this found in the source of the black bile in the spleen on the left side, for from it are generated every evil and severe sickness, such as consumption, and the fourth fever, and all kinds of madness, and fear, and trembling of the limbs.

And just as the clouds ascend, for they are like the smoke which ascends from the earth, and just as the clouds raise up water from the depths to the air of the heavens to cause rain to fall upon the earth, so does smoke go up from the upper intestines and brings up moisture to the mouth and to the head. And from that moisture which goes up from the intestine roll the tears and the mucus of the nostrils and the spittle of the mouth. And just as in the world God created mountains, so did He create in the body of man the shoulders and the sinews of the arms and the patellas on the knees. And the joints of the ankles and all of the other sinews which unite all the limbs. And just as God created in the world stones and strong, hard rocks so did God create in man the teeth and the molars that are harder than iron and any bone. And just as He created in the world hard and soft trees, so did he create in man hard and soft bones. And just as

ORCHOT TZADIKIM — Chapter Twenty-Eight

he created in the world, earth that is thick and hard, moist and soft, so did he create in man the flesh which is similar to the soft earth and the skin which is similar to the hard earth.

And just as among the trees and the herbs there are those that produce fruit and seed and those that do not, so are there among men those who beget children and those who do not. And just as He causes grass to sprout from the earth, so does He cause man to sprout forth the hair of the head and the beard. And just as there swarm animals and creeping things in the woods and in the land, so do similar things swarm in the head of a man and in his hair. And just as God created in the world the signs of the Zodiac and stretched it in the firmament from east unto west from end to end and the stars and the constellations and all things in the world are attached to it, so did He create in the body of man the white spinal cord which is in the hollow of his spine. And it stretches from the end of the brain of the head unto the bone at the base of the spine, and the twelve parts as well and the ribs and all the limbs of the body are attached to it from here to there. And just as in the year there are three hundred and sixty-five days so are there in man three hundred and sixty-five sinews.

The end of the matter is that the work of creation and the mystic world are all hinted at somewhat in man. And one who understands the secret of this thing will understand the wonders of the Lord, may He be Exalted. Therefore, man is called a world in miniature. And because the body of man is formed in the pattern of the upper world and the lower world, Therefore, there has been given within him the soul which is somewhat similar to its Creator.

And Therefore, David said (see Lev. Rabbah 4:8), just as the soul fills the body and carries the body and outlives the body and is unique in the body and does not eat things of the body, sees and is not seen, and is pure within the body and does not sleep, so does the Holy One, Blessed be He, fill His world, as it is said, "Do not I fill heaven and earth? saith the Lord" (Jer. 23:24). And He bears His world, as it is said, "I have made, and I will bear; Yea, I will carry and will deliver" (Is. 46:4). And He outlasts His world as it is said, "They shall perish, but thou shalt endure" (Ps. 102:27). And He is alone and unique in His world, as it is said, "Hear, O Israel, the Lord our God, the Lord is One" (Deut. 6:5). And eating does not apply to Him, as it is said, "Do I eat the flesh of bulls, or drink the blood of goats?" (Ps. 50:13). And He sees and is not seen, as it is said, "Which are the eyes of the Lord, that run to and fro through the whole earth" (Zech. 4:10). And He is pure in His world, as it is said, "Thou that art of eyes too pure to behold evil" (Hab. 1:13). And He does not sleep as it is said, "Behold, He that keepeth Israel doth neither slumber, nor sleep" (Ps. 121:4). Therefore, the soul which has within it all these qualities should come and praise the Holy One, Blessed be He, who has within Himself all these qualities.

The soul sits and ponders who created it and then she clothes herself with humility and reverence of the Lord, may He be Blessed. Therefore, a man must understand himself and comprehend his duty, and know whence is his origin and his root, and how he was formed out of a fetid seed. How, after this he became a bit of flesh, how there was breathed into him a supernal spirit, and how he was provided with bones and sinews, blood and brain, and clothed with skin and flesh. How the features of his face were formed, how his brow was set up, how his nostrils were pierced from within, and how the throat was made so that man could breathe and smell. How his ears were fashioned to hear, and the sockets of his eyes to see, and how in his eye there are several colors. How he has eyelids, and a mouth and throat, and a palate and tongue, and lips to open and to close, and molars of the jaw, joints of hands and legs, the hollow of his body, and fingers with their joints and nails.

He will understand how each is different from the others and how he was imprisoned for nine months in his mother's womb and came forth naked, blind, deaf, and unable to walk. All these he will think about and say in his heart, "Who opened your eyes and your ears? Who made for you all the elements of your body? Who made your hair black in your youth and even if you should wash it with all the soap in the world you could not whiten it? And yet in the days of your old age, it grows white by itself." Upon such matters should you ponder. And then you will be modest, lowly of spirit, and reverent of God.

"The end of the matter, all having been heard: fear God, and keep His commandments; for this is the whole of man" (Eccl. 12:13).

Finished and completed, Praise to God, Creator of the World.

www.ingramcontent.com/pod-product-compliance
Lightning Source LLC
Chambersburg PA
CBHW070124080526
44586CB00015B/1553